I dedicate this book to Ferdinand,
my loving husband who made my wonderful life possible.

I also dedicate this book to our beautiful children:
Adanna, Nneka, Okechukwu Jr., and Chike.

I hope this tribute to your father is a constant
reminder of how blessed we are as a family.

My love for you continues to grow with each passing day.

Thank you for always supporting and believing in me.

TABLE OF CONTENTS

ACKNOWLEDGEMENTS

Mom

I want to thank my mother Roberta Payne for her unwavering and unconditional love and support. You have been my biggest fan/cheerleader throughout this journey. I appreciate all of the excitement and enthusiasm you demonstrated as I methodically went through each phase of the writing process.

Your weekly text messages wishing me luck before each editing session with Bruce was both motivating and encouraging. Calling me after each session to hear about his feedback, thoughts, and opinions were heartfelt. Each conversation gave us opportunities to share memories, have serious discussions, and self-reflect. Our thought-provoking exchanges helped guide the direction of my book.

Thank you for loving, empowering, and teaching me to think positively. Your constant reminder that "Life isn't fair" helped me get through difficult real-life situations by being proactive instead of reactive. You're an incredible woman and I am proud to call you my mother. I could not have gone through this process without you. You are my "rock."

Thank you for encouraging, uplifting, and validating me. Consistently hearing the words "I'm proud of you, Cynthia" is worth its weight in gold coins. I am forever thankful and grateful for all that you do for me. Most importantly, thank you for being my phenomenal mom and very best friend. You are the absolute best and I love you more than you can imagine.

Bruce

I want to thank my editor Bruce Hurd for helping to make my book, *A Marriage Made in Heaven,* a reality. After attending your Make Your Book A Reality retreat in October 2021 and having a one-on-one coaching session with you, I eagerly joined your weekly one-on-one coaching program. Within ten months I reached my goal of becoming a first-time author. Thanks to you and your writing program I can honestly say I published a book that I am extremely proud of.

Words cannot express how much I appreciate you and your commitment to the authors with whom you work. The time you spent analyzing my writing, eliciting information, and paying attention to every detail is evident and impressive. Our editing sessions became the highlight of each week as I looked forward to your edits, suggestions, creative thoughts, and endless encouragement.

I felt as though I were taking a master class in writing. You spent a great deal of the time going over each chapter with me, analyzing each paragraph and providing constructive critiques. Your ability to help me express feelings I didn't even know I had was extremely helpful and essential to writing this memoir. This experience was both emotional and sensitive in nature.

Throughout it all, you kept emphasizing, "Cynthia this is your story, this is your book." Your professionalism, positive attitude, and words of praise and encouragement made this process thoroughly enjoyable. I learned a lot from you and my writing skills improved tremendously. I can now proudly say, "I am a published author!"

Thank you for making this journey enjoyable, seamless, and life changing. Working with you has been a pleasure and I look forward to working on my next writing project with you.

INTRODUCTION

Dr. Ferdinand O. Ukah, Director of Transplantation and chief transplant surgeon at the University of South Alabama Regional Transplant Center

A Marriage Made in Heaven is a book about eternal love, devastating loss, and the profound healing that came afterward. It is a book about how trusting in God and having an all-powerful faith helped me and my family conquer overwhelming obstacles resulting from an unspeakable tragedy.

A Marriage Made in Heaven is my story, but it involves far more than just me. It is a love story between a Nigerian man – a medical student studying in America who was born into a royal family, and a teenage girl raised in Queensbridge, one of the biggest housing projects in New York City. It's a story that shows how two people from vastly different cultures beat the odds to pursue their dreams and aspirations, and how they created a beautiful family together, as they lived the American dream.

This book is also the story of my devoted husband, Dr. Ferdinand Ukah, the loving father of our four children, and an extremely gifted transplant surgeon. It's about a man who, at the peak of his skyrocketing career, demonstrated the ultimate gift of love by traveling to a remote Nigerian village to perform a lifesaving procedure on his father under austere conditions.

A Marriage Made in Heaven is also about how our lives were cruelly upended in an instant by the sudden, brutal murder of my husband in a faraway country the day before he was to leave Nigeria to come safely home to us. I describe the shock of seeing my mother, living a thousand miles away in New York City, standing unexpectedly at my front door in Mobile, Alabama, and knowing instinctively that she was bearing terrible news.

I talk about telling my four young children of their father's death. I describe the sudden realization of the difficulties I was unprepared to face as I grieved my husband. I also speak of the secrets surrounding Ferdinand's death and how it took me years to find out exactly what happened the day he died. I describe the heart-breaking experience of packing up and moving from what had been the opportunity of a lifetime, where we were living in the home of our dreams.

While this book addresses the tragedy of Ferdinand's death and the aftermath we faced as we dealt with his irreplaceable loss, it is infinitely more than that one experience. This book, above all else, is a tribute to love, and hope, and faith. It is about the powerful, eternal love Ferdinand and I continue to share even though he passed away well more than 20 years ago. It is about the generous outpouring of love and support we received from our wonderful neighbors, friends, and church community as we moved back to Iowa City and reestablished ourselves in the wake of Ferdinand's death.

A central strand that also runs through this book is the importance of hope and faith in my life and the lives of our children. My hope for a brighter future and a powerful, abiding faith in God are what have supported me throughout my life. To put it more emphatically, without faith and trust in God I would never have been able to get beyond the overwhelming obstacles I felt when I suddenly found myself without my beloved partner and without an income as the single mother of four children under the age of eight. There were countless times where I didn't know what to do, where to go, or how I was going to make it through even the simplest tasks in life. Without faith, I would have been completely lost. With faith, my family and I thrived.

My book begins with describing our individual stories and how we came to meet and fall in love. I proudly describe our journey together, with a focus on Ferdinand's medical career as a very promising young transplant surgeon, culminating in his being appointed as the Director of Transplant Surgery at the University of South Alabama Hospital.

After his death, I describe how I coped — or didn't cope — with the many challenges I faced. I emphasize how I stayed true, as best I could, to the plans Ferdinand and I made for our children, asking myself "what would Ferdinand do?" whenever I was feeling overwhelmed by uncertainty, and repeating my mantra: "Love lasts forever. Love never dies."

The end result is, blessedly, a happy, healthy, loving family I am extremely proud to call my own. Adanna, Nneka, Okey, and Chike bring me more joy than I can ever express. My career as an elementary school special education teacher has also been deeply rewarding in ways I cannot adequately describe. I have so much to be grateful for and even more joy to look forward to. I am blessed.

On a personal level, an important goal behind my writing this book is to honor my late husband, Dr. Ferdinand O. Ukah, and to help keep his memory alive. I want to share his legacy and ensure he will be remembered. I want my children, their children, and their children's children to know how special their father was. I want them to know their history and understand they come from royalty and to be proud of that. I also want them to know that with hard work and perseverance, just like their father showed, anything and everything is possible.

Writing this book has been a very special type of blessing, too. While part of me dreaded reliving these terrible events as I recalled deeply painful memories, the writing process was therapeutic beyond my wildest expectations. Unlike anything else I have tried, it helped me face the reality of Ferdinand's death. I now realize I've been in a state of denial for 25 years. I placed so much emphasis on trying to keep Ferdinand's memory alive for our children that I didn't spend any time focusing on my response to Ferdinand's death or even allowing myself to grieve properly.

Before writing this book, I also wasn't aware of the details surrounding my husband's death. While I had much of the information available to me, I deliberately chose not to look because I was afraid of what I would find. I realized that to fully tell our story in this book, I had to review the court documents related to Ferdinand's case. Although this information broke my heart, I finally know the truth, and I am grateful for that.

I am also hopeful that readers will connect with what I have written in this book. While we are all unique and each of us has a different story to tell, I know there are many women and men who have been faced with unthinkable, tragic loss and have been forced to deal with situations they never imagined, even in their worst nightmares. If reading my story can help anyone who is facing unthinkable grief and unbearable loss, I am grateful.

More than that, I hope the example of the love Ferdinand and I shared can serve as a beacon of joy showing what is possible in life. Finally, I hope I have demonstrated how faith and trust in God has served and comforted me throughout even the darkest chapters of my life.

Blessings and joy to all of you, regardless of your beliefs and circumstances.

I hope you enjoy my book.

CHAPTER 1
HOMECOMING

My four children (Chike, Okey, Nneka, and Adanna) and me. Our first family picture after Ferdinand's tragic death.

I couldn't believe it. I stood there, in my consuming grief and utter shock, trying to come to grips with what I had just learned.

How could it be that Ferdinand — my best friend, beloved husband, and father to our four young children — was here yesterday and was now gone for eternity?

As I stared at my mother in the doorway and watched the sunlight from our quiet street in suburban Mobile stream in behind her, it struck me for the very first time how deeply distressing death was, even as it appeared so suddenly in the midst of complete calm. Here I was, wrapping my head around the concept that Ferdinand Okechukwu Ukah had departed this earth and yet life continued to go on as usual.

October 8, 1996 is a day I'll never forget. After decorating the living room for my husband's return from a three-week trip to Nigeria, dropping my daughters off at school, running a few errands, and picking up groceries, I was exhausted. It was time for my two young sons and me to take a nap. This was a routine I looked forward to daily.

Approximately an hour into my nap, I was awakened by the sound of a doorbell. The bell had a slow, drawn out, echo-like tone and I was completely taken aback because it was the first time I actually heard it ring. To say I was disoriented is an understatement. Now that I'm thinking about it, I wish I could turn back the hands of time.

I couldn't imagine who would be ringing my doorbell mid-day. Our family recently moved into our new home, and we knew only a handful of people. We had developed a friendship with our real estate and insurance agent. We also became friends with our new neighbors across the street, Clarence and Charlesetta Ball. And I met Olinda Edwards, a lovely woman who became a dear friend, at one of our weekly family taekwondo lessons.

Olinda was my go-to person whenever I needed help navigating life in the South. Up to that point, I had lived in big cities most of my life and I didn't know anything about Southern culture. Olinda grew up in the South and was a great resource, answering all my questions and explaining Southern etiquette. I quickly learned that people don't visit or drop-by without being invited or providing advanced notice. I was also shocked to learn that family and close friends typically enter homes from back doors.

Still feeling a bit disoriented and distracted by the doorbell, I hesitantly walked toward the door, holding my one-year-old in one arm, as my three-year-old son continued to sleep. I peered through the sheer white fabric panels I made to cover the long rectangular windowpanes on both sides of the front door. I was shocked to see my mother and next-door neighbor Mrs. Ball standing directly in front of me. Ironically, I was initially excited to see my mother. There was an element of surprise to see my mother showing up for an unexpected visit. I had the biggest smile on my face. In fact, I thought about jumping for joy and calling out to my son to tell him, "Nana is here."

That feeling of happiness and joy didn't last long. I suddenly realized that my feelings weren't being reciprocated. My mother and neighbor were not smiling, in fact they both stood frozen-like, without uttering a word or attempting eye contact. It was then I noticed how defeated and solemn they both looked. My attention was suddenly drawn to their black clothing and dark sunglasses. I knew at that moment something was terribly wrong. My feeling of joy quickly turned to dread. Something terrible had happened and I was terrified to find out what it was.

My mind started spinning. I couldn't think rationally. My mom and I talk on the phone every day. In fact, I talked to her at 11:30 p.m. the previous night. She didn't mention anything about visiting. My mother lived in New York City, yet here she was, standing at my front door in Alabama. She would never visit without telling me. Why did she look so sad? She's usually smiling and full of life. Why does she look so stiff and why is she wearing dark sunglasses? Her body language spoke volumes. She couldn't hide her feeling of complete and utter sadness.

The front door in our house required a key to open it from the inside. Since I rarely used the front door, I couldn't locate the key to let my mother and neighbor into my home. I was scared, confused, and panicking at this point. I found myself pacing the foyer like a woman without a sense of direction. It was clear my mother was here to deliver terrible news.

Still shaking, unable to think, and unable to find a key, I just couldn't make sense of anything. Still clinging to my son Chike and noticing that my son Okechukwu had just woken up, I gave him the biggest hug and held onto his hand tightly. As I paced from one side of the foyer to the other, I kept repeating the same phrase:

"What happened to my husband? What happened to my husband?" At the same time, I felt trapped inside my own home.

Mom and Mrs. Ball waited outside ten minutes before I was coherent enough to direct them to enter through the back door. My mother didn't waste any time. She walked in the door, sat on the sofa, looked me straight in the eyes, and bluntly spoke.

"Cynthia, Ferdinand is dead."

I couldn't believe what I was hearing. I felt like I was in another world as I tried to pretend this was all a dream. I felt like I was just hit with a bombshell, the worst news anyone could get. Although I didn't notice it at the time, not one tear came out of my eyes. As unbelievable as it seemed, the reality slowly dawned on me that my dear husband, partner for sixteen years, father of my four children, and very best friend, had died in a fatal car accident in Nigeria. At least, that is what I was led to believe.

Just weeks earlier, I vividly remember the day Ferdinand answered the phone and received the devastating news that his father was dying of stage four renal failure. Although Ferdinand was speaking Igbo, his native language growing up in southeastern Nigeria, I could tell by the tone of his voice, that sorrowful look in his eyes, and the continuous use of the words "renal failure," "stage four," "transplant," and "Papa," that his father needed a kidney transplant.

Ferdinand jumped into action to find a way to help his father. He immediately called and consulted with his brother-in-law, Dr. Orjoke, the Director of Public Health with the Nigerian Federal Ministry of Health and Human Development in Lagos. There was a family meeting to discuss the possibility of Papa traveling and having surgery in the United States. Ferdinand also consulted colleagues and close friends in the United States for advice.

Having his dad travel to the United States ended up not being a viable option because of his age and health status. Even if he did make the trip to the states and had a transplant, Ferdinand didn't think his frail father would survive the one-and-a-half-day journey back home to Nigeria. After carefully weighing all the pros and the cons, Ferdinand knew exactly what he had to do. That evening, Ferdinand confirmed what I already knew.

"Cynthia, I am the only person that can save my dad and give him at least two or three extra years of a quality life. My father made sacrifices, invested in me, and made it possible for me to attend college and medical school in the United States. I was trained by the 'Father of Transplantation,' Dr. Thomas E. Starzel, and I'm the Director of the USA Regional Transplant Center at the University of South Alabama."

Ferdinand felt empowered and extraordinarily blessed. He also thought it was ironic that his dad was in need of a transplant and living in a remote place where it was simply too underdeveloped to make a kidney transplant possible. He had already proved he could build a world-class transplant center and perform transplants with successful results. It was going to be an honor and ultimate gift of love to operate on his own father.

With my support and encouragement, Ferdinand started making plans to return home to save his father's life.

Because Ferdinand felt he was on a mission to give his father a transplant, he started making plans to travel to Nigeria. He was on the phone constantly, calling hospitals all over the United States and trying to acquire outdated medical equipment stored in hospital basements. He made arrangements to have large machines and dialysis equipment shipped directly to Nigeria while some equipment was shipped to our home in Alabama. Knowing the unused, outdated equipment would eventually be discarded, Ferdinand secured everything needed for the operation. His brother, Clement, was responsible for securing a hospital and operating space in Nigeria.

Ferdinand interviewed and consulted with doctors in Nigeria, discussed the magnitude of what he was planning to do, and went over his plans for the actual transplant. He also made requests for additional materials he would need to make the operation a success. This plan was not made public. Very few people knew what Ferdinand intended to do.

Ferdinand was excited and felt honored that he could provide his dad with a few more years to live. On the other hand, I couldn't imagine how stressful operating on a loved one might be or how Ferdinand would react if the surgery wasn't successful. Apart from the deep emotions involved, the magnitude of what my husband was attempting was enormous and surrounded by uncertainty. It could go wrong in so many ways. Yet, despite my fears, my heart swelled with pride for the wonderful man I had married.

Another miracle during this process was that Ferdinand found his purpose. He had plans to build a hospital in his hometown of Mgbowo once he was established in his career. By helping his dad, he found the perfect way to give back to the community where he grew up as a boy. Once he realized how useful the soon-to-be-discarded machines and equipment located in hospital basements across the U.S. could be in Nigeria, he made a pledge to gather and ship medical equipment to Nigeria on a regular basis to help save the lives of the people in his hometown.

Ferdinand flew to Nigeria on September 23, 1996, with equipment he would need to operate on his father. He couldn't find an organ donor in Nigeria, so his plan was to remove his father's kidney, insert a device that would make dialysis possible, provide him with all of the medical supplies he would need for nine months, and then return to follow up on his dad. In addition, after the surgery, Ferdinand was prepared to donate the machines and hospital equipment worth 4.2 million Nigerian naira – over $92,000 today — to the University of Nigeria Teaching Hospital (UNTH), to help save the lives of Nigerians suffering from renal failure. More to the point, it would have been nearly impossible for UNTH to acquire this life-saving equipment, much less find the money in their budget to buy it in the first place. Ferdinand would not only be saving his father's life, but he would also be laying the groundwork to help thousands of Nigerians for years to come.

After Ferdinand spent weeks on the phone orchestrating the assembly of a team of doctors to discuss his plan of action, UNTH became skeptical and decided not to cooperate with him. Although

Ferdinand was disappointed, this did not deter him. Time was of the essence and Ferdinand had to operate on his father. He contacted a family friend who had a small private practice and made arrangements to perform the operation.

On Tuesday, October 1, 1996, Ferdinand secretly took his father to a private hospital room in Enugu and successfully operated on his dad. The room was small in size and very basic. It included an operating table, a bed, three machines, surgical tools, a basin, and operating supplies. That's it. Protected and empowered through prayer, the love he had for his ailing dad, and equipped with his brilliance and surgical expertise, the operation went smoothly and was a huge success.

Once the extraordinary medical feat caught the attention of the Nigerian media, the airwaves constantly had his story on the news. Journalists followed him everywhere. News reporters, people in the community, medical doctors and students, all waited outside of his hotel. They eagerly wanted to hear from this confident, skilled transplant surgeon, and fellow countryman. Ferdinand gave television interviews and delivered lectures to doctors, professors, and medical consultants who traveled long distances to learn from the young surgeon. In a short time, Ferdinand was hailed as a national hero.

By the end of this experience, he was exhausted. Even though he was modest and not accustomed to receiving so much attention, he didn't have a moment to himself. Everywhere he turned, medical doctors, journalists, patients, and people in the community sought him out. Ferdinand didn't turn anyone down.

On October 7, 1996, my beloved Ferdinand Okechukwu Ukah gave his final lecture. The room was packed with hundreds of people. Media and lights surrounded the perimeter of the room, positioning themselves and trying to get the best angle. He was an instant celebrity.

At the end of the evening, a chauffeur drove Ferdinand to the market to purchase souvenirs and gifts for the children and me. He later drove Ferdinand to his hometown of Mgbowo to spend the night with his mother before leaving for the United States. Ferdinand made it home safely that evening and had a wonderful time eating dinner, discussing his father's progress, and spending precious time with his mother.

The next day the chauffeur arrived to pick Ferdinand up to take him back to his hotel. Within an hour the car, driven by Mathew Nwalu, was found in the bush by the side of the highway. Ferdinand's lifeless body was in the front seat. It appeared as though the car skidded off the road. The driver, however, was nowhere to be found.

When the news broke of the untimely death....

CHAPTER 2
DESCENDED FROM ROYALTY

Igwe L. N. Ukah, the Ohaire 1 of Mgbowo

Ferdinand's father, Igwe Lawrence Nwosu Ukah, known as Lawrence, was a profound influence on my husband throughout his life. "Igwe" is a term of reverence that comes from the Igbo language. Igbos are an ethnic group currently numbering over 45 million people, mainly residing within southeastern Nigeria. Igwe is a royal title used to address traditional rulers who control autonomous communities in

Nigeria. In 1976, Ferdinand's father was elected as the first traditional ruler in Mgbowo, the village in which he grew up. Along with the title of Igwe, his father also became Ohaire 1 of Mgbowo – first king of Mgbowo.

This designation was a result of a governmental declaration in 1976. That year, the government of Anambra State in Nigeria required every autonomous community in the state to select a traditional ruler. Although numerous successful, wealthy, and popular individuals were interested in the position, the Mgbowo community knew exactly what type of ruler they needed. They searched for a candidate who was selfless, honest, humble, and business-minded. They wanted an individual who had already established himself in the community, invested in the community, and proved himself by making significant contributions.

Throughout his life, Lawrence took great pride in Mgbowo and believed in doing everything in his power to make it great, not just "better." Although Lawrence had no interest in politics, he was one of the highest monetary contributors to development projects in Mgbowo. As an ordinary man, Lawrence quietly helped fund the development of the local church, community bridge, and civic center. He didn't make a big deal of his contributions or advertise them. He simply provided a check and continued with business as usual.

Lawrence contributed in many other ways as a trader of beers, oil, and gas, along with providing trucking services. As a prominent businessman, he hired many people in Mgbowo, providing them with an income in an economy with a very high unemployment rate. After his death, the family found records in which he assisted several less fortunate families with shelter and financed the education of many underprivileged children. When the time came to elect an Igwe, the election committee approached Lawrence on several occasions and tried to convince him to seek the nomination. Each time, he politely declined, stating he had no interest in politics and wanted to focus on his family and business.

On the day of the election, December 31, 1976, the people of Mgbowo gathered in the town square to select their first traditional ruler. Five people were nominated, and community members noticed with disappointment that Lawrence Ukah was not on the list. Someone in the crowd quickly added L.N. Ukah to the nomination list. As people searched the crowd, they noticed he wasn't in attendance.

Lawrence had stayed home deliberately, hoping someone else would win the election. Once his absence was noted, however, highly respected members of the community went to his home and persuaded him to attend the election. He agreed to participate, even though he had no desire to seek or hold office. The Mgbowo community did not take no for an answer. L. N. Ukah won the election and became the first traditional ruler of Mgbowo.

Although Igwe Ukah wasn't happy with the results, he felt it was his duty and responsibility to serve the Mgbowo community. He ruled for more than 18 years and continued to make significant contributions to the development of the Mgbowo community throughout his reign as Igwe.

My husband Ferdinand revered his father and learned a great deal from him. He not only learned the value of integrity and hard work, but he also saw firsthand how a man with no formal education, whom many predicted would fail, believed in himself, worked extremely hard and achieved greatness. Prior to his election, Igwe Ukah had become one of the wealthiest men in Mgbowo. Because of his integrity, wisdom, and business skills, he ensured that Ferdinand and his eight siblings would be productive, highly capable members of society by sending all of them to college. This was an extraordinary achievement, and it was something Ferdinand always remembered and admired about his father.

Lawrence Ukah had an extraordinarily difficult childhood. He was an only child, born to a very young mother, Mrs. Ogbonne Udenwude. His father died of kidney failure before he was born, and Lawrence faced many challenges as a youngster.

His mother remarried when Lawrence was very young. As a result, he often had to fend for himself. He attended school up to the fourth grade, but by the age of ten he had to leave home to serve as an apprentice wine tapper to help provide income for his older relatives.

In later years, Lawrence described this as a very difficult period in his life. At a time when most boys were still living at home and focused on learning the basics of reading, writing, and arithmetic, Lawrence left his village and family without any clothing on his back. He spent two years away from home, where he climbed palm trees in the jungle as many as three times a day to harvest the sap to make wine.

By the time Lawrence turned fourteen, he became interested in trading. He was determined to make a better life for himself and took advantage of every opportunity to learn from businessmen who took interest in him. He eventually became skilled, well liked, and highly respected. As young Lawrence began to thrive, people enjoyed conducting business with him. They appreciated his honesty, work ethic, and integrity, and he eventually went into business for himself. As his business grew, his confidence did as well. He purchased land, owned gas stations, sold cars and became very successful.

Many people encouraged Lawrence to marry early, so he could have many children and raise a family of his own. As he was the only son in his family, his lineage was in jeopardy. Instead, Lawrence waited until he was 27 years of age and successful before marrying Benedette Lewechi Ukah in 1948. Lawrence had five children with his first wife, Benedette, including Ferdinand. Lawrence also married a second wife, Ekumalo Kama, in 1950 and had four children with her. Having more than one wife was legal in Nigeria and was often associated with great wealth. This practice was even admired, because it meant having the means to support more than one wife.

As you might imagine, Ferdinand's and my early lives were worlds apart. I was born in 1961 in New York City and grew up in a thoroughly American environment. Ferdinand was born in 1956 and grew up in Mgbowo, a small village in Nigeria where his entire childhood centered on the compound where his family lived. His home was huge — a gated, two-story home with an open courtyard and balcony encompassing the entire upper level. The girls lived on the left side of the home and the boys lived on the right side. Igwe Ukah and his wives occupied the middle space.

There was a steady flow of people coming and going at all times. Due to Igwe Ukah's importance in the community, there was even a bank at the front entrance of the home. Members of the community assembled outside his home to commune and chat. Others stopped by to discuss issues, problems, or concerns. Numerous cars were parked in front of the home with drivers waiting to take family members wherever they needed to go. Most impressive of all was an outdoor meeting space with two huge wooden, traditionally carved chairs fit for a king and queen to hold court.

Ferdinand was born on July 26, 1956, and often laughed as he recounted the story his mom shared about the events that occurred on that day. His mother went into labor while walking through a grassy field. Ferdinand was born so quickly, she delivered him alone under a tree. Too nervous and afraid to carry him home alone, she decided to leave him by the tree while she quickly ran home to get help and find something to wrap him in. In all of the excitement and stress, once she returned to take her son home, she couldn't remember the exact location where she left him. She would often tease Ferdinand by saying she literally lost him in a field the day he was born. In the end, she located him within 20 minutes and, although it was very scary at the time, Ferdinand loved talking about it.

Ferdinand was the second son born to Lawrence Ukah and his first wife Benedette. He was the fifth child in the family when children from the second wife are included. It's important to note, the entire family lived as one unit. All the kids were raised together and observed both mothers as mom equally

After calling Ferdinand's brother Clement ("Clem") in Nigeria to get more information about Ferdinand's childhood, I was surprised to learn he couldn't provide any details. He had to call his older brother Godwin – the first son from Lawrence's second wife. Lawrence deliberately paired two sons from different wives and had them attend two separate boarding schools for their elementary and secondary education. He didn't want the children to feel he favored one mother's children over the other, so he paired them in an equitable manner to avoid complaints of unfairness or favoritism.

According to Godwin, Ferdinand was a quiet, well behaved, committed child. He always did what was expected of him, and he was peaceful, hardworking and had a good temperament. He didn't talk much but tried to tell jokes occasionally. Ferdinand spent a great deal of his spare time reading and was an excellent student. He didn't spend a lot of time playing with other children, though he enjoyed watching other children play, and he was quite observant.

He also had a very disheartening condition as he grew up, which contributed to his shyness. Ferdinand spoke with a vocal stammer that was accompanied with uncontrollable hand movements — Ferdinand slapped his leg repeatedly each time he tried to get words out. He often thought people felt sorry for him and was most comfortable spending time with his mother who felt protective of him as a young boy.

People in the community referred to Ferdinand's mother as Mama Okey. Okechukwu is Ferdinand's traditional name and Okey is the short version. That title alone demonstrates the bond Ferdinand had with his mother. Fortunately, by the age of 14, he grew out of the vocal stammering and uncontrollable tics. Even though those difficulties were behind him, he never forgot how challenging that time was and always remembered how patient and sympathetic his mother was during that time.

Though he never explicitly said this to me, I always got the sense that Ferdinand's early communication challenges and physical tics are part of what made him an excellent communicator as a partner and physician. When I'd watch him speak at medical school functions and later accompanied him to work banquets and formal events, I would watch as others would lean in to catch every word Ferdinand would say in his accented English. I was proud of the way he made each person feel heard and valued.

Many Nigerian families believe their children will take care of them in their old age and the oldest son is often groomed to take over the family business. Ferdinand's oldest brother Godwin helped his dad with the family business because that was the role of the oldest male sibling. Clem, the second oldest son, wanted to attend college after high school. Entrance into the relatively few high-quality colleges in Nigeria were very competitive in those days and, unfortunately, Clem didn't get into any of them. He decided to apply to college in the United States, and to his surprise, he was accepted at Portland State University.

After Clem convinced his father to let him attend school in the United States, his brother Godwin thought it would be too expensive and might hurt the family business. Once Clem converted Nigerian naira to U.S. currency, they ran a total for a college education in the U.S. and saw that it would cost five thousand dollars. Clem soon realized he could also get grants and financial aid, and the cost of education was reduced even further. Because of the lowered cost, his residence in the U.S. and familiarity with the American education system, Clem was able to help Ferdinand enroll at Portland State University, too.

Ferdinand's transition to Portland Sate was relatively smooth. He lived with his brother Clem the first year and was laser focused on his studies. He attended class, went to the library until nine o'clock, ate, took a shower, studied some more and went to bed. He repeated the same cycle day after day. Fiercely focused on his goals, Ferdinand didn't let anything distract him from his studies.

According to family members, Ferdinand always wanted to become a doctor. They remember a family member, Dr. Okelu, frequenting their family home throughout Ferdinand's childhood. He always addressed Ferdinand as Dr. Okey, much like Ferdinand's mother was nicknamed Mama Okey after her close relationship with "Okey" (Ferdinand). It is likely that his early introduction to medicine, a positive strong role model, and supportive tone from his family set the stage for Ferdinand's future profession.

After four years of study at Portland State, Ferdinand earned a joint Bachelor of Science degree in Biology and Psychology and graduated with honors, on June 8, 1980. Ferdinand's big goal, though, was to attend medical school and become a doctor. Despite graduating with outstanding grades, Ferdinand didn't get into any medical schools in the U.S. He was, however, accepted into a Canadian school, so he packed up his belongings and headed north to start his medical career in the fall of 1980. However, on his way to Canada, he stopped by Howard University College of Medicine while visiting a friend in Washington, D.C. Out of curiosity, Ferdinand connected with the Director of Admissions to find out why his application to medical school had not been accepted. His timing couldn't have been better. He learned that someone had just dropped out of the program the very same day.

Much to his delight and surprise, Ferdinand discovered he still had a chance to go to Howard. His originally rejected application was still on file, and he reemphasized his desire to attend Howard. Before he knew it, his plans had changed and he was enrolled as a first-year medical student at Howard University, a Historically Black College located in the heart of the "Chocolate City," Washington, District of Columbia.

Ferdinand asked his friend if he could stay with him for a few weeks until he could find an apartment. Meanwhile, he attended orientation sessions, purchased books, received his white coat and was prepared to attend classes a mere five days after he discovered he had been accepted into Howard Medical School. Even though his life had changed dramatically in just a moment, Ferdinand was thrilled. He was excited to be going to medical school and to be attending Howard. The environment would be so completely different from Portland, yet he knew it would be perfect for him.

CHAPTER 3
BORN IN QUEENSBRIDGE

My mother Roberta, my father James, my brother Darryl, and me in 1975

"I'm going to divorce your father."

My mother's words seared my soul as I began to understand what this might mean to me and the life I was living. I was a sophomore in high school, and I knew things would be changing. It was frightening, especially after I had just spent years being bused to a neighborhood far from home, where I spent my days in an elementary school with children I did not know and who did not look like me.

Yet, my childhood was so very much more than these traumatic events. There was joy, and friends, and a thriving, loving neighborhood where I felt very much accepted. It was home, and I loved being there. Most of all, there was my family: Mom, Dad, and brother Darryl. The love we shared is unbreakable, even to this day. Even now, decades later, I know this unconditional love has helped support and sustain me through the years, even as the unspeakable tragedy of Ferdinand's death forced its way into my life years later.

I was born September 26, 1961 at a time when Ferdinand was navigating the early years of primary school. My parents, James and Roberta Payne were two native New Yorkers. My father was a shipping clerk in New York City's Garment District and my mother was a teaching paraprofessional who had met and married in 1959 when they were in their teens. They already had one baby boy, my brother Darryl, one year before getting pregnant with me.

My mother described me as a placid, calm baby. I never woke up in the middle of the night, started talking at nine months, and spoke in complete sentences by the time I was one year old. This was a great relief to my parents, because my older brother Darryl was the total opposite. He had colic and cried all night for five months. So, while they loved us both dearly, I was a breath of fresh air.

My mother had a beautiful, cocoa-brown complexion. She was tall and slender, with stunning long black hair extending down her back. I should have been jealous of my mom's beauty, but I wasn't because she was as beautiful inside as she was on the outside. She looked like a model who should have been on the front cover of a magazine. Men smiled and respectfully complimented her on her beauty as she walked by. Horns constantly honked, acknowledging her beauty, with men taking a second look as she passed them by. Whenever we were in public and I called her mommy, people looked in disbelief, publicly stating, "I can't believe that's your daughter." They thought she was my sister.

My mom was family oriented, with my father, brother, and me always being her priority. My mother was also my best friend. While I had friends my age, my mother and I just really enjoyed each other's company. We did almost everything together. We'd go shopping, have lunch at restaurants, and attend Broadway plays together. She even let me accompany her when she traveled to other boroughs to visit her girlfriends in Brooklyn or Manhattan. We loved watching soap operas, too. After school I'd get off the school bus as fast as I could to watch *Dark Shadows* with her. On top of all that, I couldn't believe she let me read her True Confession magazines when I was in junior high school.

Warm, kind, and thoughtful is how I would best describe my mom. We had an affectionate family, with all four of us expressing our love by saying "I love you" throughout the day, accompanied by frequent hugs, kisses, and reprimands when necessary. I remember getting a spanking because I called a girl an inappropriate word while riding in a car with my parents and two adult family members on our way home from a family reunion. It was pitch black and as we drove through a dark alley, we almost hit a teenage girl riding her bike

It was then I yelled the curse word.

My dad quickly and angrily turned around and asked, "What did you say?"

I repeated the statement and he demanded, "Where did you hear that word?"

"I heard it from you daddy, I was just repeating what I heard you say."

There was complete silence in that car. You could hear a pin drop.

When we arrived home, he located a dictionary and asked me to read the definition of the word out loud.

He then looked my way and said, "This is going to hurt me more than it's going to hurt you."

He spanked me three times and I could see tears coming from his eyes. I believe he felt he had to teach me a lesson — however, I believe he ended up learning a more powerful lesson than I did.

My mother also had a very close relationship with her grandmother, Bertha Sewell, who raised her and whom she called Mama. Her biological mother wasn't in the picture during her childhood years. I have numerous memories of them talking on the phone at least once a day, laughing, joking, and having so much fun. Having a close-knit family was all I knew. I had a loving, nurturing, childhood and my family felt comfortable talking about anything and everything.

There were no holds barred. My mother had a great relationship with her mother Bertha – this was a bond my mother and I duplicated.

Outgoing, outspoken, and curious by nature is how I would best describe my brother Darryl. He was tall, suave, and good looking, too. Yet from the very start, we were total opposites. Rarely seen without a basketball in his hand, Darryl loved sports, spending every spare moment at the Boys Club of America, playing basketball in a neighboring town after school and on weekends. Often leaving our house at eight-thirty in the morning on weekends, he would arrive home at six o 'clock sharp: just in time for dinner. Our parents insisted we eat dinner together as a family — no excuses allowed. Darryl always made it home on time — he was never even one minute late. He knew this wouldn't be acceptable. My father loved his family and wanted to spend time with us when he came home from work.

Darryl was also on a Little League baseball team called the Silk Sox. My dad was an amazing father and an active participant in both of our lives, especially Darryl's. Dad grew up without a father in his life, so he made it a point to serve as a positive role model. He would often take Darryl across the street to River Park to practice baseball as I looked forward to his Sunday afternoon baseball games. I was pretty much guaranteed a New York City dirty hot dog from a nearby stand during the game — complete with sauerkraut, mustard, and cream soda, my favorite drink.

Our parents encouraged us to be very independent and taught us not to rely on others to achieve happiness. As an example, Darryl frequently went to Yankee Stadium alone, even as a young kid. Feeling self-assured and independent, he enjoyed going to sporting events by himself. By the time Darryl entered junior high school, he started becoming interested in music, too.

I believe my father, James Raymond Payne, was a deeply frustrated musician. My dad played in bands before he met my mother and performed on weekends during the early years of married life. He had musical talent but lacked the opportunities and resources to make a living at it. My father wrote a hit song – and was the lead singer on the record "Love Me Tenderly" by the DelRoys, a 1950s era doo-wop quartet. Dad had a unique tone to his voice that was quite powerful. His greatest accomplishment was seeing his hit song on Billboard Magazine and performing on the Clay Cole Show; a rock music television show based in New York City. He was known as "The Dream" by Jerry Love, a well-known record producer at that time.

Dad playing the organ

Once my father started playing at nightclubs on weekends, patrons would leave drinks on his organ – I assume it was to show their appreciation. Initially, my dad would take a sip of each drink; he didn't want to offend anyone or appear unappreciative. My mother thought it was funny initially, as my dad would come home feeling a little tipsy. He would be in a good mood, laughing and sharing the audience's reaction to his music.

As time went on, my dad's drinking increased. He would come home feeling agitated and unhappy, complaining and being confrontational about every little thing. Eventually, my mother made it a point to go to bed before he came home. This was her way of reducing the possibility of conflict and keeping this family secret at bay. My brother and I had no idea that my dad was an alcoholic. My mother was trying to protect her children as well as my father's image.

I remember my parents coming home from a New Year's Eve party, arguing about the difference between paper and confetti. It was the first time I heard my parents argue and I must admit it seemed kind of comical

Did it really matter whether it was paper or confetti?

What was the big deal?

My mother kept repeating "It's confetti" while making distorted faces – mimicking my dad's intoxicated state – which I wasn't aware of at that time.

"It's not confetti, it's paper!" my father responded.

My mother finally reached her boiling point. She was tired of protecting my father, trying to maintain peace, and keeping her mouth shut at the expense of exposing him. She decided that very day, she had a voice – and she was going to use it!

After repeating the same phrase one last time, my mother took the cup she had in her hand and threw the contents up toward the ceiling of our living room. The liquid splattered everywhere; I couldn't believe my eyes.

"It's confetti!" she yelled.

She left my dad standing in the middle of the room, bewildered. She slammed the bedroom door and didn't come out of her room until the following morning. I was shocked to see my dad slumped on the sofa when I woke up the next morning – I didn't know what to make of the situation, but it felt terrible. He always slept in the bedroom with my mom

That afternoon, my mother walked with my brother and I across the street to River Park. While sitting in our parked car under the 59th Street Bridge, she admitted that my father had a drinking problem and was an alcoholic. It was painful for her, and my head was spinning. What did this mean? Why was she telling us this? She said she tried to hide it from my brother and me as long as she could, but she could no longer keep up the façade.

She felt his drinking was out of control. He wasn't drinking just on weekends anymore. He was also drinking alcohol during the week. She referred to my father as a "functioning alcoholic." This meant he depended on alcohol even as he managed to go to work and fulfill most family responsibilities. My mother had decided she could no longer deal with his mood swings and belligerent state of mind. She confided in both of us about her plans to divorce my father, but she knew she had to be patient. She felt she needed to save money before she could make her plan a reality.

I was shocked because I didn't have a clue what was going on in my own house. My mother emphasized that my father was a good man who genuinely loved his family. She encouraged my brother and me to maintain a close relationship with him. My mom emphasized he was addicted to alcohol and, although he tried to stop several times, he just couldn't do it. She had given him an ultimatum if he wanted to save their marriage. He either had to go to Alcoholics Anonymous or marriage counseling. He attempted both one time and refused to go back. After almost 20 years of marriage, my mother made the decision to leave my dad.

She had a two-year plan to save enough money to move and live independently. She told my brother and I we may have to go on welfare, but she would try to save as much money as she could to prevent that from happening. My mother encouraged me to share this information with my best friends at the time, just in case I needed someone else to talk too. Surprisingly, when I told my friends about my father being an alcoholic, they both laughed and said, "I thought you had some big news to share." They both shared that their fathers were alcoholics as well. Once again, I was clueless.

One of my friends took me to the Plaza, because she wanted to show me where our alcoholic fathers most likely hung out. Although this was new to me, I had an amazing support system and coping mechanism. I certainly didn't feel alone, and my friends assured me I had nothing to worry about. Each month my mother would share details from her secret bank book that showed how much she was accumulating for her big move. My mother finally left my dad two weeks after I moved to Washington D.C. to attend college. She remained in the marriage longer than expected to make sure I grew up in a household with both a mother and father.

Throughout his life, music flowed in Dad's blood. We had an organ in our living room throughout my childhood. My father replaced the organ every three years for a bigger and better model. Playing the organ was pure joy for my father. Every time he sat down at it, he perfected his soulful voice as he sang day in and day out. I remember watching my dad carefully holding his composition book where he would write lyrics to his songs as if it were a precious work of art. He would carefully place it on the organ stand, drawing musical notes on each line, and then playing the notes in succession as his creation evolved.

The pride he took when he created something beautiful elicited so much joy. My mother was always his first audience as she listened intently, praising his latest composition. In my mind, he was a musical genius. I loved the way he sat on the stool, back hunched, legs spread apart, with his long, outstretched fingers straddling the keys as he sang with delight. I was surrounded by the sound of music.

My father also had a band called the Bill-Ray Trio. My Uncle Bill was also in the band, where he played drums. They practiced at our house every other weekend. Because they were so loud and the walls were so thin, everyone in our three-building section was exposed to the music. Passersby often stopped outside our window to sing, make music requests, and dance to the beat. Over time, the drum set became another permanent fixture at our house.

Because it was difficult to transport drums back and forth, my brother became fascinated with them and started fooling around with his uncle's drums during the week. Before we knew it, Darryl became an outstanding drummer. My mother decided to invest in music lessons twice a week. She felt that if he was serious about music, it was important for him to learn how to read music and play correctly. Darryl became so skilled he occasionally served as a back-up drummer whenever my Uncle Bill couldn't make it to practice or performances. Darryl caught the music bug without anyone really noticing and he is now a record producer in Las Vegas with a list of hit records of his own. Ironically, he's living my father's dream.

Our parents also taught us to be responsible, self-confident, independent thinkers. A term I remember hearing often from my mother was "life isn't fair." Mom was not a pessimist; it was just that she didn't want either of us to expect anything from individuals or to blame anyone for misfortunes we may experience. She stressed that we are in control of our own destiny, and we can only depend on ourselves. This was her way of empowering both of us to take responsibility for our own actions as well as anything that happens to us.

Since this belief was indoctrinated into us at such a young age, it became our family mantra. To this day, we don't have unreasonably high expectations of others. We accept people as they are, don't pass judgment, and try to be as empathetic and understanding as possible. My brother and I don't worry or stress about anything we cannot control, and I credit both of my parents for modeling that for us.

I grew up in a two-bedroom unit within the Queensbridge public housing development located in Queens, New York City. Queensbridge was enormous. At that time, it was the largest public housing development in the country. The development consisted of ninety-six buildings, incorporating three thousand, one hundred and forty-two units. It was divided into six blocks, and we had access to everything we needed. This included grocery stores, a recreation center, and, most importantly, the candy store, all just a five-minute walk away.

People often associate living in the projects with negative images or connotation. I remember Ferdinand accompanying me to Queensbridge to meet my father. He stopped me in the hallway, leaned on the banister, took a deep breath, and looked me in the eye before he spoke.

"Is this really where you grew up?"

"Yes," I answered. I was confused by the question. What did he mean?

His eyes started to water as if he wanted to cry.

Now I was getting concerned. Why was he asking such a silly question?

Finally, it came to me. *Oh, I get it.*

He didn't realize his girlfriend grew up in the projects. It was probably his first time in a setting like this. And for the first time in my life, as a sophomore in college, I was able to see firsthand an outsider's negative perception of project life.

In my experience, this outsider perspective couldn't be further from the truth. In fact, I found it to be quite the contrary. Growing up in Queensbridge was a wonderful experience and I wouldn't change anything about my childhood. I had the freedom to explore, participate in a variety of activities and observe interactions with many different people. My community was rich in every way, and by all accounts, I lived an abundant life. Queensbridge was my home and my parents provided me with everything I wanted and needed. We functioned as a unit – community members supported each other through good times and bad. There was always something going on in our neighborhood and there was no time for boredom. From my perspective growing up, I lacked nothing.

Queensbridge was located on prime real estate, also. I woke up to the view of the New York City Skyline and lived across the street from River Park. I had access to nature, trees, and playgrounds on each block. On weekends I had the option of attending weekend musical, cultural, and festive events. The 59th Street bridge was directly behind my apartment building. At night, it was the most beautiful sight, as it was adorned with lights outlining the shape of the bridge.

Like my future husband Ferdinand, I was a shy child who had to be persuaded by my mother to socialize, or even just engage with new people outside the four walls of our home and the children in my building. Queensbridge was also a community in which most other children my age would excitedly venture out between buildings and cross city blocks to walk to nearby stores or parks independent of their parents. I, on the other hand, was my mother's shadow. I felt content to spend time with her at home. I typically had one or two solid friends and avoided large groups of people whenever possible.

My home at 41-13 Vernon Blvd. was my world growing up. My best friend, Arlene Rodriguez, lived in the unit beneath me with her two sisters, Phyllis and Celeste. I spent a lot of time at their house playing, singing, dancing, and watching television. We even played in the hallway. Their mother, "Mrs. Mary," was a feisty woman who was proud of her Puerto Rican heritage. I loved listening to her accent as she talked. Always animated and expressive, Mrs. Mary intertwined English and Spanish as she spoke, all the while showing various expressions with the movement of her eyes and the changing inflection in her voice whenever she talked. Her house was full of life and energy. My neighbors attended St. Rita's Catholic School; however, most of the children in my neighborhood were Black and attended public schools.

One of the major influences on my life took place well before I was born. In 1954, the Supreme Court determined "separate but equal" racially segregated schools were unconstitutional. As part of the landmark Brown vs. Board of Education ruling, it was decided conclusively that schools with a high percentage of Black students were almost always inferior to schools intended for white students. This was in large part due to states giving more funding to predominantly white schools.

As a result of the Supreme Court's ruling, desegregation busing, commonly shortened to "busing," was introduced. Busing was the practice of transporting both black and white students to schools outside of their local districts to help alleviate racial segregation. Ironically, the school children on my block were the only students in Queensbridge selected to try this new concept. As a result, I left the comfort of my surroundings and peers to attend a far-away, mostly white school during my elementary school years.

I found that going to school wasn't particularly enjoyable. I had to walk to the bus stop, typically sitting alone on the twenty-five-minute commute to a neighborhood that was foreign to me. I entered classrooms in which I was usually the only Black female in just about every class. I was an average student, and this environment made my tendency to be a passive learner even more pronounced.

I didn't go out of my way to make my presence known. I simply paid attention, wrote down copious notes, complied with instructions, completed assignments, and spoke only when teachers singled me out to ask specific questions. I felt invisible at school, never raising my hand or voluntarily sharing any of my thoughts or opinions. I felt like I was just filling space. I looked forward to the end of each school day so I could return to familiar surroundings. It was a sad, lonely, and isolated life in so many ways.

Despite all of this, I do remember two very special girls at that school who became my good friends. Josephine Aguedello, an outgoing Hispanic girl, befriended me the first day of school. We sat next to each other in most classes and our parents occasionally gave us permission to go out for lunch at a nearby White Castle. Inez from Brazil was another friend. I initiated that friendship because she arrived midyear and looked terrified on her first day at school. Her English was limited, and kids made fun of her, but I invited her to sit at my lunch table. She caught onto the English language very quickly and moved to another school before the year ended.

By the time I was in fifth grade I was also much taller than almost everyone else. I was 5'9" in height and already wearing a size ten shoe. I really stood out at a time when I would have preferred to blend into the background. I lacked confidence because I towered over almost everyone my age, including and especially the boys. I felt awkward and out of place. I was like a giant among my peers. Shopping was a nightmare, too. Because I couldn't find pants long enough to fit my long legs, I wore "highwaters" all the time. My pants were short in length and only reached my ankles.

I also ended up wearing the ugliest shoes imaginable. Most size ten shoes at that time were designed for adults and teens, not for school children. They also had high heels, which were a complete non-starter since my mother forbade me to wear them. At the other end of the spectrum were size-ten shoes designed for senior citizens – these were what I usually had to wear. I remember distinctly having a pair of shoes made of fake leather that looked like a patchwork quilt, complete with black zigzag stitching and patches from every color of the rainbow. In my mind, I felt I looked like a clown. My mother noticed my frustration and taught me how to sew. I took sewing very seriously and, as soon as my parents purchased a sewing machine for me, I started making all of my clothing, including pants long enough to reach the tip of my shoes.

My parents were extremely social, and strongly encouraged me to participate in extracurricular activities, as they felt that would improve my confidence and self-esteem. I went to dance school every Saturday, where I took ballet, tap, and jazz classes. I also became a majorette and practiced twirling my baton every other Thursday evening. I even participated in competitions on weekends. As the years went on, the wall next to my bed became a timeline reflecting the stream of 60s- and 70s-era Americana activities for young girls. These displays ranged from Brownies and Girl Scouts recognitions to dance and performance ribbons and trophies I earned as a teen for being a majorette and combo ballet/jazz/tap dancer at Cathy's Dance Studio.

While I typically downplayed my accomplishments whenever my friends came over and they saw my ribbons and trophies, I was secretively very proud of what I had accomplished. And I was so very grateful to my parents, family, and friends for being so loving and supportive. Yet, I recognize even now my childhood at Queensbridge was not completely perfect, with busing to a school far from my neighborhood and with parents who eventually divorced over my father's alcoholism. I also realize that as all of us grow older, we often tend to remember the love and special experiences we had as a child, while suppressing traumatic events in our lives that also shaped who we are. Still, I can't help but feel warm and loving inside as I remember the love my family shared and the extraordinary experiences I had in that special and sacred place. Yes, it was not perfect. But I would not change it for the world.

My loving family in the 1970s

CHAPTER 4
NEAR DEATH AND REBIRTH

Me at age 16 in 1977

This is what heaven must feel like, I thought.

I was 16 years old and, for the first time in my youthful life, the prospect of my death crossed my mind. The feeling was so overwhelming that I sensed I was going to die, and I didn't want to be alone.

Amid all the schoolwork, socializing, and after-school activities, two moments from my teens stand out in particular: I received a Bible as a Christmas gift at the age of thirteen, and I contracted a severe case of spinal meningitis when I was sixteen. The first was deeply inspirational. The second was life-threatening.

In 1976, I received a Bible as a Christmas gift from my mother, and I have treasured it ever since. I ended up reading it cover-to-cover. Prior to that, religion hadn't been a focal point in my life. While God and religion were very prominent in Queensbridge, religion had not been a central theme of my life until I began studying my new Bible. The church is a central gathering space in many Black communities and even before I received my Bible, I frequently attended events at neighborhood church services.

The neighborhood church, like many churches throughout America, was very active, periodically providing dinners, children's activities, and family events in an effort to get members involved outside of Sunday services. My neighbors downstairs attended Catholic School, and I occasionally accompanied them to church services at St. Rita's. I had also attended church with my family on occasions such as weddings and funerals. My mother describes herself as a spiritual person and although I didn't have a strong religious foundation in terms of attending church on a regular basis, she often made references to God and encouraged my brother and me to believe in God.

I wasn't an avid reader at that time, but something about the Bible drew me in. The story of creation and the Garden of Eden fascinated me. The very human and fallible decisions made by the women of the Bible felt familiar to me. Mary, giving birth to the Savior as a teenager; and Ruth, making the decision to follow her mother-in-law after her husband's death, struck me deeply. I was also impressed with Rachel and Hannah, and the list goes on. By the time I reached the New Testament and the final few books of Jude and Revelation, I felt like I had a compass and guidepost in life — the world and my own universe with God at the center was starting to make sense. I felt like my life was starting to take shape, and from that point on, I decided to use the Bible and my Christian faith as guides. I felt I was on a journey, and I wanted to live a life with God at the forefront.

As I entered tenth grade, I attended Long Island City High School, a twenty- minute walk from my neighborhood. I remember feeling faint one day, while sitting in the back row of chorus during the end of my sophomore year.

The feeling that day was both scary and surreal. What initially started off as a feeling of extreme calm — my mind in a daze, feeling like I was floating on a cloud — suddenly turned into sheer panic. My vision progressively blurred, and the fear of blacking out set in. I was straining my eyes, constantly looking at the clock, counting down only eight more minutes until the end of chorus. I felt the class couldn't end soon enough.

As soon as class was over, I went directly to the nurse's office and arranged for my mother to pick me up and take me to a clinic to get checked out. The doctor at the clinic examined me and concluded I had a virus but predicted I would be feeling better before the official lab results came back. He prescribed rest, lots of liquids, and Tylenol as needed. I followed the doctor's instructions and slept most of the day.

During the evening, that soothing feeling reemerged. Once again, I simultaneously experienced both calm and fear. My body felt weightless, and my head spun in circles. I revisited the feeling of my body floating on a cloud. Even though I feared what was happening to me, I felt such a sense of peace. I thought about dying, too, and I was afraid to face it by myself.

The fear of dying alone prompted me to go into my mother's room and ask if I could sleep in her bed. Although my father protested, my mother knew something had to be terribly wrong and gave me permission to join her. She knew I wouldn't make such an odd request unless it was one hundred percent warranted. Thank God she did. A few hours later I was delirious with a high fever, flapping my hands uncontrollably and waking her up from a deep sleep.

My mom felt the heat from my body and knew my temperature was very high. She immediately called the emergency room and was told to put me in a tub of cold water to try to get the fever down. Unfortunately, I was practically unconscious, and my body felt like dead weight. I was almost too heavy to lift, and it was impossible for my parents to get me into the tub. The dead weight was too much for them to manage. Instead, my dad grabbed my shoulders while my mother grabbed my feet. Struggling, they carried me outside, shoved me into the car, and took me directly to the emergency room.

When I arrived, the doctors assumed I was on drugs based on my almost lifeless, incoherent state. My parents tried to convince them that I wasn't using drugs, but they had a difficult time getting through to the staff. Thank goodness the doctor I saw earlier that day was the on-call physician. He vouched for me, stating he examined me earlier during the day and confirmed I had a virus, and that my condition wasn't a result of drug use.

After further examination and administering additional tests, the doctors gave my parents devastating news. I was diagnosed with spinal meningitis, an infection of the fluid and membranes surrounding the brain and spinal cord. Once the infection starts, it can spread quickly. Without treatment it can cause brain damage in a few hours and can be fatal within twenty-four hours.

Doctors confirmed I was in a coma and probably wouldn't come out of it without serious after-effects if I even emerged at all. They predicted I would be severely brain damaged if by some chance I survived. My parents learned that approximately 10% to 15% of people infected with spinal meningitis die. For those who survive, one in five experience a variety of long-term disabilities.

According to my mom, family members and many people in my neighborhood prayed for me. Strangers and hospital employees also prayed. Once I recovered and heard testimonies from those who prayed for me, I understood the power of prayer and felt I personally experienced God's intervention and presence in my life.

I remember waking up, not knowing the extent of my illness. One of the first things my mom did was hand me a box full of cards, prayers, letters, and well-wishes. She shared stories about people who were praying for me, lighting candles at church, and holding candlelight vigils. I can vividly remember the look on my doctor's face and his expression of sheer disbelief when I came out of the coma. He saw me talking to my parents and shouted.

"I can't believe you're alive!"

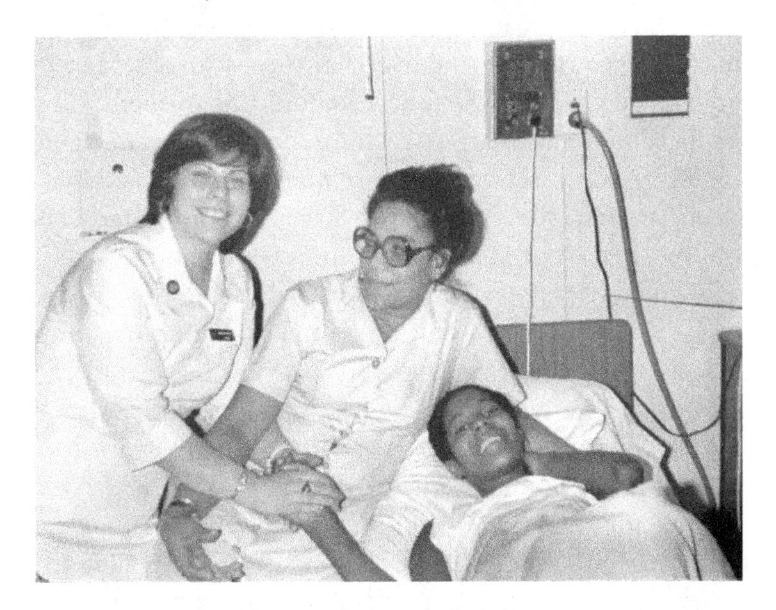

Me recovering from spinal meningitis at
LaGuardia Hospital in 1978
I am shown here with two of my wonderful nurses.

Several doctors, nurses, medical students, and housekeeping staff peeked into my room. They were completely astonished. I felt like I was a modern medical miracle. My illness and recovery affected me spiritually, too. I experienced God's mercy and grace and it is something I will always remember. I knew I was close to death, and yet I wasn't afraid. As a result, my relationship with God became more intimate. Even now, as I pray each night, I thank God for allowing me to survive spinal meningitis and giving me a second chance in life. With my health restored and faith in God strengthened, my final years in high school went smoothly.

As I moved into my senior year, I realized it was time for me to start making plans for life beyond high school. I knew I wanted to go to college and was inspired to become a teacher for the hearing-impaired. There was a girl in my neighborhood I admired and observed from a distance. Her name was Simone, and she was deaf. She was beautiful, too. She had a great smile and one of the best-looking afros on the block. I loved the way she lived her life — just like her peers. I took advantage of any opportunity I could just to spend time with her. We had fun, even though we didn't completely understand each other. Despite being deaf, Simone attended school, was popular and had an active social life. I wanted to learn American Sign Language because I wanted to be able to communicate with her.

I also had a friend, Crystal Granger, whose mother was hearing impaired. I loved going to her house and watching her mother as she navigated life without being able to hear. I wanted to be a part of their world. This was also a catalyst for my career choice.

Making the decision to attend Howard University is one of the best choices I've made. Even before high school, I remember overhearing my mother and my Cousin Dianna talking about a predominately Black college in Washington, D.C. called Howard University. Although I lived in a Black neighborhood, I didn't have an opportunity to attend classes with many people who looked like me. When I heard about this revered Black college in our nation's capital, I couldn't believe such an institution existed. I remember sitting on a bench in front of my building in Queensbridge when my brother's friend George Williams sat down next to me. While chatting, I mentioned what I learned about Howard University and to my surprise he had a cousin who was attending Howard. He offered to take me on a day trip to tour Howard University. He wanted to leave right then and there — on the spot!!

One minute I'm sitting on the bench in front of my apartment building and the next minute my mother is giving me permission to accompany George on the four-hour drive to Washington. On the way to Howard, we talked so much about what we were going to see, it didn't feel like a four-hour trip. I was in awe when we arrived at the school. The campus was impressive, and it was nice to see so many people who looked just like me walking to and from class in an educational setting.

There were so many young adults talking or debating, with each individual exuding extraordinary confidence and pride. I was hooked and just knew Howard University would be the best college for me. Midway through my senior year, though, I became nervous about moving so far away from home. I even told my mother I had decided not to attend Howard. The truth is, I didn't want to leave my mother or the security of my home. My mother calmly persuaded me to apply, and later that spring I was accepted. I am now a proud alumnus of Howard University.

CHAPTER 5
HOWARD UNIVERSITY

Celebrating my graduation from Howard with my mother and my grandmother Esther

Over my dead body, she thought.

My mom realized she had done me a huge disservice when, at the age of sixteen, I told her I would never leave home and would stay with her until the day I died. It was abundantly clear that I was dependent on her, and it was at that moment she decided it was important for me to go away to college. I needed not only to gain an education, but it was also very clear I had to become independent and learn life skills.

After reflecting on my proclamation, my mother realized I wasn't emotionally equipped to do much of anything on my own. She had been my spokesperson whenever I faced major challenges or obstacles. I remember seeing a help-wanted sign and having the desire to apply for a job at Lynn's Clothing Store when I was 15 years old. I was afraid to walk into the store by myself to ask the manager for an application.

My mom tried to help by driving me to the store on three separate occasions, hoping I would have enough nerve to walk into the store and ask for an application. I didn't have the confidence to do it and out of frustration my mother asked the manager to hire me. I lacked confidence because I was shy and not accustomed to initiating conversations with anyone, much less an adult. I was also afraid of being rejected. I knew I would feel embarrassed if the owner didn't hire me. My mom eventually expressed her frustration by putting her foot down.

"This is the last time I'm going to speak up for you. You must learn how to do these things on your own."

Thankfully, the manager hired me, and I worked at Lynn's Clothing Store after school, on weekends and during the summer for a little more than two years. When I made purchases, had to return an item, or needed to handle a difficult situation, after trying to encourage me to speak for myself, my mother more than likely solved the problem for me. Although my mother assisted me with awkward situations out of love; the reality was, she was hindering me. She realized I was, indeed, correct. She was concerned I would end up living with her until the day I died if she didn't do something drastic and force me to gain some sort of independence.

My mother strongly encouraged me to apply to Howard University, which I did because she kept making the request to do so. I was an average student and not strong academically. I didn't think I would be admitted, so filling out the application wasn't really a big deal. Most of the young adults in my community enrolled at the nearby

LaGuardia Community College and I was fully prepared to follow in their footsteps.

I remember walking into my apartment one hot summer day. My mother was holding a white envelope and an opened letter in her hands. Based on her expression, I assumed she won the lottery.

"Guess what I have in my hand?" she said.

"A letter?" I guessed cautiously.

"It's addressed to you. Can I read it?"

"Sure." I still didn't know what it was about. Whatever was in it was definitely exciting to Mom.

Mom's face was glowing, and she was all smiles; barely able to keep her hands from shaking as she read it out loud.

"Dear Cynthia,

"Congratulations, you have been accepted to the freshman class at Howard University."

I suddenly found myself standing there, speechless. Deep down inside, I couldn't believe I was accepted.

My mom raised her voice. "Did you hear me?"

"Yes."

I was still stunned. I honestly didn't know how to react. The possibility of attending a Historically Black College or University seemed out of my league. I remembered my favorite teacher in high school asking students where they were applying for college. She deliberately skipped over me, and even though she hadn't asked, I spoke up and volunteered information for the first time ever in her class.

"I'm applying to Howard University," I said in a low voice.

She looked directly at me and, without even giving it a second thought, she matter-of-factly responded.

"Oh, you'll never get into a school like that."

What she said may have angered or discouraged other students. Instead, that statement taught me how important it was to believe in myself. I adored that teacher and thought she felt the same way about me. It was at that point I decided I wouldn't let anyone's opinion affect or deter me from accomplishing my dreams, goals, or aspirations. In fact, that statement made me want to prove she was wrong.

It was a wonderful lesson for me to learn. Often, the people closest to us don't necessarily have our best interests in mind. They don't even realize how extremely damaging and limiting their low expectations are.

This eye-opening experience is most likely the primary reason I'm rarely concerned when people have negative things to say about me. Once I graduated from college, I even went back to Long Island City High School to visit the teacher who tried to discourage me from achieving my dream of attending Howard. Unfortunately, she had retired and was no longer teaching, so I may never know if she ever became aware of what I accomplished. As an educator, I wanted to let her know how damaging her words could be to the students she teaches. I also wanted to address her as a proud graduate of Howard University.

As my mother stood there with my acceptance letter from Howard, I started thinking about my Uncle Jimmy, a lawyer who later became a judge; as well as my Cousin Dianna who was a teacher. It was at that moment I began to put two and two together. Before then, I was almost oblivious to the varied professional and educational accomplishments of individuals in my family. I was having too much fun being a kid and not paying attention to my environment. I began comparing the lifestyles of family members and realized many of the successful people in my family most likely had a college education. They lived in well-to-do neighborhoods, single-family homes, and frequently went on family vacations. I was beginning to make a connection between college and opportunity

"Cynthia, aren't you excited?" she wondered.

"Not really." There was hesitation in my voice.

"Why not?"

"Because I'm not going," I insisted.

Despite starting to understand the importance of getting an education, I was still reluctant to move away from home. The bottom line was I didn't want to leave my mom or familiar surroundings. I was afraid of the unknown.

As frustrated as she was, my mother knew that moment wasn't the time or place to push the issue. She was confident that over time she'd be able to convince me to attend Howard University. She knew I was excited about the prospect of attending Howard, stemming from the time I visited just a few months earlier. She also knew I was afraid to spread my wings and jump into the unknown far from home.

Later in life, Mom even confessed that she was "going to soup her up like Campbell Soup and make her feel so excited about attending Howard, she'll be more than ready to leave her home."

In spite of my reluctance to leave home, my mother was also on a mission to get me out of the house. She felt she needed me to depart so she could execute her plan to divorce my father. She wanted to complete her goal of raising me in a home with both parents present. My mother left my father three weeks after I moved away to college. Thankfully, my parents' divorce had little effect on my bonds with either of them individually. I continued to have a wonderful relationship with both. We talked on the phone frequently and my dad wrote letters every week with $20 or $50 for extra spending money. My mom and dad remained friends the entire time. My parents were married for 20 years, and my mother always loved my dad. She just couldn't live with him under the circumstances. My father didn't stop drinking and had a few serious relationships. Neither one of them remarried; in fact, my mother took care of my dad and visited him in the hospital every day after work for a year before he passed away in 2003. I love my dad.

The summer of 1980 was spent preparing for my big move to Washington D.C. My grandmother surprised me with a five-piece set of light blue leather luggage so I could travel to college in style. She didn't want me going to college with random boxes and an assortment of mismatched suitcases, looking improvised. My mother also purchased a black foot-locker trunk with a key and metal butterfly latches.

After seeing all of this, I was beginning to get excited and started feeling grown up. I practiced locking and unlocking the locker several times a day; packing and repacking items as I daydreamed about my next adventure. I slowly purchased necessities for dorm living in addition to a few new outfits for special occasions. My mother's plan worked. She made me feel that attending Howard University was the opportunity of a lifetime. I was also very eager to attend college on a predominantly Black campus. The summer seemed to fly by quickly and before I knew it, I was ready to begin my journey.

I casually told a few friends I was going away to college but didn't really understand what that entailed. This decidedly casual perspective of mine comes from how I approach life — I basically take things one step at a time. I don't make predictions or assumptions; I simply follow directions and take the steps necessary to accomplish my goals. My brother attended LaGuardia Community College for one semester and my mother took a few classes as well, but neither of them earned a degree. Moreover, I wasn't close to anyone who went away to college. The few people I knew who did go to college were far removed from me. I felt I was about to enter unknown territory, so I kept a low profile.

The day I left for Howard, my mother and her friend Bill drove us four hours to Washington with all my earthly possessions packed strategically in the car. I wasn't nervous, mostly because I didn't know what to expect. I knew Eaton Towers, my assigned dormitory, was in the heart of D.C. I also knew this was going to be my home for the next four years. Eaton Towers was an impressive building; approximately a 30-minute walk from the White House. Due to increased enrollment, Howard University had recently purchased a hotel and converted it into a dorm. This was where I was going to live.

My dorm was an all-female unit and was the first time Howard allowed freshman students to live off campus. I had access to a shuttle to and from campus and there was an all-male dorm, Sutton Place, directly across the alley. After carefully examining Eaton from the outside, I had a feeling my accommodations would be nice. I must admit, Howard didn't disappoint. Each room was spacious with a full kitchen and bathroom in every unit.

As it turned out, moving day was on one of the hottest days in August. I believe the temperature reached 95 degrees. I was one of the first groups of students to arrive at 9:00 a.m. and as students were lining up to get checked in, I stood in the corner of the room taking it all in. My mother and Bill were sweating profusely, waiting for me to get in line. The lobby was full of parents, students, luggage, and boxes galore. Everyone was jam-packed, with aggressive parents and students jumping the line trying to get the attention of residents. They were all rushing to get checked in to expedite the process and get keys to our dorm rooms. I continued to wait in the corner. Furniture, lamps, and fancy home decor was passing by each second. I was overwhelmed.

I refuse to come to her rescue, my mom thought as all of this was going on.

The Howard University parental handbook specifically stated how important it was for incoming freshman to navigate their first experience away from home independently. Students were required to approach residents to ask for help, fill out paperwork, and secure keys to dorm rooms themselves. My mother had to remind herself numerous times not to intervene and to focus on the end goal of helping me establish my independence.

The head resident gave a speech, stating, "Your children will be on their own from now on and they will be treated like adults." She went on to emphasize that "parents must cut the cord and give their children the freedom and opportunity to make decisions on their own."

Not being able to help me was definitely a struggle for Mom. My mother was hot, sweaty, and frustrated. Deep down inside, she wanted me to get into my dorm room as quickly as possible so she could get back on the road for the four-hour return trip to New York. Not only that, she needed a cigarette, but didn't want to give up her seat because she knew she would have to stand up for the remainder of the time I was checking into the dorm. I give my mother a lot of credit. She was a trouper. Although she was frustrated, it wasn't apparent to me.

My mother remembers thinking "I'll wait until the end of the day if I have to."

Unfortunately, she did. I was one of the first students to arrive at 9:00 a.m. sharp and the last freshman to get the keys to my room. This early bird doesn't always catch the worm.

Once we made it into the room, she appeared to be happy for me. She helped to set up my room, and we even went shopping to make a few purchases. Importantly, she let me know how proud she was of me. At the end of a very long day, she left and gave me the biggest hug and kiss. It wasn't until I spoke to her the next day that I found out how frustrated and upset she really was about the events that took place the previous day.

We ended up laughing about it, even though to her, it wasn't a laughing matter. She said she had never sweated so much in her entire life and was happy that I seemed to be adjusting well.

I was in utter shock when Cathy (not her real name), my roommate, entered the room. I didn't have any preconceived notions of who my roommate would be. I just wasn't expecting to see a bubbly, blonde, white girl moving into the room. Our freshman class was 95% Black, and she was the only white resident in the entire dorm. I didn't mind rooming with her, it was just completely unexpected.

My new roommate was from Maine and, according to Cathy, there weren't any Black people living in her community back home. The racial composition of her town is currently a little over 94% white and just under 4% African American. I'm pretty sure the percentage of white people was even higher 40 years ago.

Cathy told me her parents were older and had no idea she had been accepted to and was planning on attending a predominantly Black university. She only told them she was attending college in the nation's capital. When her family found out more about Howard, they were not happy at all.

Later, I even overheard Cathy telling her parents, "Don't expect me to be the same person when I come home. I'm one of them now. I might not come back."

The two of us were cordial but didn't establish a close friendship. She would wake up early and leave shortly after grabbing something quick to eat. She returned to the room at night, with just enough time to shower and get some sleep. Cathy spent most of her time on campus at the gym with football players. Rumor had it she was some sort of volunteer trainer, wrapping athletes' legs for practice.

I also felt she was gullible and somewhat naive. She gravitated toward athletes, and I sometimes worried about her. I didn't see her studying or spending time with friends. We lived together for only one semester, and I found out she was indulging in or possibly selling marijuana. After looking around, I found marijuana in the room – this was highly illegal at the time, and we could easily be expelled for breaking the rules in the dorms. I made a request to move out because I didn't want to get in trouble for her actions. I don't believe Cathy graduated from Howard. The last I heard, she was still living in D.C.

School was challenging, especially the prerequisite classes. I spent a great deal of time studying and simply trying to figure out the college grading system. I was a first-generation college student in my family, and I was learning the school system step by step. I failed a math class three times and dropped an African American Studies class ("Black Diaspora") three times as well.

I studied and worked very hard at math; however, it was difficult because I lacked basic foundational skills. Math is based on building blocks and there is a systematic way of solving equations. I understood the math concepts that were being taught, but I consistently lost points because there were gaps in my prior knowledge and there were several skills I was missing.

I didn't feel bad, I simply kept studying and filling in the missing pieces by getting help from graduate assistants, tutors, and taking advantage of extra help after class. Eventually, I mastered the skills and passed. I wasn't concerned about my GPA because college was new to me, and I didn't understand its significance or impact on my grade. I received an A in every other class, so my grades were still pretty good, considering the circumstances. My mindset was, if at first you don't succeed, try, try again. Practice makes better and I proved that to be true.

My experience with the "African American -Black Diaspora" class was shared by many students. It was considered one of the most difficult classes at Howard. I wish I had known that at the time. I believe fifty percent of the students dropped the class the first time they took it because it was so challenging. Very few students received an A grade, and the average grade was a C with a huge bell curve. It was the most challenging class I've taken. The professor wanted to make sure Howard students knew every aspect of our rich African history. The test consisted of vocabulary, multiple choice, fill-in-the-blank responses, and essay questions. She forced us to analyze, compare, and contrast. Prior to taking this class I studied by memorizing material. I had to learn how to study critically. I finally passed with a "D" and I was totally satisfied with that grade. It's not always the grade that counts, the most important result of the class was that I learned a lot, including how to think critically and analyze information as well.

Once I started taking education classes, I began to thrive. The professors were passionate and extremely knowledgeable. After going through the challenges of trying to pass classes and getting the needed support to succeed, I made the decision to minor in special education.

Gallaudet, a college for the hearing impaired, was also in Washington, D.C. Although my primary interest of going to college was to learn American Sign Language to teach deaf students, I quickly realized how limited my options would be in terms of employment. I didn't have plans to reside in D.C. after graduation, and schools for the hearing impaired are few and far between.

It was then my academic advisors suggested minoring in special education. That way, I would have the best of both worlds. I would be able to work with students who have a wide range of challenges and disabilities, including hearing-impaired students. I would also have more options and flexibility to work in schools wherever I decided to live. Once I started taking education classes, I became an A student, was on the Honor Roll and made the National Deans List.

CHAPTER 6
DANCING THE NIGHT AWAY

Ferdinand and me when we began dating in 1981

In 1980, most girls received two pieces of relationship advice as soon as they stepped foot on the Howard campus. Number one is that "many girls attending Howard have the specific intention of meeting and marrying a doctor or lawyer, so the competition is really stiff if that's what you want." The reasons for this are obvious: financial security and status frequently come with that type of union.

The other piece of information was more of a caution: "If you want to get married, stay away from African men. They will never marry an American woman. Oh, they will date American women, but their families will pressure them to marry someone from their own culture. It's a no-win situation, and you'll be left all alone."

While I heard and understood both pieces of advice, I wasn't concerned. I didn't fit into either of those two situations. I wasn't interested in meeting a doctor or a lawyer – I had my own professional career as a special-needs teacher to pursue. I also didn't even know any African men, so why would I worry about meeting or dating them? I didn't have a care in the world, and I certainly didn't need to focus on any of that. I had more important things to spend my time with, like studying. Little did I know my life would change dramatically one September evening.

I met Ferdinand at Howard University in 1981. He was a second-year medical student in the general surgery program, and I was a sophomore studying to become an elementary-education teacher. Although Howard was known as a party school, I was focused on my studies during my first year in college. I didn't attend a single party, but did go to a few basketball games, talent shows, and theatrical events.

I even met my good friend Ruth at an archery class that year. She was an older student; I believe she attended community college before transferring to Howard. She was hilarious and it didn't hurt that she was a New Yorker. With her outspoken ways and opinions about everything, she was very different from me, which was part of the attraction, of course. We were both terrible at archery; however, we enjoyed each other's company and spent a lot of time with one another after our class was over.

I remember someone calling my name from outside my window during the first weekend of my sophomore year. It was Ruth, asking me if I wanted to go to a Med-Dent (Medical and Dental School Party) at the dental school. I love to dance, and didn't have anything to do, so I agreed to go. We decided to meet in the dorm lobby at 9:30 p.m. and we took the school shuttle to the dance.

We arrived at the dental school around 10 p.m. and the place was packed. The room was a large hall, and there were people on the dance floor and surrounding the four walls. It was dark and the music was very loud. Being the shy person I was, I quickly stood behind two of my friends as soon as we walked through the door. Keep in mind I'm 5'9", so standing behind two women who are 5'4" and 5'6" was pretty silly. It was useless – I completely stood out.

Within a few minutes of my walking into the room, a gentleman strolled behind my two friends and asked me to dance. The music was awesome, and I hadn't danced in a long time, so I was excited. I accepted his invitation, and we had a blast. I was into leopard prints at that time. I typically wear jeans, a simple top and flats. This was my basic attire, and it hasn't changed, even now. That evening, though, I was dressed up well beyond anything I'd typically wear. Of course, I wore my standard jeans. The camel-colored vee-neck, form-fitted top with dark blue tiger stripes, heels, and bright red lipstick were flashy additions. I felt like stepping out of my comfort zone. And this is something I almost never do.

I've been told I'm a pretty good dancer, and that night I certainly felt like it. Let me clarify. I have a unique style in which my long arms take on a life of their own. I was pleasantly surprised when I saw that my new dance partner was quite amazing on the dance floor as well. We didn't talk at all, at least not during the first hour of nonstop dancing.

After an hour, the gentleman did ask what my name was. The music was so loud, I don't think he heard a word I said. I asked for his name, too, and I also couldn't hear a thing. We stayed on the dance floor an additional hour. In fact, this man danced so well we eventually had a crowd encircling us because he took dancing to another level. He was so outstanding that people enjoyed watching his creative, one-of-a-kind moves. Oftentimes, I learned later, he was incorporating traditional native moves with modern dance styles. The result was spectacular.

After two hours on the dance floor my feet started to hurt, and I was getting tired. I politely thanked this gentleman for the dance and went back to join my girlfriends. My brother Darryl was already a successful music producer and after I returned to spend time with my friends, my brother's hit record came on. I excitedly called my brother to tell him his song was playing at a Howard party, and I quickly searched the crowd to find my dancing partner. I found him and described how my brother produced the song we were listening to. We returned to the dance floor and stayed for an additional hour.

Ferdinand was his name, and he eventually asked if I wanted to get some fresh air. It was extremely hot, so we went outside to the front entrance of the building and talked for a while. Ferdinand was tall, handsome, and had a million-dollar smile. He wore beige khakis, a white shirt, and a tie. It looked like he came to the party directly after work.

My girlfriends joined us outside. Ferdinand was a complete gentleman and asked all of us if we wanted a drink. I declined because I don't drink. Ruth and her friend responded yes; and Ferdinand quickly left to get something to drink. During his absence, Ruth asked me so many questions.

"Where is he from?"

"Is he a medical student?"

"Is he a doctor?"

"Is he married?""

"Does he have a girlfriend?"

"Does he have a car? Maybe he can give us a ride home."

I couldn't believe she was asking so many questions. I told her I didn't talk to him at all and wasn't interested in anything besides dancing. Once Ferdinand returned with their drinks, Ruth interrogated Ferdinand with her questions.

It turned out my dance partner was from Nigeria, and was a second-year medical student in the surgery department. He wasn't married and didn't have a girlfriend, but he did have a car. My girlfriends were impressed because he was a medical student and was going to be a surgeon. Ruth wanted me to ask for a ride home and I flat-out refused. We came to the party by ourselves, and we could certainly make it home with no problem. It's a good thing I wasn't the jealous type. Ruth spent more time talking to Ferdinand than I did. They laughed, joked, and had wonderful conversations while I stood there and listened.

Ruth eventually felt comfortable enough to ask Ferdinand for a ride home, which he agreed to provide. He had a small orange beetle Volkswagen that was full of medical books. He moved his books around and came up with a configuration that would make it possible for all three of us to squeeze into his little car. Two of my friends sat in the backseat while I laid across the two of them with my knees upright. We were packed like sardines, but we made it home safely.

Ferdinand wrote his phone number on a small piece of paper he requested from the resident assistant in the lobby. He gave it to me and asked if he could take me out on a date the following day. I put the number in my back pocket, went to my room and immediately fell asleep. I was exhausted from all the dancing.

I woke up the next morning feeling conflicted. I started thinking about the telephone number and the possibility of calling Ferdinand. Life at Howard was going extremely well. I had the perfect number of friends and acquaintances. I wasn't interested in dating or having a relationship. I ultimately decided to leave the decision to chance. I took two pieces of paper; I wrote the word "yes" on one piece of paper and "no" on the other. I threw them both in the air and whichever one I selected would be my decision.

Fortunately for me, I selected the piece of paper with the word "yes" on it. I called him and Ferdinand and I went on a date the next evening. We quickly became boyfriend and girlfriend, and we dated from that moment on until his untimely death. I recently shared this story with my twenty-six-year-old son Chike, and his jaw dropped. He couldn't believe what I was telling him.

He said, "I can't believe that my existence was based on a flimsy piece of paper.

"Mom, I wouldn't be alive if you chose the word 'No'" he said.

Chike was absolutely right. I feel extremely lucky and blessed.

Things didn't get off to the best start, though. Our first date was a disaster. We went to a movie entitled *Caligula*, an erotic historical drama focusing on the rise and fall of a corrupt, decadent Roman Emperor. Not only did we arrive 30 minutes late, but the theater was packed. We had to sit in the front row, which was awkward enough. To make things worse, the movie consisted of several scenes in which the screen was full of nude women in the background. At least, that's my recollection. I felt extremely uncomfortable and, to a certain extent, disrespected.

What was Ferdinand thinking?

I wondered if this type of movie was a "first date" show in Nigeria?

Perhaps he wasn't thinking.

This is not how anyone should try to impress a woman on a first date. To top it off, he slept or should I say "snored" throughout the entire movie. It was so embarrassing. It was obvious he was sleeping. He couldn't control the nodding of his head. I had to hold his head in place by allowing it to lean on my shoulder to make his sleeping less obvious. I couldn't do anything about the snoring, though. It was there for everyone around us to hear.

Whenever I attended a movie and noticed a couple with a sleeping partner, I automatically assumed the nodding individual was either rude or doesn't care about the person he or she was with. In my mind, it's the ultimate form of disrespect. Between the movie and the snoring, I knew for sure this was going to be our first and last date.

Surprisingly, Ferdinand redeemed himself by taking me to a lovely restaurant after the movie. He was a perfect gentleman, opening doors for me and holding my hand at the appropriate times. I love holding hands. Ferdinand was personable and down to earth, and our conversations were free-flowing and spontaneous.

As time went on, I got to know Ferdinand and the grueling demands of medical school. I learned to appreciate his willingness to spend any of his free time with me. His demanding schedule consisted of challenging classes, lectures, and morning rounds at the hospital. In addition to studying for exams, Ferdinand was also in a competitive pyramid surgical program.

This meant that of the approximately fifteen medical students accepted into the surgical residency program, only nine retained their spots at the completion of the program. Each year, students were cut based on academic performance. Ferdinand worked extremely hard because he understood that "legacies" were guaranteed spots. A "legacy" student is defined as someone whose parents attended or graduated from Howard University Medical School. Ferdinand persevered by being hardworking, laser-focused, and determined to make the grade. He became one of the nine special students because he consistently worked hard to achieve his goal.

Despite his busy schedule, Ferdinand made it a point to take me out every weekend for a three-hour date. Occasionally, I would also meet him for lunch or dinner at the hospital cafeteria. Sometimes, I would stop by to see him at his "second home," the third-floor cubicle at the medical school library where he studied until 2 a.m. daily. As time went on, I realized how lucky I was that he took me out at all.

As time passed and I got to know Ferdinand better, I no longer had a problem with him falling asleep during dates. I knew it wasn't personal; he was just mentally and physically exhausted. Ferdinand told me he loved me while sitting across the street from the White House after we were dating for only three months. I didn't make a big deal of it because I didn't think anyone could fall in love in such a short period of time.

I did know we worked well together as a team, and we supported and encouraged each other during good times and bad. I also knew he was a brilliant, humble, caring human being and even then, I felt our relationship was something very special. Time would prove this true beyond any expectations I had as a college student, and I feel blessed to have had the opportunity to share my life with him. I would also learn, as our relationship grew stronger and our love for each other deepened, there would be more surprises than I could have ever imagined. The wild ride was just beginning.

CHAPTER 7
BECOMING CLOSER

Ferdinand visiting for Christmas holiday at home in Flushing, New York (1983)

It was the middle of the afternoon one day during my junior year. I was at Ferdinand's apartment to get away from my dormitory roommate and her boyfriend. I needed to study and that was impossible with the two of them constantly making out with each other.

Suddenly, I heard a loud and powerful knock on the door. Not only did that surprise me, but it also startled me to the point where I was actually scared of who this was and what he might represent. I tiptoed quietly toward the door and peeked through the peephole. I saw a gentleman wearing traditional Nigerian attire. I could also see he was holding a large suitcase.

This was very unusual, especially since Ferdinand hadn't told me about anyone who might be visiting. I was suspicious and I didn't want the stranger at the door to know I was even there. I knew he couldn't see me, so I acted as though no one was in the apartment. I decided to just let the gentleman continue to knock until he gave up and went away.

One thing was for sure: I wasn't going to let this strange man into Ferdinand's apartment.

So many thoughts ran through my head. My mind was racing.

Who on earth is he?

I know all of Ferdinand's friends and I don't recognize this guy at all.

I must call Ferdinand right away.

I was scared as I walked quietly to the kitchen and dialed the phone.

Months before, Ferdinand and I had settled into something of a routine as our relationship grew deeper. We continued to spend time together every weekend. I think he looked forward to our dates as much as I did because it was the only time he left the confines of the hospital, library or his small one-bedroom apartment. Ferdinand was very disciplined, and he allocated a specific amount of time to break free from his studies, visit with me, and simply enjoy fresh air.

Living in Washington, D.C. was the perfect place to be. Ferdinand always found something interesting for us to do and we took advantage of the National Mall and Memorial Parks. The always-packed events calendar provided us with lots of options and the best part was that most of the activities we indulged in were free. I particularly enjoyed the Smithsonian National Zoological Park, the fascinating array of museums, and walking through the mall during the Cherry Blossom Season each spring. Our weekends were full of adventure.

We occasionally spent time hanging out with Ferdinand's friends, too. This was a challenge for me at the beginning of our relationship. Ferdinand's close friends were mostly Nigerian medical students, and they talked about life in Nigeria and their medical school experiences. I couldn't relate to either of those topics and they were of very little interest to me. They also preferred to speak in their native language, and I didn't understand a word of Igbo.

Especially at the beginning, I sat quietly smiling, nodding, and pretending to be engaged. I found myself staring into space; hoping they would conclude so I could leave. Ferdinand tried to comfort me by holding my hand, periodically asking if I was okay and occasionally interpreting. He eventually realized I wasn't enjoying myself and we shifted from spending time with his single friends and began spending more time with young Nigerian couples. His rational was that I would at least have a female to converse with, while he enjoyed speaking Igbo and spending time with his friends from Nigeria.

I would learn throughout our life together that this type of experience would become commonplace whenever Ferdinand and I attended Nigerian gatherings. By observing Ferdinand with his Nigerian peers, I could easily see it brought him so much joy. Watching the excitement in his eyes, animated hands and huge smile on his face as he conversed and expressed himself made attending each event totally worth it. This was the life I was beginning to choose, and I was willing to feel a bit uncomfortable because it made Ferdinand so happy. Over time, I was treated as an honorary member of the Nigerian community, and I was able to understand the gist of most conversations. In addition, members went out of their way to interpret or speak English whenever I was around.

As time went on, we became very good friends with Ifeoma (Ify) Obenwa and her husband Peter. I refer to Ify as my Nigerian sister because she welcomed me with open arms and taught me everything I needed to know about Nigerian culture. She taught me common Igbo terms, how to prepare traditional meals, and how to wear traditional clothing. Often giving me an opportunity to choose from a variety of vibrant, colorful, fabrics with detailed prints, Ify would transform a long rectangular piece of fabric into a beautiful skirt or traditional dress.

She would dress me up in her expensive traditional clothing, head-wraps and jewelry, transforming one piece of fabric into three different styles. It was a lot of fun and Ferdinand loved it when I wore traditional clothing. As time went on, I appreciated Ify far beyond her introducing me to Nigerian customs and the wonderful community in Washington. Ify and I have continued our friendship to this day. She is the godmother of my first-born child, Adanna. Ify also named one of her daughters Cynthia after me. I treasure our relationship and we are Nigerian sisters to this day.

I soon discovered there was a strong, close-knit Nigerian community in Washington. As I learned more about them, I was impressed to see the dedication and commitment of everyone in this group. For example, there were monthly Nigerian meetings where we would exchange news, support each other, and bond over Nigerian meals. Unfortunately, Ferdinand didn't have the opportunity to attend many of them because of his busy schedule.

They welcomed new Nigerian families into the area by inviting them to meetings, and the community as a whole attended, organized and cooked food for major events such as weddings, christenings and birthdays. Committee members also provided support to families that experienced the death of loved ones back home in Nigeria and in the U.S. Since it was expensive to travel to Africa, the Nigerian community would collectively raise enough funds for that person to travel home to attend the funeral. If a Nigerian died in the United States, funds would be raised to fly the body back home. Nigerians believe in burying their loved ones in Nigerian soil, underneath or in close proximity to the family home.

Each year the women carefully selected traditional fabric and created a stylish outfit to represent a unified group for special occasions. I was extremely impressed by this solidarity and creativity. Women would also gather at a moment's notice to help individuals or families in need. It only took one phone call, and the phone tree would begin. Members would assemble to provide support or assistance when needed. This was something else I really admired. As I moved to Iowa, Alabama, and elsewhere, I found this was a common thread throughout the United States. There was always a supportive, welcoming Nigerian community — even if it was very small — when we moved to a new location and rapidly assimilated into their group.

Apart from the Nigerian community Ferdinand introduced me to, I also made close friends at Howard. Vicky Mardre was one of my best friends in college. She was from Philadelphia, and we became roommates during my sophomore year. Vicky was a Human Ecology major, and our beds were situated side by side in our triple dorm room. We had another roommate Marché, a pre-med student, who was extremely popular and social. We didn't see Marché much at all. She spent her time studying at the library and was rarely in our room.

Vicky and I were both quiet and reserved. We spent a lot of time together by default because we were always in our room. At one point, Vicky started noticing me making educational materials and preparing lesson plans for class. This was because I had to prepare a different lesson and create books, games, and activities each week designed to meet the needs of students in various subject areas. Vicky observed what I was doing and frequently asked what I was making. After explaining how I was going to teach certain concepts; she became intrigued. Vicky eventually changed her major to education and our friendship blossomed. Vicky is now a special-education teacher, also. She lives in D.C., and we continue to be good friends.

Vicky was also an avid reader, and she was the only student I knew who had friends outside of the university setting. She wanted to explore the entirety of D.C. and didn't limit her social interactions to Howard students. Additionally, she was a straight shooter, expressing her thoughts, views, and opinions with no regrets. Loyal, supportive, and Afrocentric is how I would describe Vicky. She delved into the community by patronizing Black businesses and attending community events. I was interested in what she was doing, and we attended many campus events together.

Our last semester at Howard was the best. We couldn't believe we were only a few months away from becoming proud graduates of Howard University. One of my favorite memories was sharing the excitement of our upcoming graduation by going out to eat and shopping. We wanted to be unified, so we decided to wear all white clothing on graduation day. We found the perfect outfits at Dress Barn. Vicky purchased a sharp white pant suit, and I selected a white asymmetrical dress. We helped each other pick out shoes and accessories; it was all so much fun. It was extra special for me because I typically hate shopping. Not this time. This memorable shopping experience even felt like a rite of passage. It was our way of celebrating friendship and transitioning from college students to adults.

As much as we were good friends in college, Vicky's friendship became more important later in life after Ferdinand's death. The love and care she showed me was instrumental to my well-being and she was extremely supportive as I made it through an extraordinarily painful and difficult experience.

Not long after Ferdinand and I began seeing each other regularly and were growing closer, he made plans to travel home to Nigeria for a visit. It had been three years since Ferdinand had visited his family and he finally had some free time. He was going home for a couple of weeks, and he was so excited. I was at Ferdinand's apartment when he started packing. After filling his suitcase and leaving it open to add last-minute items, I decided to write a few notes to put in his luggage. I strategically placed six folded pieces of paper in his rolled-up socks, shirt pockets, and undergarments. He forewarned me that communication would be scarce since he would be spending most of his time in the village with his parents where electricity was inconsistent. I wrote those messages because I wanted Ferdinand to know I was thinking about him and would miss him during his absence

Once Ferdinand arrived in Nigeria, his older brother Clem snooped through his luggage and was surprised to find love notes signed by a girl named Cynthia. He immediately wanted to know who I was. Ferdinand didn't mention anything about a girlfriend and, being a protective older brother, Clem didn't want anyone or anything to interfere with Ferdinand's studies.

Clem did some investigating by calling Ferdinand's friends in the United States. After making some inquiries, Clem learned that Ferdinand had been dating me for quite some time. Complicating things further, Clem learned that not only was Ferdinand dating, but the girl was American. This concerned Ferdinand's brother and it was at that moment Clem started making plans for a surprise visit to D.C. He wanted to go directly to the source to find out exactly who this girl was. More importantly, he wanted to know what her motive was.

Ferdinand came back to Washington after three weeks in Nigeria feeling well rested and rejuvenated. He had a fabulous time with his parents, family, and friends. He was also happy to report that his parents were healthy, the family business was thriving, and he finally had time to rest, relax, and eat delicious traditional foods. He felt ready to continue where he had left off at Howard University Medical School.

Each year Ferdinand's schedule became more rigorous. Whenever we had plans to go someplace or do something as a couple, Ferdinand's attendance was never a guarantee. I learned early on that I needed to be prepared to attend many events by myself. I simply could not depend on Ferdinand to accompany me at most gatherings. If he showed up, it was considered a bonus. I had to be independent and confident from the start. Our relationship became so close I represented Ferdinand in his absence when he wasn't present.

As I continued my studies during my junior year, I was spending a great deal of time at Ferdinand's apartment. At that time, I was still living at Eaton Towers and had two random girls as roommates. Despite having the option of rooming with a friend, I chose not to do that. Based on what I observed in previous years, rooming with friends often ruined relationships. As an observer, I witnessed good friends moving in together as roommates at the beginning of the year and despising each other by the end of it. I didn't want to make the same mistake.

Living with more than one female can be challenging on a good day. I simply wasn't willing to lose a friendship over jealousy, envy, or frivolous misunderstandings. I decided to room with girls I didn't know. One of my roommates was homesick. She went home practically every weekend and eventually dropped out of college. My other roommate entertained her boyfriend every day. In fact, he practically lived in our room. I often found myself leaving my room at the most inconvenient times because they were always making out and that made me very uncomfortable.

Because of this, I asked Ferdinand if I could stay at his place during the day because his apartment was empty at that time, and I would be free to focus on my courses without any distractions. He agreed and I was so appreciative. It was the perfect solution for me because I could study in peace and walk to and from class with no problem. For the longest time as I studied at Ferdinand's apartment, no one stopped by or knocked on his door.

The man wearing traditional attire returned and knocked loudly. I was suspicious and scared at the same time. I quietly made my way to the kitchen to call Ferdinand.

As I spoke to him in a low voice, I told him about the man dressed in traditional Nigerian attire that showed up at his door. While I was on the phone, the man knocked again. At that point, I'm pretty sure he heard me talking on the phone. Since Ferdinand was on the other end of the phone, I felt comfortable asking for his name.

"Who is it?" I called out to the stranger.

The man on the other side of the door confidently replied, "My name is Clement, I'm Ferdinand's brother from Nigeria."

Ferdinand was surprised and asked me to let him in. Clem introduced himself as Ferdinand's older brother and briefly talked to Ferdinand on the phone. Ferdinand told me to make Clem comfortable and that he would make an exception and come home at midnight instead of his usual 2 a.m.

My mind was still racing.

How can this man show up without prior notice?

He's coming all the way from Africa. This isn't a casual trip.

What would he have done if I wasn't in the apartment?
This is really blowing my mind.

I eventually learned that it's not uncommon for Nigerian family members to show up unannounced. Despite that, it still seemed strange that Clem would surprise Ferdinand while he was absorbed with medical school. It just didn't make sense to me. I'm not a suspicious person by nature, but I believed Clem had ulterior motives.

I later learned that his plan was to catch us off guard so he could accurately assess our relationship. Of course, at that point I was the one available to entertain Ferdinand's visiting brother because of Ferdinand's rigorous schedule. Normally, this might have bothered me but my perspective at that time and throughout life has been to go with the flow and do what needs to be done. This was just another one of those situations. Clem stayed in D.C. for a week, and we spent a great deal of time together. After the initial shock of the visit, we got to know each other better and eventually enjoyed each other's company. We had fun dancing, going out to eat, and spending time with friends from his hometown.

Clem kept asking if I was for real. I didn't understand what he meant at the time but figured it must be a good sign.

He continued to say, "You're such a lovely girl."

Clem would sometimes even ask, "Do you always act like this?"

I thought these were very strange comments. I was being myself and if that impressed him, oh well.

Even at that early stage of our relationship, I appreciated how Ferdinand and I worked well together as a team. I admired how hard-working, goal-oriented, and focused he was. He was extremely thoughtful and caring, too. I also knew he could not make a commitment to me while he was a medical student, and that we would date until he completed school. I was perfectly fine with that. I just figured we'd enjoy each other's company as long as it lasted and once he finished his program, we would go our separate ways. I understood what the rules were based on the advice I had been given about dating African men during my freshman year. I would be a fool to count on anything other than having this wonderful relationship with Ferdinand while he was here.

Why would I set myself up for failure and think we could have some type of future?

Nigerians don't marry Americans.

The fact is this relationship won't last forever.

We'll just enjoy being together as long as we can.

After spending a week with us, Clem decided to visit his college friends in Oregon but promised to come through Washington before returning to Nigeria. When he did return a month later, he made a proposition. Clem invited me to an all-expenses paid trip to Nigeria. He said it would be a vacation. The thought of a vacation in another country certainly appealed to me. It would be my first experience traveling internationally.

"Cynthia, I would like you to come to Nigeria for a vacation," Clem stated with a serious tone.

He continued, "I will pay for your ticket and all of your expenses. The only thing you will need is spending money for gifts and souvenirs."

I couldn't believe what I was hearing. I've never traveled out of the country and this man is offering me a free trip to Nigeria!

The semester was going to end in a few months and, after I had told Ferdinand what his brother said, he encouraged me to take advantage of this opportunity. Clem asked how much money I planned to spend on souvenirs. I was a struggling college student, so I said two-hundred dollars, at the most. In the end, I agreed to give Clem two-hundred dollars before he left.

In return, Clem would convert the two hundred dollars into Nigerian naira and would give it to me upon my arrival in Nigeria. At that time, the dollar was very powerful. I believe the exchange rate was one hundred and five naira to one American dollar. Clem was a businessman and I suspected he could get a better exchange rate in Nigeria than I could in the U.S. or at the government exchange banks in Nigeria, though I didn't know exactly what he planned to do with the money. This arrangement worked out perfectly for me because I would be able to travel to Nigeria with little or no money at all in my pocket. I set a travel date, secured a passport, and took malaria and yellow-fever shots. Within a few months, I was on my way.

Ferdinand and I didn't spend a lot of time discussing the logistics of the trip. He was busy and I was preoccupied with school and preparing for finals. Ferdinand did give me some advice, though:

"Don't do anything you don't feel comfortable doing. There are many cultural differences and I trust your judgment.

"People will complain that you are too skinny and will want to fatten you up. Don't let that happen."

"Stay close to my family, they will take very good care of you."

I clearly wasn't thinking about the enormity of this trip; my mother was in shock, even though she wondered, "How can this girl who is afraid to do anything by herself, suddenly pick up and travel to Nigeria?"

We were all going to find out ....

CHAPTER 8
NIGERIAN WELCOME

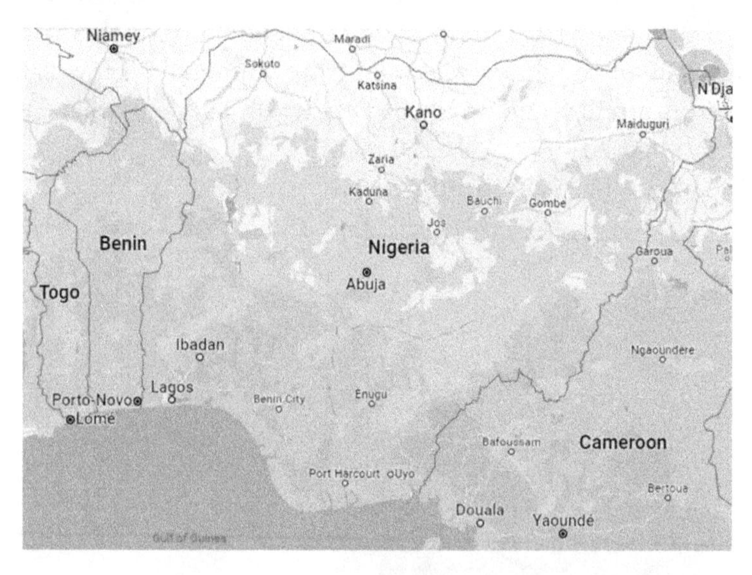

Map of Nigeria
Lagos, where I landed, is in the southwestern corner of the country on the coast.
Enugu, where I spent much of my time, is about 350 miles due east of Lagos.
(Source: Google Maps)

Immediately after deplaning at the chaotic Lagos Airport, I noticed two large signs. American citizens were sent in one direction while Nigerians were sent in another. The only people walking toward the American section were a young newlywed couple and myself. I walked to the podium first and was asked to show my passport. The man at the podium wore a military uniform and quietly asked me to give him one hundred American dollars. I told him I didn't have that kind of money. He looked at me sternly and replied.

"You better find it or I'm going to send you right back on that plane to America."

I tried to explain how I exchanged money with my boyfriend's brother in America and didn't have cash because he was going to reimburse me in Nigeria. I also stated they should have informed American citizens about this requirement beforehand. This guard wasn't having it and did not care about anything I had to say. He nodded his head toward a group of men and within seconds four additional military men with guns and rifles escorted me to a small room that resembled a cell.

Now I was scared. These soldiers meant business and I had no way to get myself out of this situation. I didn't even know what I had done to deserve this, other than being an American. Ferdinand's brother Clem was nowhere to be seen. A million thoughts raced through my head.

Do I even remember what Clem looks like?

I only met him on two occasions

Honestly, all the men dressed in traditional attire are beginning to look alike.

After an already exhausting, difficult day traveling from the U.S., I had no idea what was going to happen next, and I was afraid to find out.

Years later, as I look back on this pivotal event in my life, I can't believe I traveled to Nigeria by myself. What was I thinking? Obviously, I wasn't focused on the importance of this trip or what it might mean to me and my entire future. I was just living in the moment without a care in the world.

Ferdinand wasn't thinking either, because he failed to tell his brother the exact date and time I planned to arrive in Nigeria. Miraculously, Clem called the day before my flight was supposed to land. Ferdinand thought Clem called to confirm my time of arrival. Instead, Clem called simply to chat. He was stunned when he found out I was already en route to Nigeria. According to Ferdinand, Clem screamed, slammed the phone, and quickly made arrangements to board a plane to Lagos, the booming, bustling capital city of Nigeria.

Unfortunately, Clem didn't arrive on time.

Nigeria Airways flew out of Kennedy Airport in New York City. I asked my mother to meet me there, thinking we'd be able to have lunch and spend some quality time together before my flight. I decided to check in early and it's a good thing I did. Even though I was checking in five hours before boarding, I wasn't prepared for the chaos that entangled me at the Nigeria Airways terminal. There had to be at least two hundred people there, all needing attention from the airline's representatives.

Like most Americans, I was accustomed to airlines that had one or two long lines; one person standing behind the other, waiting their turn to check into flights. Instead, I saw hundreds of people. There were men, women, and children sandwiched together in huge crowds. I could barely see the airline attendants quite a distance away. I did notice that everyone was well dressed, displaying designer outfits, tailored suites, and fashionable traditional African attire.

I, on the other hand, was accustomed to traveling in comfort. Once again I stood out, as I wore blue jeans, a simple top, and flats. I couldn't stop staring at all the beautiful women and children. The hairstyles in particular were stunning. There were beautiful braids in different styles, and elaborate head wraps adorned the heads of many women. I also loved seeing the vibrant colors and wide variety of traditional fabrics. I felt as though I were already in the Motherland: Africa. No one was speaking English and the heat was unbearable. As it was, I was just getting a glimpse of what lay ahead.

Being five feet, nine inches tall had its advantages at that moment. I was able to see above the crowd and strategically move in the direction of the attendants. It was so crowded; people were being shoved and pushed in all directions. Each person was trying to get closer to the front, in an attempt to get checked in. The number of suitcases, boxes, and trunks was insurmountable, and I'm pretty sure they outnumbered people five to one.

I assumed people purchased gifts for every member of their family. Later, I discovered it's common for Nigerians to give gifts to family members when they travel abroad. I'm also sure some people purchased large quantities of unique and hard-to-find items to sell for profit. A few people noticed I had only one suitcase and asked if I would check their luggage in with mine, since they wanted to avoid paying extra fees. Ferdinand specifically warned me about this and told me not to do that.

"Cynthia," he cautioned me, "don't offer to help anyone at the airport and do not hold, take, or check-in anyone else's luggage."

Despite Ferdinand's warning, it was difficult saying no because people were very persuasive. In the end, I trusted Ferdinand knew what he was talking about, and I politely declined.

I eventually checked in and was told I had to go through security right away. Even though I was hours early, I didn't realize I had to board so quickly and was disappointed that I didn't get to spend quality time with my mom. Instead, we spent two and a half hours navigating Nigeria Airways. Looking back, I'm surprised my mother wasn't nervous. Clearly, we both trusted that God would look over me. She kissed me good-bye and made me promise to call when I arrived in Nigeria.

The airplane was the biggest aircraft I've ever seen! There were four rows of seats, instead of the typical two rows that I was accustomed to. The journey was long; the flight to Brussels took eight hours and there was a six-hour time difference. After the four-hour layover in Belgium, I proceeded to Nigeria, which took another eight-and-a-half hours. Between the long plane ride and time difference I felt as though I were traveling two consecutive days. Almost everyone on the plane was Nigerian.

I did notice one woman around my age. She appeared to be shy and nervous. The woman was sitting next to a gentleman wearing a dark blue suit. I guessed they were a married couple and this girl, like me, looked like she had never been to Nigeria. I smiled and said "hi" to her, because I couldn't really talk to anyone else on the plane. It was difficult sitting in silence for such a long period time. The young woman barely said a word, however the gentleman next to her announced they had just married, and he was moving to Nigeria with his new wife. That explained the nervousness. As I sat there, I could only imagine what she must have been thinking.

I was relieved when the flight attendant announced forty minutes to arrival in Nigeria. My legs were cramped by that time, and I was tired of sitting in one place. I was also very hungry. Nigerian food was served on the flight and the only thing I ate was chicken, plantain, and rice. While there were other options, I preferred to eat what was familiar to me. I couldn't wait to get off the plane and was excited once we finally landed.

Once the soldiers demanded their 100-dollar bribe and escorted me to a small cell at the airport, I should rightfully have been terrified. I wasn't, however, because I hadn't done anything wrong. The American woman I met on the plane also joined me in the same room a few minutes later. She looked traumatized at this point. The men kept demanding one hundred American dollars; when converted to naira, it was a large sum of money for the men to split. Of course, it was basically another bribe.

Apparently, the newlywed's husband came up with the money because his wife was released thirty minutes later. I continued to explain I only had thirty-five dollars and offered to give it to them. The guard kept yelling and demanding the total amount in cash. I promised that Clem, the person picking me up, would have the money. Every fifteen minutes, they would escort me to the waiting area so I could try to locate Clem, but each time they let me out of the room to look for him, he wasn't there.

Now I was beginning to worry, and Clem was nowhere to be seen.

I didn't realize it at the time, but I had another more pressing problem. Clem didn't have a clue I was arriving in Nigeria. I was wondering whether he forgot, or Ferdinand failed to tell him. Perhaps there was miscommunication between Ferdinand and his brother. The guards were starting to get angry and frustrated. They said they thought I was playing games with them. At this point I was becoming really afraid. I was scared.

I'm in another country.

I'm in a room that resembles a cell.

I'm the only girl in here with four men and four guns.

This is not looking good.

Lagos is the capital of Nigeria. Nigeria's population at that time was seventy-seven million people, and Lagos was a huge city with more than five million people and a chaotic, bustling airport. After Clem's connecting flight, he had to drive a few more hours to get to The National Airport. Ferdinand was extremely nervous; he knew I was an inexperienced traveler and would most likely freak out by what I would be encountering at the airport. More ominously, he knew there was a possibility of danger. And, yes, Ferdinand had every reason to be concerned.

Clem arrived at the airport two hours after my arrival. Once the guards made their demands to him, Clem spent the next two hours asking people if they had American currency; trading Naira (with interest) for dollars until we had a total of one hundred American dollars. The exchange rate for the dollar was high at that time and people were not willing to depart with it unless the rate was better than market value. Finally, the customs guards were satisfied, and I was approved to leave with Clem.

Leaving the airport was a blessing and I was relieved to see daylight. Clem's driver met us in front of the airport and the long and drawn-out journey continued. We drove a few hours to a smaller airport, and boarded the final flight to Ferdinand's hometown of Enugu. Once we landed, I was so happy that we finally made it to our destination, I took a photo to commemorate the occasion.

That was another big mistake. Once again, a group of men dressed in military uniforms surrounded me and wanted to confiscate my camera. I had no idea it was against the law to take photos at an airport. I later learned that airport security is on high alert for suspicious or out-of-the-ordinary behavior. Taking the photo made me stand out, and the fact that I had an American accent didn't help. I was devastated when they took my camera. After an extremely long day and the horrible experience at the Lagos airport, and now this: they've taken my camera. It was the straw that broke the camel's back. I broke down and cried. I couldn't help myself.

How will I be able to document this trip?

Traveling this distance and not being able to take pictures is breaking my heart.

They've taken my camera.

My trip is ruined, and it had hardly started.

Clem tried to his best to reason with the military men. After much arguing, persuading, and finally bribe money, I was able to keep the camera as long as I was willing to relinquish the film. We felt vindicated and couldn't wait to leave the airport.

It was late and I was exhausted by the time we made it to Clem's home. We drove thirty more minutes and it was pitch black outside. There were no sign of lights anywhere. The building we entered resembled a warehouse only because it was such a long building. I was greeted by two youngsters. I later determined they were house helpers. They greeted me, bowed, and called me Aunti; a term used to show respect to elders. They took my suitcase into the house, and I remember walking down an extremely long hallway.

As I got closer to the end of that hallway, the aroma of delicious food encompassed the room to the left. I was introduced to Clem's first wife Oge, and to my surprise, I was also introduced to a priest. I assumed the priest was a close family friend but would later discover the priest was on a mission. There was an assortment of traditional foods laid out. There was fufu, chicken, chin-chin, and my ultimate favorite, plantain. I must say, I was impressed. That was quite the spread, especially considering Clem had no idea I would be arriving that day.

The subject of religion came up right away. After blessing the food. Clem gave a speech about how important religion was to his family. He wanted to know my views on religion. I confidently stated I was a proud Christian and my faith and my belief in God were core values for me. That statement was followed with a speech from the priest talking about the core beliefs of the Catholic church. The priest asked if I would consider converting to Catholicism.

Without hesitation I said, "I would not." I could tell by their reactions they were very disappointed. I also couldn't understand why they looked that way. I could tell Clem was trying to contain himself. When he asked why I wouldn't convert, I simply said. "I am not one to judge, that's God's job."

I also told them I believe in divorce and a woman's right to make decisions regarding her body. Based on what I knew at the time in Nigeria, divorce was almost non-existent. If a man was dissatisfied with his wife, the husband could marry another wife, although he would continue to financially support the first wife. She wouldn't have the option of developing another relationship or remarry. I didn't think that was fair at all. They later asked me to just "say" and "agree" to convert verbally. I clearly told them I couldn't do that. Many thoughts raced through my head.

I wouldn't ask Ferdinand to convert to my religion.

I accepted him the way he was, and I felt confident he accepted me.

I was really surprised at the length Ferdinand's brother went to try to get me to change my religion. It was then that Oge escorted me to my room. I didn't realize how exhausted I was until my head hit the pillow. I slept like a baby and woke up to the sound of roosters crowing, leaves blowing in the wind and the sound of the heaviest rainfall I ever heard.

The rain lasted only fifteen minutes, but it was powerful. Since the roof was made of tin, the heavy rain sounded like hundreds of nickels pounding on the rooftop. Again, the aroma of delicious food flowed beneath my bedroom door. I didn't rush to get up, as I was taking this experience in and honestly didn't know what to do at that point.

I heard adults in the house speaking Igbo, and children running through the hall. Before, I knew it, there was a knock on the door. Another woman opened the door carefully to look in on me. It was Clem's second wife, Uche. I recognized her from the pictures Ferdinand showed me when he returned from his trip to Nigeria.

She asked me to get up because they were expecting a visitor. I got up quickly and went into the dining room. Clem and Uche ate with me during breakfast. It was then I was told that I was going to meet Ferdinand's father. Everything was fine until Clem explained I had to bow when I greeted him.

Bow?

Is he kidding?

Why would I have to bow?

They both laughed.

"Our father is a Chief. Ferdinand comes from royalty. Every time you greet him, you will have to bow. It's a form of respect."

I was shocked and couldn't believe what I was hearing.

Why didn't Ferdinand explain this to me?

This is a big deal!

Ferdinand vaguely mentioned something about his dad being a Chief, but he didn't elaborate or make a big deal of it. It was at that point Clem told me Ferdinand was a Prince.

By this time I was flabbergasted. Ferdinand was very humble, something I always loved and admired about him. He wasn't interested in titles or proving anything to anyone. And while I appreciate that about him, I was still reeling from what I had just learned. This was all so much to take in. My head was spinning.

What do I do now?

I also remember having one other, very specific thought.

Ferdinand should have shared this vital piece of information.

As I would soon learn, the "vacation" was just getting started.

CHAPTER 9
WHEN IN NIGERIA ...

A wonderful Nigerian celebration thrown in honor of my visit. I am in the back on the right in the orange top.

My mind was still reeling.

Ferdinand is a prince? What?!

I also knew the next few moments were very important. Meeting my boyfriend's father for the first time under any circumstances was, of course, both important and nerve-racking. The fact that he was Nigerian royalty upped the ante tremendously. I wanted to make a good impression. If I was in America, I would have known how to behave.

But here, there were so many unknown customs, I didn't know what to do at all, and I for certain didn't want to make any mistakes. The first thing I needed to learn was how to greet Ferdinand's father ("The Chief"). Even for a laid-back person like me, I wanted to make a good impression, and I knew I had to get this very first part right.

Clem saw my discomfort and he taught me how to bow. After practicing a few times, Ferdinand's father was announced. We walked toward the end of a long hallway, and in the parlor stood Ferdinand's dad. I don't remember what he had on, however I do remember he wore a red cap, which I later learned is only worn by chiefs. He was holding an intricately carved wooden staff. I believe he used it as a symbol of position and prestige. Ferdinand's father was very handsome, with his fair skin, light-brown eyes, and white hair. He was shorter than I expected; especially considering Ferdinand was 6'3" tall. He wasn't intimidating at all.

Clem gave me the signal to bow, which I did as he instructed me. I was surprised when I didn't get the response I expected. As I stood in front of him at the conclusion of the bow, Ferdinand's dad laughed at me. Because of his serious demeanor, though, his laugh wasn't obnoxious. His laugh consisted of a full-blown smile accompanied with a raspy "ha, ha, ha." Clem cracked up, too, thinking I was hilarious. I didn't know exactly what I did that was so funny, however, I'm sure I got an "A" for effort and made a good first impression. Ferdinand's dad also had a calm demeanor, which instantly made me feel comfortable and at ease.

Ironically, while I was in the process of writing this book, I watched an interview in which Meghan Markle shared an experience on Oprah Winfrey's special about being asked to curtsy when she met Queen Elizabeth. It was at that moment I understood why Ferdinand's father laughed at me. Clem taught me how to bow like a man. I was supposed to learn how to curtsy like a woman. I would have also laughed if a man walked up to me and curtsied like a woman.

Our meeting didn't last long. I quickly understood Ferdinand's dad was a man of few words. I was surprised to learn he didn't speak English. This was something I didn't factor into the equation when I decided to visit Nigeria. I didn't realize there would be so many communication barriers with him and other members of Ferdinand's family. As I sat in the parlor, Clem spoke to his father in Igbo. Clem later informed me that I was invited to spend a few days at Ferdinand's childhood home in the village. Plans were made for me to visit the very next day.

As I walked toward my room, I noticed Clem's wife Oge preparing lunch in the kitchen. Of course, I offered to help. It was the first time I experienced someone grabbing a living chicken, breaking its neck, boiling it to pluck feathers, and cooking it right before my eyes. I wasn't mentally prepared for that and was proud of myself for not fainting right there on the spot. Instead, I tried to act like it was an everyday occurrence. I was, at that moment, very grateful for my typical shopping experiences at the grocery store back in the United States.

Just about every part of the chicken was prepared, cooked, and consumed. Nothing was discarded. I wasn't accustomed to seeing a person eat the head or the feet of a chicken. Clem laughed as he noticed my discomfort as he ate the chicken's feet, informing me that it's the tastiest part of a chicken. Needless to say, I didn't eat chicken that afternoon. I just couldn't wrap my head around eating something I saw alive just a few hours earlier. I did eat lots of salad, rice, and plantain, as I still had to give myself a little more time to process what I just witnessed.

Later that afternoon, Clem drove me around town to meet family members and friends. I'm not materialistic, but I couldn't help but notice the Mercedes Benzes and BMWs in front of the house. Clem lived in the city and on our excursion to check in on Clem's business ventures, I saw lots of homes, businesses, and children selling pop, fruit, and gift items along the road.

We even stopped to purchase chin-chin. Chin-chin is a tasty biscuit treat, cut into little squares that I learned to really enjoy. Some streets were adorned with hand crafted statues that were for sale. They were stunningly beautiful wood and ebony art pieces representing the sculptured faces of people and life in Africa.

The thing that surprised me most was that no one followed driving protocol. Speed limits, traffic lights, and driving on the right side of the road were ignored by all. Everyone was negligent, it didn't matter what their status was. As Clem drove, I either closed my eyes tightly in fear or kept my eyes wide open in disbelief. This adventure was a frightening and new experience. Clem laughed at me as he zig-zagged through traffic, drove at top speed, and avoided numerous potholes and accidents. As we sped toward our destination, I swore to myself there was no way I was ever going to drive in Nigeria.

I eventually became accustomed to the very haphazard driving and felt more comfortable as time went on. There were also checkpoints along the way in which uniformed officers would ask each driver questions. They would then request bribe money and send drivers on their way. I noticed Clem rarely stopped. He simply zipped right past the officers. He seemed to have a free pass because of the type of car he was driving or some other indication of wealth and status.

It was also interesting to see motorbikes and motorcycles designed for two people transporting three or four people sitting in various configurations so they could all fit. For me, it looked like an accident waiting to happen. Clearly, this was a way of life and it worked for them. The motorists drove seamlessly through the traffic.

Our first stop was Uncle Benjamin's house. If Clem was trying to make a good first impression, he most certainly succeeded. Uncle Benjamin lived in the grandest house I had ever seen. It was impressive on the outside and equally impressive on the inside. There was a huge sunken living room that was elaborately furnished and a dining room that could have been on the cover of an interior design magazine. The dining room was elaborately decorated, and fit for a king.

After sitting down to eat, a house attendant carried a huge bowl full of water so that each one of us could wash our hands before the meal. Another attendant provided hand towels to dry our hands. Fufu and egusi soup was being served – I learned this is the most common staple in Nigeria. Fufu is a dough-like food made from fresh cassava and usually formed into a round ball. Egusi Soup is a kind of soup thickened with ground seeds, okra, palm oil, and other vegetables. Seasoned meat is also included and there are many variations.

I remembered the first time I tasted egusi soup back in Washington. Ferdinand's friend invited us over for dinner. It was the first time I met one of Ferdinand's friends outside of the hospital setting. I remember when Ferdinand found out egusi soup was being served, he was extremely excited. He hadn't tasted it in quite a while and said it reminded him of home. Once I spooned it into my mouth, I realized I couldn't bite into it. I felt like I was chewing it forever; and as much as I tried, I just couldn't bite into it.

I tried to bite it into small pieces but found it was impossible due to its consistency. I was embarrassed whenever someone asked a question, I basically slid the food to the corner of my mouth and provided short responses so no one would notice my struggle. At the end of the evening, I told Ferdinand I had to secretly put a tough portion of the meat into a napkin. Ferdinand laughed at me and confessed egusi soup is not supposed to be chewed. It can only be swallowed.

Can only be swallowed? What type of food is this?

I wish he had told me that beforehand.

I guess he somehow assumed I would have known.

Uncle Benjamin was very kind and down to earth. He spoke English most of the time and that was very welcoming. His wife Josephine was beautiful and sophisticated. She was dressed up from head to toe with fashionable jewelry to match. They had nine children and I clearly saw the love and respect they had for each other even though our interaction was brief.

We then stopped by Ferdinand's oldest brother Godwin's and his wife Grace's home. They also had an impressive house and four beautiful children. The landscape and house design were ultra-modern. The entryway was stunning, with native flowers and greenery in front of the house. I'm sure Americans would be shocked to see the lifestyles of many Nigerians; I clearly was. The wealth that I witnessed in this short span of time is something I haven't seen in America. Grace and Godwin were polite, quiet, and somewhat guarded. Clem had already told me Godwin was quiet by nature. I wasn't sure how they felt about me, though, and I understood if they were suspicious. Thankfully, Clem did most of the talking.

Whenever I'm at a loss for words, talking with any children present is often my default. That day, I ended up communicating with and spending more time with the children than with the adults. That was my comfort zone. As it turned out, everyone in Ferdinand's family was thoughtful, kind, and welcoming. They went out of their way to make me feel at home and I felt honored that they were comfortable enough to introduce me to their family and friends. Importantly, I was able to see first-hand that Ferdinand came from a close-knit family. They worked together as a unit and treated me like a member of their family. I knew I was in good hands, and I was having a wonderful time.

The next morning was a whirlwind! We woke up early, ate breakfast and went out to see as many people as we could before we headed out to the village, Mgbowo. I met many family members and friends as the day went on, and I could tell status was paramount in Nigerian culture. Education, profession, even parents' occupations, meant a great deal. After each introduction, the typical questions that followed were:

"What do you do for a living? "

"What type of degree do you have?"

And "What do your parents do for a living? "

Initially, I was taken aback by the directness and personal nature of the questioning. I eventually realized this was the norm. It was nice connecting faces with names of people Ferdinand told me about and those I heard him talking to over the years during phone calls. It was also nice meeting Ferdinand's brothers and sisters. Each of them identified Ferdinand as the favorite child in the Ukah family. I remember thinking "If that isn't a compliment, I don't know what is."

It was clear everyone adored Ferdinand and listening to stories and experiences people shared about him brought so much joy to my heart. Ferdinand's appreciation of others and his ability to bring joy to our friends is something I already knew; however, it was nice to hear everyone else felt the same way I did. After meeting with many friends and family members, Clem gave me a quick tour of life in the city where I experienced the hustle and bustle of a thriving community.

I met young professional men and women working hard, striving for excellence, and living the life of luxury. While driving I noticed gas stations, car dealerships, and other businesses bearing the L.N. Ukah name, too. After stopping at a restaurant to grab a drink and a quick bite to eat, we were finally on our way to the village. It seemed that everywhere we went, people knew Clem and the Ukah family. Driving to the village was certainly surreal, too. It was way beyond anything I had anticipated. So many thoughts kept running through my head.

I still can't believe I made it to the motherland.

Here I am, Cynthia Payne, from the Queensbridge projects, experiencing life in Africa.

Driving to the village was like an out-of-body experience. I realized this was the place where my ancestors were born and, thanks to Ferdinand, I was having the adventure of a lifetime. I was deeply moved and so grateful for the opportunity to experience all of this. Extreme heat and abundant greenery is also what I experienced as we traveled on an empty road.

As we moved closer toward Mgbowo village, the houses became smaller and smaller. I noticed more children spending time outdoors, where they were working or playing. Animals such as chickens, cows, and goats were visibly fenced in backyards of homes. I could smell a variety of foods women sold at the edge of the road, along with kids flagging cars down to sell cold drinks, fruit, and a variety of treats. There were women selling food and wares from baskets on their heads while at the same time carrying children on their backs.

I was also surprised to see women carrying a table and chair on their heads to set up shop at a nearby road. The sound of children's voices, talking and singing in a variety of dialects, was music to my ears. As we entered a dirt road, I figured we must be getting closer to the village. It was then I saw a wooden sign that read "Mgbowo," and I knew I would soon be there.

There were quite a few people outside the chief's compound when we arrived. When I asked why there were so many cars and people in front of the main house, Clem matter-of-factly stated they were drivers. He explained that each family member had a driver who waited outside in case someone had an errand or appointment.

Wow!

That's all I could think of. Just "Wow."

Before exiting the vehicle, I asked Clem how I should address his parents.

Should I say Mr. and Mrs. Ukah? Chief Ukah and Mrs. Ukah? I didn't have a clue.

He insisted I address them as Mama and Papa. I thought that was strange, but it was easy to say, and I was thankful for his guidance.

The first person I met when we walked into the compound was Mama. She walked up to me, grabbed my two hands and said what sounded like "Welcome, mommy." She had a high-pitched voice and a lovely, warm smile. I understood that words have varied meanings and I focused on her mannerisms. I didn't want to be misunderstood. She stared at me as she held my hand, and she smiled and communicated with Clem in Igbo. I kept hearing the name "Okechukwu" in the conversation and assumed she was clarifying I was Ferdinand's girlfriend.

The first thing she commented on was my weight. Clem laughed as he translated by saying his mother thought I was too skinny. Ferdinand warned me about this, telling me that his family would want to fatten me up. I was tall, thin, with just a hint of hips. In Africa, beauty is often associated with being curvaceous. Curvy and voluptuous women were celebrated. I think bigger woman were more desirable. It was assumed they were healthy and well cared for. Ferdinand specifically told me to ignore such statements, as he felt I was perfectly fine the way I was. Mama also kidded me about my clavicle, stating she could pour water into it.

Ferdinand's mother was beautiful, with dark flawless skin, narrow eyes, and a lovely smile. Tall and endearing, she wore a casual Nigerian outfit. Watching her, I saw where Ferdinand had inherited his humility. She was a prominent woman who obviously felt she didn't have anything to prove. That impressed me a lot.

Mama had a high-pitched voice, too. She was definitely a woman in control. As we walked through the compound, she sounded like a drill sergeant, giving orders to every individual she passed. Mama became my teacher, and every chance she had she taught me something new. She taught me how to wrap traditional fabric around my waist like a skirt. She also taught me how to tie a head wrap. Mama allowed me to help prepare certain dishes and, yes, she taught me how to curtsy properly.

We ate another big meal and that is when I met Ferdinand's younger sister, Beatrice. She was my age and we clicked right away. Beatrice was a very sweet, strong-willed, funny girl with a great personality. I slept in a room across from her and we had so many interesting conversations at night during my visit. She reassured and comforted me, telling me about the personalities of members in the family and teaching me about the family dynamics.

Clem drove me around the village as he showed me the various properties belonging to the family. He also made a point of taking me to see all the land the Ukah family owned. Furthermore, he explained that Ferdinand could choose one of the properties to build a home in the village so that when he marries, his family would have a place to stay.

I felt as though Clem was giving me a glimpse of the type of lifestyle I could have if I was selected to be a member of the Ukah Family. At this point I could tell Clem was thinking about the possibility of marriage between Ferdinand and me. However, I didn't take what he was saying personally because I felt that would be close to impossible. His statement did surprise me because Nigerian family members are usually the first to frown upon or resist this type of union.

Under other circumstances I might have been taken aback but I didn't feel that way at all. I was very comfortable with this thought because this was nothing Ferdinand and I decided or even discussed. I didn't feel like I was committed or had an obligation to consider anything at this point. Since I didn't hear anything about marriage from the horse's (Ferdinand's) mouth, I didn't feel that what Clem was saying applied to me.

Nigerians are proud, distinguished, and confident people. They are goal-oriented and feel comfortable sharing their dreams and aspirations and displaying their accomplishments. It wasn't unusual for Clem to show me or any other visitors his family properties. The Ukah family worked very hard to achieve success, and Clem checked on each property whenever he was in the village. Work was being done on several properties, with each at different stages of construction.

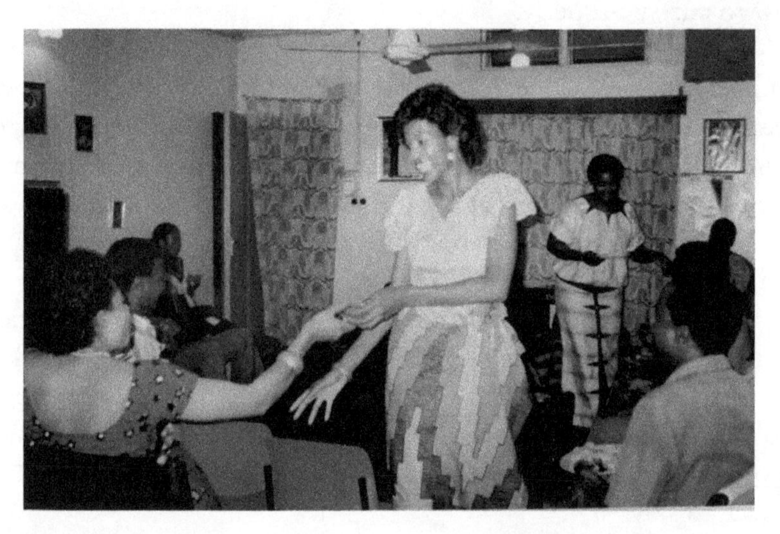

My future sister-in-law Mary hosts a gathering in Nigeria

We also visited Ferdinand's oldest sister Mary, where she lived with her husband, Dr. Orjioke. They also welcomed me with open arms. Mary was stunning and had a beautiful smile. She was also confident, outgoing, and opinionated. Often ending each conversation with a laugh or joke, she made me feel like part of the family. That helped me feel like I was welcomed and belonged.

When I woke up the next morning, I felt extremely blessed. After growing up in New York and living in DC, nothing can compare to waking up and listening to roosters crowing in the morning. I thought that only happened in movies. I also loved waking up to women singing, praying, and talking to neighbors, with the sound of pots and spoons clashing as women prepared food in their common areas outside. I loved listening to children giggle as they walked to the stream to gather water for their families. All of this was such a joyous time for me.

About an hour later, I was told to get dressed because I had visitors. I quickly got up and got ready for the day. I was confused, though. Who would be visiting me? To my surprise, there was a long line of people waiting outside to meet me. I could not believe what I was seeing.

I'm not a celebrity.

Why are so many people standing in line to see me?

I sat in the parlor and one by one people would come in, sit across from me, and hold my hand and smile if they didn't speak English. If they did speak English, they would welcome me and share how they knew Ferdinand or share a special moment or story about Ferdinand. There had to be at least fifty people in line that morning. This wasn't the end, though. The greeting line continued for two more days.

When I did venture outside the compound, people would call me "Onyocha." They would just point and call me by that name. When I asked about the meaning of "Onyocha," I was told it simply meant "white woman." Most people in the village had never seen an American. Onyocha was the term they used to describe a foreigner or American. The people in the village were curious and just wanted to see me – that's why they had all lined up for three days.

Once the visitors all left, I sat with Papa for breakfast. He was the only one in the dining room at the time. Since we couldn't really communicate, we just smiled, stared at each other, and attempted to have conversations by pointing and using hand gestures. Whenever he did have a question, he would signal for a house helper to interpret for him. He used an interpreter to ask me some very direct questions.

"Why don't you want to become Catholic?"

"Why are you so simple?"

At this point, I had long since gotten over being taken aback by questions that would have been seen as very personal or even offensive in America. I explained my reasons for not becoming Catholic and didn't understand what Papa meant by the term "simple," so I asked Clem to come in and clarify.

"Papa thinks you look like a poor African and we look like rich Americans. You wear jeans every day, and you don't dress up at all. Why is that?"

I told him I was a college student and there was no need to dress up where I come from. I explained that most Americans dress casually unless there is a special occasion. Wearing casual clothing was comfortable for me and I was perfectly happy wearing jeans. Later that day, Oge arrived with a tailor to take my measurements. I'm accustomed to walking into stores and selecting clothes on display. That day, the seamstress measured every part of my body before we ventured out. I was really impressed.

We then went directly to the market to select and purchase fabric. Oge located her designer and explained in detail exactly what type of outfits she should make for me. Within two days I had an entirely new wardrobe. I couldn't believe it. Everything was tailor made, and each outfit was stylish and beautiful. Oge had the seamstress make traditional outfits and professional attire I could wear for special occasions back home. I ended up with ten stunning outfits and I was extremely appreciative. Even so, it caused me to think.

I guess my attire isn't appropriate or fancy enough for Ferdinand's family. They must think I'm an embarrassment.

If that was true, though, it didn't bother me in the least. There were important events coming up and the Ukah family wanted to make sure I fit in and was properly presented as Ferdinand's girlfriend and as an important member of their community. When in Rome ....

I was having the adventure of my lifetime, full of the most incredible sights and sounds and exotic foods. I was being attended to and pampered like I had never been before. Most important of all, I was meeting the most wonderful, enjoyable, and loving people. I decided to embrace the situation and as has always been my philosophy, to go wherever this adventure takes me.

I also knew there was so much more to come. Far more than I could imagine.

CHAPTER 10
PAPA ARRIVES IN AMERICA

Papa and me before traveling to America.
From Left: my future sister-in-law Oge, Papa, me,
our very close family friend Julie Azionu,
and Ferdinand's sister Beatrice.

Wait a second. What's going on now?

I had been on my Nigerian vacation with Ferdinand's family for several weeks and it wouldn't be long before I was heading back to

America. I loved the adventure I was having in this foreign and exotic place, and Ferdinand's family could not have been nicer. Despite language barriers and cultural differences, I was sorry to leave what I would easily describe as the "experience of my lifetime."

Yet, at the same time, I was anxious to get home. I missed Ferdinand and couldn't wait to see him. As the time to depart got closer, I wanted to savor every moment. My trip to Nigeria was full of new experiences and fascinating surprises. Each day presented a unique situation that was totally out of my realm; Ferdinand's family always had exciting adventures in store. This time it was something I absolutely wouldn't have expected. And when it happened, I knew it was time for me to "roll with the punches" one more time.

Staying with Ferdinand's father (known to us as "Papa") at his royal residence was extremely fascinating and enjoyable. It was an entirely different world from what I had been used to, and I was amazed at all the wonderful new experiences I was having. Not everything went smoothly, though.

Whenever Papa needed something or had a question to ask, he would ask someone in the house to "fetch" me. I heard the word fetch quite often in Nigeria. It was used the same way I used the word "get" when I wanted something. Hearing "fetch" reminded me of a time early on in our relationship when Ferdinand asked me to fetch his shoes. Growing up, I associated the word fetch with a dog fetching a ball or newspaper. I almost lost it and was highly offended when he asked me to fetch his shoes.

Does he think I'm some type of dog?

Who does he think he is?

I expressed my concern to Ferdinand and made it clear that using that term was inappropriate. With his typical calm demeanor, coupled with the fact that Ferdinand didn't believe in wasting time debating or arguing, he apologized even though he didn't see anything wrong with saying "fetch." Ferdinand was a great listener and an even better problem solver. Out of respect for me he made a commitment not to use the word "fetch." That meant a lot because every relationship requires a little give and a little take. It was clear that Ferdinand understood me and valued my feelings and what I had to say.

I appreciated that Ferdinand didn't mind making adjustments for me. It's the little things that often count the most in relationships. Communication, acceptance, and forgiveness are key. This is especially true when dating someone from a different culture. The same words can frequently have much different meanings and can easily lead to unnecessary misunderstandings. I learned a lot about Ferdinand and his culture during my visit to Nigeria and, as a result, my love and appreciation for him grew even more.

I ate breakfast with Papa most mornings. He was an early riser like me, and we woke up before everyone else. Although we didn't communicate efficiently all the time, we certainly tried. Each day I noticed Papa feeling a little more comfortable attempting light conversation. Instead of simply smiling and staring at each other in between bites, we transitioned to pointing at objects with our fingers and using simple hand gestures to get our point across.

I remember one interaction I had with Papa regarding children. I was getting ready to leave the kitchen area when he asked me to sit down, which I did. He put one hand up and said "Okechukwu" (which is Ferdinand's traditional name), then put the other hand up and said, "Cynthia." Next, he clapped both hands together and said what sounded like "picking."

Picking?

What does picking mean?

Papa repeated the hand motion several times, which didn't really clear things up. It took a while for me to figure out what he was trying to say. I eventually realized that "picking" was Papa's way of saying "children." He was trying to describe Ferdinand and me having children. He also said the words "afraid" and "no see picking." It was then I finally understood what he was trying to say — he was afraid he wouldn't see Ferdinand's children if we had kids, because we lived far away in America.

This was something I never considered before that. I saw Papa's gesture as more of a hypothetical question than anything else. Marriage wasn't something Ferdinand and I thought about or had discussed. This question, coming from Papa, deserved a response from me, though. I used an interpreter as I explained.

"I don't think marriage is on Ferdinand's mind. However, if I did marry someone from another country, I would definitely embrace both cultures."

I also affirmed my children would visit long distance family members during holidays and summer vacations. I knew Papa was satisfied with my response because he patted me on the back and left the room with a huge smile on his face.

Papa seems to understand everything I'm saying, I remember thinking. *Wow, that's interesting.*

I often joined Papa in the parlor during the evening around 5:30. He stayed in his room at the royal palace most of the time and basically made appearances for breakfast, lunch, and dinner. During the evening, like clockwork, he would enter the parlor to watch his favorite American shows on TV. I joined him because I enjoyed watching the sheer joy, fascination, and glisten in his eyes as he took in the sights, sounds, and adventures of the big city on the television screen.

I soon became aware that Papa had a lifelong dream of someday traveling to America. He was most vocal during the time he was in the parlor watching television. He would often speak out in one-word phrases. For example, he would watch a show and say things like "America, kill" or "lights" and point at me as I sat across from him. He would then wait for my response. I tried to explain that people in the show weren't real. I also pointed out that killers on show were not real murderers, they were just actors. He loved looking at the lights from high-rises, bridges, and marquees. Papa was especially fascinated with the New York City scenes.

Unbeknownst to me, a family meeting had been held to discuss Papa's desire to visit the United States. Clem thought my journey back home would be the perfect opportunity for Papa to visit America. They determined I would be able to accompany Papa, and this would allow him to visit for an extended period of time. In addition, they saw that Papa would get a well-deserved vacation. Most importantly, though, he would be able to spend time with Ferdinand.

I remember Clem joining me in the parlor and casually telling me Papa wanted to travel with me on my return to America. He explained Papa was getting older and this would probably be the only time he would be able to take advantage of this opportunity. I had already established a great relationship with Papa and would do anything to make him happy. I also witnessed first-hand how close-knit Ferdinand's family was and how they collaborated as a group to make family decisions. No decision was made lightly and if Ferdinand's family trusted me to take Papa on this journey, I felt honored to do it.

Ferdinand spent years away from his family in his quest to become a doctor and he worked tirelessly to achieve his goal. I'm sure there were times he felt lonely and missed his family tremendously. Clem was right, his father was getting old, and this might be Ferdinand's only chance since his childhood to show his appreciation, share his lifestyle with his father, and bond with his dad for an extended period of time. Ferdinand made so many sacrifices and I knew that spending time with his dad would be a wonderful gift. Once Clem confirmed the entire family was on board and approved Papa's trip to the United States, the family started making travel plans

I wasn't aware of everything that was happening behind the scenes, either. Because Papa was the chief, people in Mgbowo did not want him to leave. Not only that, Papa also had to temporarily remove himself as ruler of Mgbowo and select someone to take his place during his absence. This was not a simple decision and needed to be handled sensitively. Papa planned to be gone for a month. Since there was a lot of resistance, there was a lot of convincing and planning to be done. I wasn't privy to the details, but I suspect finding someone to take Papa's place for a month caused some discord.

The first order of business was to get a visa from the American Embassy in the capital city of Lagos. We traveled the very next day on the long journey. Clem dropped us off outside the American Embassy as we joined the long line of what seemed like over more than 100 people. I couldn't believe the number of people that wanted to travel abroad. We stood in line for three and a half hours in extreme heat, with sweat constantly dripping down our faces. The worst part for me was not being able to talk to anyone to help pass the time. Papa and I resorted to looking at each other periodically and smiling as usual.

Thank goodness Lagos was a very busy city with a lot going on. In many ways Lagos reminded me of 42nd Street in New York City. I entertained myself by observing people wearing a myriad of fashionable Nigerian clothing. I was intrigued by the heavy traffic, traffic jams and minor accidents that occurred left and right in front of me. I observed women and children carrying baskets in their hands or balancing them on their heads with little or no effort. Once again, I loved smelling the aroma of a wide variety of African foods. I also admired the outdoor markets and marveled at the goods men and women were selling.

As the line moved closer to the front of the Embassy, my heart broke because I saw so many people leaving the building in tears, looking helpless, overwhelmed, and defeated. Many of them were denied visas and it was sad to see their reactions. I have to admit after watching this I was worried about Papa's chances of getting a visa. However, Clem reassured me that Papa had a very good chance of getting a visa because of his age and status in Nigeria.

Getting an approved visa to travel could be very difficult. There was a fear on the part of the Nigerian government that its citizens traveling abroad would likely not return to Nigeria once their foreign travel was complete. This has always been a big concern based on years of experience. After all, Nigeria had only been independent since 1960 and it was still very much a developing country. There were many places in the outside world that offered opportunities far beyond what was available to many Nigerians.

In Papa's case, though, he was a chief who relinquished his title for a specific amount of time to conduct this travel. Because of these circumstances, his return was pretty much guaranteed. Papa's entire life revolved around his community in Nigeria and there was no reason for him to leave other than to go visit his son in the U.S.

Once we finally made it inside the building, we were given a number and sat for an additional two hours. I was bored out of my mind. Then, out of nowhere, Papa looked at me and asked, "Where is the bathroom?"

I couldn't believe the words that came out of his mouth.

Is Papa really speaking English in a full sentence?

Startled, I replied, "Excuse me … What did you say?"

Papa calmly repeated, "Where is the bathroom?"

Flabbergasted, I stood up, and looked right at him.

"Do you really know how to speak English?!" I pointedly asked. "Do you mean to tell me, I just spent six and a half hours standing in line with you, totally bored out of my mind, keeping my mouth shut because I didn't think you spoke English?!"

He laughed at me with his typical ha-ha-ha. He then got up and left for the bathroom. From that point on, after he returned, we communicated flawlessly. Papa did get a visa and when I shared my experience with Clem regarding our lack of communication, Clem explained his father was afraid to speak English because he lacked practice using the English language. He wasn't sure I would understand him. Once Papa got to know me and felt comfortable being around me, he felt confident talking with me.

A week before my journey home and Papa's upcoming trip, I had opportunities to attend church services, community events, and weddings in Nigeria. Nigerian couples typically have two weddings. The first is cultural and incorporates most of the traditional Nigerian customs. The second is usually a religious ceremony. The ceremonies can be days or weeks apart. Traditional ceremonies take place outdoors and are typically open to the public. Everyone is welcomed and it seemed as though there was a wedding celebration taking place every weekend. The first thing I noticed when I attended church was that men sat on one side of the church and women sat on the other side. During my entire trip, I rarely saw men and women walking or congregating together. People either walked in alone or in separate groups of men or women. I didn't see children walking around with their parents, sitting with them, or playing with them, either. I am accustomed to seeing parents with their children in all settings. Especially walking in neighborhoods, shopping, and at family gatherings. This lack of family togetherness was very surprising to see.

It was the result of children from wealthy families being attended to or cared for by house helpers, servants, or extended family members. I also noticed couples didn't hold hands or show public displays of affection. I couldn't tell who was married to whom unless the couple wore matching attire. More than that, I couldn't imagine going to church or a large gathering with Ferdinand and not being able to sit with him or hold his hand. There is another major cultural difference I wish I was aware of prior to my visit, too. I didn't realize it was considered disrespectful to shake hands with your left hand. While attending one community event in particular, a few elders gave me a hard time because I would shake hands with my left hand. These men would get upset and say, "I won't accept your gesture unless you shake with your right hand."

I couldn't understand why it was such a big deal, especially after I explained that I was left-handed and was proud that I was born that way. I apologized but insisted I wouldn't change any part of me. I politely declined to make the accommodation, remembering Ferdinand's words: "Don't do anything you don't feel comfortable doing. I trust your judgment."

I later learned that in many cultures the left hand is seen as unclean, usually because the left hand is often associated with the process of self-care. Now I understand why offering my left hand was considered rude and disrespectful. If I knew then what I know now, I would have made it a point to shake with my right hand. I just wish I had been given more of an introduction to the basics of Nigerian customs and traditions prior to my visit.

I believe this important cultural tradition never came up because we attended Nigerian events with our peers in the United States. I didn't have an opportunity to shake hands with Nigerian elders at formal events and the situation never presented itself. Despite this one significant oversight in my cultural education, I'm grateful for all the preparation I did have before I left the United States. Without it, I would have been completely lost. I'm particularly thankful Ferdinand integrated me into the Nigerian community from the onset of our relationship. I used each cultural experience with our wonderful Nigerian community back home as my guide as I navigated life in Nigeria.

I was nearing the end of my journey when I was introduced to the rest of Ferdinand's family members. I briefly met Ferdinand's sister Patricia and brother Christopher, though we didn't talk too much. I didn't have a chance to see Ferdinand's younger brother Basil, who lived in London at the time. Basil called Ferdinand frequently throughout the years and I felt I knew him well. The one exception to these final introductions was Ferdinand's younger brother Vincent. I didn't have an opportunity to meet him during my visit.

Finally, the day came, and Papa and I boarded a flight to the United States without any hiccups. It was an entirely different story on the arrival end of the flight. Everything was new and exciting for Papa. Watching Papa experience America for the first time is a memory I will always have etched in my mind. Papa was impressed from the moment he landed at JFK. The first thing he noticed was the infrastructure at Kennedy Airport. He was impressed with the huge airport surrounded by windows with high ceilings. He couldn't believe the indoor shops, stores, and restaurants. He kept stopping among the crowd to look around in amazement. People continually bumped into him as they hurried to get to wherever they were headed. As a result, Papa had difficulty keeping up with the walking flow of the airport traffic.

The population stunned Papa, too, since diversity was something he had never experienced. This was the first time he saw so many people of different races, colors, and hues. He often stopped to point and stare each time he saw someone that looked different. He wondered why there are so many "Onyochas" (foreign people). I'm sure he could have counted the number of white people he saw in his lifetime prior to this trip on one hand. He would also wonder, "Why are people naked?" He was referring to scantily clad men and women wearing shorts, tube tops, and very short dresses.

Papa was also fascinated by the elevators and escalators at the airport. We stood and watched people go up and down the escalator for a little more than thirty minutes. He tried to time each movement until he was ready to go down the escalator himself. The look on Papa's face when we walked through the airport was one of amazement and wonder. He had the same expression I saw when he was watching American television back home in the village.

All the while, he kept chanting, "I'm in the U.S.! I'm in the U.S.!"

He was displaying the biggest smile I have seen. "I am in America! Ha, ha, ha!"

I LOVED his laugh. He couldn't believe what he was seeing. Of course, it was at that moment I realized how much I took for granted living in America. Life is so easy and convenient here.

Papa was shocked every time he saw a man holding a woman's hand, couples touching each other, hugging, or kissing. He would ask "Why are men handling women that way?"

He stared at the families, with moms and dads traveling throughout the airport. At times, his behavior made people feel uncomfortable. I sometimes had to explain to strangers that this was Papa's first experience in America, and he was staring because everything was so very new and unfamiliar. I emphasized he was just very curious. It was so much fun sharing these experiences with him, watching him marvel at all the new and unexpected sights.

Papa also wanted to meet my parents. Because we landed in New York, I asked my mother and father to briefly meet us at the airport. I didn't understand why he wanted to meet my parents. By the same token, I didn't think it would be a big deal. This meeting also gave me an opportunity to see my parents before going back to DC.

I forewarned my parents about the language barrier and asked them to speak slowly. When they met, I tried to interpret as best as I could. At one point, Ferdinand's dad wanted to talk to my father alone. They both walked to the opposite end of the seating area, and I was somewhat confused.

What could they possibly be talking about?

After a while, I was starting to feel a little unsettled. I intentionally hadn't told my father or my mother that Ferdinand's dad was a chief and a very wealthy businessman. After talking what seemed like only five minutes, my dad rushed back to me with a huge smile on his face. He was unable to control himself or his movements. Instead of standing still, his feet resembled a slight jogging motion. His hands were moving up and down with his palms up. Dad was stuttering as he tried to get his words out.

"Cynthia, Ferdinand's father just asked me how much money I wanted for you!" Dad was really excited.

"He asked you what?!" I responded in shock.

"Ferdinand's father told me if you agree to marry Ferdinand, he will give me money for you."

Marriage was the furthest thing from my mind. I wasn't thinking about marriage in any way, shape, or form. I had been with Ferdinand for almost four years, and I was totally aware of the unwritten rule I learned as a freshman at Howard: "Africans marry Africans and most African families wouldn't accept an American."

I also was beginning to realize that the difference here was that Ferdinand's family appeared to support the idea of a marriage between Ferdinand and me.

My father asked me how much he should request. Ferdinand's dad had assured him he was fully prepared to pay "any amount of money." In Nigeria, this payment to the bride's family is known as a dowry. Based on my father's reaction, you would have thought my dad just won the lottery. My response was quick and definite.

"Ask for a penny, Dad."

"But Cynthia, I can ask for any amount I want!"

My father was shocked. He couldn't believe what I just said. My father wasn't happy at all, and I could see the disappointment in his eyes. Papa later shared he never understood why we didn't take advantage of that opportunity. Papa was willing, ready, and able to pay a high price for a bride for his son Ferdinand. I suggested a penny because I thought it would be an insult not to accept anything at all. Even though my father didn't understand my rationale, in the end, he respected my wishes. He asked Papa for a penny and the transaction was settled. After we left the airport and drove to Maryland, the adventures were just beginning. Papa would find more and more to be delighted by and amused with on his whirlwind trip to America.

Chapter 11
THE ENGAGEMENT … OR NOT

Relaxing with Ferdinand at his apartment in D.C in 1986

"Do you want to get married?"

A week after Papa's departure, while sitting at the dining room table in our typical late-night fashion, Ferdinand casually asked if I wanted to get engaged. We were both exhausted at the time and I matter-of-factly said "yes." That was the end of the conversation; at least until his study partner Michael arrived at our home a few days later. Although there were no romantic pronouncements, elaborate planning, or a toast among friends and loved ones to celebrate our next chapter, it didn't bother me in the least. I already had two friends who had huge engagement celebrations and I didn't admire either one of their relationships. I certainly didn't want to be in their shoes.

One friend was engaged to an older man, simply because he was well established and could wine and dine her. She boasted a huge diamond engagement ring that she flaunted in front of her family and friends. I knew deep down inside their relationship was more of a business arrangement than anything else. It clearly wasn't based on love. Another friend had an elaborate surprise engagement party with all the bells and whistles. Within days of the party that relationship disintegrated and was followed-up by dishonesty and infidelity. It was easy to see that all that glitters isn't gold.

Prior to meeting Ferdinand, I concluded that marriage wouldn't be in my future. This perspective was another factor that influenced my decision to go to college. Growing up, I didn't see marriages I wanted to emulate. Not that I saw them as bad per se. I just didn't observe men treating women the way I felt I would want to be treated. Even though I was young, I was a keen observer. I paid close attention to the way couples treated each another.

I also listened in on my mother's telephone conversations when family members and friends called to complain about issues and problems in their relationships. I decided early on that I would be much better off by myself as opposed to having a husband adding stress to my life. I saw that going to college would give me an opportunity to be financially independent. This independence would also enable me to someday have a test-tube baby, which was a new phenomenon at the time.

With Ferdinand, things changed dramatically. I was able to put things in perspective and focus on the foundation we already built. I didn't need an impressive formal event for Ferdinand to prove his love for me. He demonstrated his love on a daily basis and I wouldn't have traded it for the world. I've always appreciated simple, genuine, practical ways of doing things. I knew without a doubt that Ferdinand would be an amazing husband and father. He was already my best friend, and I was thrilled and honored that he wanted to marry me. I felt it was a match made in heaven.

I prepared a meal for Michael and Ferdinand near the end of their study session; after serving them, I asked Ferdinand if he shared the BIG news with Michael.

"What big news?" Ferdinand replied.

"You know, the news we discussed a few nights ago." I responded, with some question in my voice. How could he forget this?

"We don't have any big news, Cynthia."

"Ferdinand, you asked me to marry you!" I was now feeling a bit shocked.

"I didn't say that," Ferdinand responded.

Here we go again, I thought, as I rolled my eyes while rolling my head from side to side. *Another language issue.* I handed Ferdinand his trusted Webster's Dictionary and asked him to look up the word "engagement." I frequently had to rely on his dictionary for clarification. I asked Ferdinand if he knew what the word engaged meant. He looked at me and seemed perplexed.

It's a good thing I'm confident and have great self-esteem because his initial response could have cut like a knife if I felt he didn't want to marry me or if he didn't understand what he was implying when he asked me to get engaged. Once Ferdinand read "a formal agreement to get married," he laughed and happily shared our big news with Michael. Perhaps he was nervous, tired, or maybe there even was a true language barrier when we had the engagement conversation days before. I learned not to sweat the small stuff because things eventually work out. They certainly do for me.

Later that evening, Ferdinand told me about the conversation he had with his father concerning our relationship and how he was advised to marry me or let me go. It's a standing joke for me and whenever people ask about our relationship, I usually respond by saying "Ferdinand only married me because his father made him do it." I knew Ferdinand loved me and I loved him as well. Culturally, he knew he couldn't marry me without his family's blessing.

Ferdinand gave me full control of wedding planning. He wanted to be responsible for his tuxedo and the groomsmen's attire. Ferdinand was particular about the music that would be playing at our reception, so he also wanted to make sure we had an amazing DJ. Beyond that, it was all up to me, and I was happy with that.

One of the constants during our courtship and marriage was that Ferdinand had a lot of friends. Throughout our years together he would have hour-long conversations with at least one friend every other week to catch up on everything that was happening in their lives. He frequently talked to Iloba, a very good college friend who still lives in Portland. Iloba visited us a few times before and after our wedding and he instantly felt like family to me. He still does.

Ferdinand also had three godchildren at that time. To be named as a child's godfather is a huge honor in the Nigerian community. It is no surprise Ferdinand was chosen for this coveted and influential role numerous times in his life. Ferdinand interacted with every child he saw. Everyone knew Ferdinand loved children and would be a great role model and support system for their children.

After looking at our calendars and busy schedules; we came up with a wedding date that was a year away. We finally decided on August 8, 1987. Once the date was selected, I slowly but surely started to make plans. I purchased the book "How to Plan the Perfect Wedding in a Year," and clipped out photos of various wedding gowns from bridal magazines. Although my family didn't have a lot of money to pay for an elaborate wedding, my mother reassured me I would have a lovely wedding I would enjoy and be proud of.

I also had to decide who I wanted to be in our wedding party. I asked my best friend Monique to be my maid of honor. She was my brother's first serious girlfriend and spent a lot of time at our house in Queensbridge. We got to know each other very well and when she broke up with my brother, we became the best of friends. Years later, I was the bridesmaid in her wedding as well. Monique was very stylish, which was a major benefit since I disliked shopping. I made it a point to invite her to go wedding-dress shopping with my mother and me.

The end result was that I tried on one dress, I liked it, and my mom purchased it. Mom was disappointed because she wanted the total mother-of-the bride experience. Trying on one dress and being done was definitely not that. Mom expected I would try on many dresses, so she could "ooh" and "aww" as I showed them to her. Unfortunately, I wasn't interested in trying on a bunch of different dresses. The first dress I chose looked good to me, and that was that. Mom never quite got over this, as she would continue to say "you're no fun" throughout the wedding planning experience.

Monique took the lead on selecting the bridesmaids' dresses, and I was pleased with her choice. She decided on lavender strapless gowns with detachable sashes. I loved that the sash was versatile and could be worn in many ways. The dresses were so sophisticated looking and gave each bridesmaid an opportunity to make each dress look unique based on how they wore the sash.

Ferdinand, also known as "Dapper Dan," went to the tuxedo shop and selected the shiniest dark gray suit he could find. I was surprised because I assumed he would have selected a typical black tuxedo. He picked it because he loved the way the tux shimmered and shined. I must admit, he looked great, and the tuxedos complemented the lavender bridesmaid dresses nicely.

Although Ferdinand was hands-off as far as the wedding planning was concerned, he was all-hands-on-deck when it came to outlining plans and expectations for our newly developing family. When I met Ferdinand, he made it very clear that he wanted a lot of children. He originally told me he wanted nine, which seemed a bit excessive. Once he realized how expensive raising children would be, that number decreased each year. Even though I love kids and was up for the challenge, I was a bit relieved when the number went down.

We also had extensive conversations about raising Black kids in America. We knew life would likely be difficult because we faced many cultural challenges. Ferdinand and I were committed to do everything in our power to make sure we raised kind, intelligent, self-confident human beings who were steeped in the Christian faith. Having been raised in two completely different cultures, we had many thought-provoking conversations and debates regarding religion, race, education, and child rearing. We built on our different cultural perspectives, rather than pushing against each other.

God and religion were at the very top of Ferdinand's list of priorities. Prayer and our belief in God were central to our relationship, and we wanted our children to be raised in that environment. It was such a blessing to learn early on that this central belief in our faith was a beautiful reflection of who we are. We both realized we are blessed in so many ways and we thanked God for our blessings and relied on God for strength during those times we faced challenges.

Yet, when it came to which specific religion would be the central focus of our children's upbringing, we had to come to an agreement. Ferdinand was adamant about raising his children to be Catholics. Although I expressed reservations with this approach, as I first did in Nigeria, I also shared that I had difficulty with the repetition and routine of Catholic Mass.

I was accustomed to attending church services that included worship singing, and active participation from the congregants. I also enjoyed reading, listening, and breaking down Bible verses to help me to understand their true meaning. I looked forward to sermons because I learned valuable lessons that reinforced the importance of putting God first. I explained that I attended church because I wanted to be a good steward and I needed accountability. In the end, Ferdinand and I compromised. We agreed I would take our children to Catholic church if he accompanied me. I also insisted that we attend church services as a family.

Once we agreed on our approach, I needed to become comfortable with what I was being asked to do. I wouldn't be true to myself, and I would feel like a hypocrite, if I took my children to a church service I didn't truly support. Prior to getting married in a Catholic ceremony, I was required to go to marriage counseling. The priest who advised us informed me that I had to raise my children as Catholics, even though I was in a different Christian denomination. I emphasized I would honor that as long as Ferdinand accompanied me to church services. For me, our mutual belief in God was the most important piece of the equation. Since Ferdinand and I were on the same page, where we specifically worshipped wasn't an issue. Ferdinand tried to attend church services with me before we got married but that was short-lived due to his grueling schedule

Ferdinand also wanted his children to speak Igbo along with English. He tried to teach me Igbo and purchased many Igbo beginner books for me to study. The problem I had was with dialect and pronunciations. I learned the vocabulary, but when I tried to speak Igbo with our Nigerian friends and Ferdinand's family, they didn't understand a word I said. Speaking Igbo with my New York accent is nearly incomprehensible. This experience was often discouraging for me. The main benefit I derived from this whole exercise was that I could understand Igbo much better than I could ever speak it. Ferdinand also wanted our children to spend every summer in Nigeria without me. He wanted me to stay with him, while the children spent those months in Nigeria with his family.

He wanted them to become immersed in the Nigerian culture. We had many conversations about this one specific request because we both knew I would be a very protective parent. I didn't want my mother in New York to keep my children over an extended period, unless there was an extreme emergency. This is completely apart from allowing my children to travel to Nigeria alone for an entire summer. Again, we had some very interesting, lengthy conversations.

Ferdinand also talked about the importance of education and how he expected our children to go to college. He wanted our children to become doctors or lawyers, which is a common theme in many Nigerian communities. I also wanted my children to go to college, but differed as to what they should study because I don't think parents should dictate what their children should do as a profession.

I also knew that my focus on studying education and becoming a teacher would make me a better parent. I saw I was being exposed to the latest research regarding best teaching practices, as well as learning the latest educational teaching techniques and strategies. In this way I felt I wouldn't have to completely rely on teachers to educate my children, and that I would be able to have more of a direct influence on their education myself.

Raising our Black children in a discriminatory environment came up multiple times. Racism is continually present in the United States. It's something Black families deal with on a daily basis. Ferdinand was often close to tears thinking about the pain and discrimination his children would more than likely have to face growing up here.

We both wanted children, and we knew we had to be fully present, readily available, transparent with our values and beliefs, and ready to advocate for them at a moment's notice. We also felt it was such a shame we had to have so many conversations regarding race and the children we didn't yet have just to be ready for their arrival. Yet, I came to treasure those conversations we had as much as anything we ever discussed. It was because of these deeply meaningful and heartfelt talks we had prior to having kids that I had the blueprint I needed to navigate life without Ferdinand at the time of his untimely death.

As we prepared for my wedding, my mother and I attended numerous wedding shows until we found a good deal for my wedding reception at a nice hotel. We had a package deal that included meals, drinks, table settings, and waiters – everything we needed for the big event. I am also very grateful to my very successful and generous brother, who contributed financially and helped to make my wedding day a huge success. The wedding invitations were mailed, and we received responses from relatives and friends from Nigeria to London and throughout the United States. We were excited that Ferdinand's mother was going to be in attendance, as well as the members of the Nigerian Consulate in Washington.

We found little cottages for our out-of-town guests to stay at, which was perfect so we could all be in close proximity to one another. Ferdinand secured an amazing DJ; that was essential since Ferdinand and I loved to dance.

The final thing on our to do list was very unconventional for an American wedding and at first I wasn't really sure how we were going to do this or if I even wanted to do it. We needed to kill a goat or cow to feast upon, which is customary for Nigerian weddings.

Ferdinand was actually excited about this because he was training to become a surgeon. He saw that he would be able to practice his newly learned skills for this uniquely Nigerian tradition.

I, on the other hand, wondered how my American family and friends used to living in urban New York City and Washington would take to this. I remembered all too clearly the whole live chicken experience I had in Nigeria, and I didn't want something like that to be on everyone's mind as they were looking at their dinner at the reception.

CHAPTER 12

OUR NIGERIAN WEDDING IN AMERICA

Wedding day (August 8, 1987) with my parents, Ferdinand's mother and brother Clement

Why does Ferdinand want to kill a goat?

Ferdinand seemed just as excited about the thought of killing a goat as he was about getting married to me. Whenever Ferdinand had conversations regarding our wedding plans, he beamed with excitement every time he mentioned the goat he was going to slaughter and serve at our wedding reception. Initially, I thought he was kidding. I later found out his excitement was very genuine. While I was quite aware of the cultural differences between us and I almost always supported his interests, I wasn't sure how to react to this rather strange focus. So many questions crossed my mind.

Where on earth would Ferdinand find a goat to slaughter?

Is that legal?

I can understand killing a goat in Nigeria, but here in Maryland? That would be close to impossible, wouldn't it?

I understood that marriage in Igboland was between families. When I agreed to marry Ferdinand, I knew I was essentially making a commitment to marry his family as well. This meant they would have an open invitation to our home and could show up unannounced and stay for extended periods of time. Ferdinand and I worked collectively as a team. We also knew if there was a concern or need, his entire family would chip in to help. Family meetings continued long distance and I didn't question any decision Ferdinand made regarding his family. My experience traveling to Nigeria helped me understand how his family decisions were made, and I respected that.

It was during this time I learned the sharing of goat meat in Nigeria is used to symbolize unity. According to my brother-in-law Clem, "Goat killing is associated with the mark of a sumptuous banquet in an African setting. It is the essence of a successful and colorful celebration. It is just like turkey is used in some celebrations in the western world. "

Ferdinand was excited because it was a huge honor to serve goat meat at our wedding reception. Not only that, but he would be able to demonstrate his newly developed surgical skill by cutting the goat meat properly for this special occasion. He was also excited to be able to practice his surgical technique without having a senior doctor looking over him or critiquing his every move. He had complete autonomy.

Ferdinand did his research and found a small family farm that sold goats in rural Maryland. The drive to the little town in Maryland is a bit fuzzy because I was fixated on trying to prepare myself for this repugnant task. Although I wanted to support Ferdinand, the thought of slaughtering a goat was horrifying and I wasn't looking forward to it at all. I remember driving a long distance that took approximately an hour and a half. After leaving our apartment, it wasn't long before we were traveling along dirt roads, driving up and down steep hills, with homes spaced out three to five miles apart. We eventually arrived at a makeshift shanty with a small pen of ten to twelve goats off to the side.

After discussing the price and bargaining for the best deal, Ferdinand selected a goat and asked for a discount because he was going to do most of the slaughtering and preparing the meat. I decided to leave once I noticed the noose in the corner of the shack. I could only imagine what was going to happen next and I didn't want to be anywhere near what I knew was about to happen. I remembered all too vividly the chicken lunch in Nigeria.

I told Ferdinand I would wait for him in our parked car, and I tried to distract myself by listening to music, looking at the landscape in the opposite direction, and admiring the never-ending beauty of the clear blue sky. After waiting in the car for 45 minutes, Ferdinand returned with three black bags full of goat meat. Thank goodness he put the bags in the trunk of the car. I didn't want to have anything to do with them. With his mission accomplished, Ferdinand smiled and listened to his favorite Nigerian tunes all the way home while I tried to get this whole scene out of my mind.

When we arrived at our apartment complex; Ferdinand asked me to carry one of the bags full of goat meat.

"Ferdinand, what do you intend to do with these?"

"We have to put the goat meat in the freezer," he replied.

"Wait. What?! What freezer are you talking about?!"

"Our freezer," Ferdinand replied casually.

"You can't be serious!" I said in complete shock.

"Where did you think I was going to put it?" he said matter-of-factly.

Once again, I hadn't really thought this whole thing through. Our wedding day was two weeks away. I had never expected I would have to live in a house with three huge garbage bags full of freshly butchered goat meat in our freezer.

The things I do for love.

It was then I discovered the goat meat was still warm. I could feel the heat as the bag moved back and forth and occasionally touched my leg. I felt nauseated. This was getting to be a bit too much, Nigerian family custom or not. I could feel my gag reflex as I thought about what was probably in store next. It was then Ferdinand announced that he wanted me to help clean the goat meat.

After taking one look at what was left of the poor animal, I knew I wouldn't be able to even be present for the cleaning, much less be a participant in the activity. I saw all sorts of different animal body parts in our sink, and it was unnerving. I saw a goat's eye, half a nostril, and various teeth among the pile of meat. I could even see hair on the goat. I had to excuse myself and leave because I had flashbacks of the goat that was alive just hours earlier. Ferdinand was in his element, though. He played Nigerian music and sang along as he cleaned and packaged goat meat in clear zip-lock baggies.

Since our reception at the hotel was catered, we couldn't bring in additional food. Therefore, we couldn't serve our homemade goat meat at the wedding reception. Our plan was to invite family and friends to our home the night before our wedding to partake of the traditional meal. I tried not to look in our freezer for the remaining two weeks. It was like looking at frozen goat puzzle pieces each time I peeked out of curiosity.

My mother-in-law arrived from Nigeria a week before our wedding. It was challenging at first because she wanted to correct everything I did. I understood that it was a cultural norm to teach soon-to-be daughters-in-law how to set up house. The biggest difference in our situation was that Ferdinand and I had been together for six years and already had established routines. By that point, I knew Ferdinand's likes, dislikes, and preferences very well.

When Ferdinand saw my discomfort, he politely told his mother "This is Cynthia's house, and it is her kitchen. Please leave her alone and let her run the house her way." I knew that was a difficult conversation to have because he loved and respected his mother dearly. I also realized how protective he was of me, and I appreciated Ferdinand even more because I knew he would always look out for me.

The day before the event at our apartment, women in the Nigerian community came over with huge pots, pans, and a variety of seasoning to prepare a celebratory meal. Every gathering included Nigerian music, turning each event into a party of sorts. The yearning for goat meat is very strong in the Nigerian community and the goat hanging out in the freezer automatically bought joy and smiles to everyone's face. The women laughed, sang, and spoke Igbo as they worked together to create a delicious meal. Huge pots of boiling water were used to get the hair off the goat meat. The fragrant aroma of onions and hot peppers sizzling in frying pans spread throughout the entire apartment. The women shared their treasured spices from Nigeria as they prepared the pre-wedding feast, and I was forever thankful and grateful.

Once the goat meat was added to the pot, the smell took a turn for the worse. I don't want to come across as ungrateful because I deeply appreciated what the women were doing for me. The pungent scent of cooked goat was unfamiliar to me, and it was particularly offensive. I believe every piece of the goat meat was cooked and prepared, including the small intestines, as is tradition in Nigeria. The smell was awful and reminded me of the African-American tradition of celebrating the New Year by eating greens, black-eyed peas, and chitterlings (animal intestines). Even though I didn't practice this tradition, I remember hearing comments confirming chitterlings do have a foul smell, but many people enjoy what is surely an acquired taste.

The spectacular meal at our home the day before our wedding was a huge success. Out-of-town guests had an opportunity to congratulate Ferdinand and me, as we chatted and enjoyed a traditional

Nigerian feast. This event set the tone for our upcoming wedding, and we couldn't wait to become husband and wife.

Knowing without doubt I was marrying someone whom I loved, honored, and trusted was one of the best feelings in the world. Knowing also that Ferdinand loved and accepted me unconditionally was worth its weight in gold. We had spent six years together solidifying our relationship. I felt as though we were fully prepared for this journey. We left no stone unturned and felt fully prepared to embark on our new journey together.

I remember waking up early Saturday morning on my wedding day to get my hair done at a salon. This was something I did twice a month, however, I hadn't told anyone at the beauty parlor I was getting married. My approach to life is that I don't volunteer information easily. If anyone asks me a question, though, I will gladly answer. I developed this behavior because I get turned off when people brag and boast. By keeping things inside without being standoffish, I hold myself accountable and only provide information I feel is necessary.

That morning, my hairdresser Tony casually asked if I had any plans for the day. When I stated I was getting married in four hours he couldn't believe it. He wanted to know where my bridal party was and could not understand why I didn't have my mom and family members around to support me. He turned toward the other beauticians and made a huge announcement for all to hear.

"Can you believe this girl is getting married today? She's so calm, I can't believe it! She's the calmest bride I've ever seen!"

He was right. I knew I was marrying someone I loved, trusted, and respected. To me, Ferdinand was the most amazing person I had ever met. That statement stands true to this day.

I planned for the bridesmaids to meet at my apartment two hours before the wedding ceremony. My mom and dad arrived thirty minutes before them so I could take photos with my parents. Getting dressed for my wedding took only fifteen minutes. I slipped the dress on, added the veil, applied eyeliner and lipstick, and voilà! I was ready.

My mother thought I would be an emotional wreck on my wedding day. I calmly explained to her that I knew exactly what I was getting myself into and I was ready and excited to spend the rest of my life with Ferdinand. The years we had already spent together were wonderful and I was looking forward to the next chapter.

My bridesmaids arrived looking amazing. They were all stunning. I purchased a beautiful pearl necklace for each one of them to show my appreciation. It was at that moment everything became beautifully crystal clear and very real. I had support from Ferdinand, my parents, family, and friends. So many thoughts entered my mind.

How did I get so lucky?

I'm really getting married.

Never, in a million years did I think this would ever happen to me.

God is so good!

I feel so blessed.

The limousine arrived to take my parents and the bridal party to the church. As I sat between my mother and father, I thought about the two pieces of paper I threw up in the air the day after I met Ferdinand. I'm so thankful I chose the word "yes." That day will stand out as a pivotal moment in my life. It's interesting how something that seemed so unimportant in the moment, years later turned out to be a tipping point that changed the trajectory of my life. I learned a great deal from Ferdinand during our time together. Observing our relationship and sharing my life with him reinforced my already strong belief in God.

It also provided me with many examples of the importance of humility and gave me an opportunity to watch Ferdinand move mountains. Ferdinand's faith, hard work, and dedication taught me that anything and everything in life is possible. I soon learned that once Ferdinand was determined to do something, he would be successful. It didn't matter what his odds were, how inexperienced he was, or how extraordinarily difficult the task was, he made it happen. When Ferdinand said he was going to do something, there was no stopping him. That mindset rubbed off on me and together we felt as though we could conquer the world. Our four children have the same mindset as their father. To this day, they also move mountains.

I discovered that the most challenging part of Ferdinand's job had to do with him coming to terms with a patient's death. As a teacher, if I make a mistake, it may cause a student to get a lower grade, miss an assignment, or cause a misunderstanding. As a surgeon, a mistake can often have extremely serious, perhaps even fatal, consequences. Watching a patient walk into a hospital appearing to be totally healthy, getting a diagnosis and having an operation and not surviving takes a serious mental toll on a doctor. I had a positive attitude prior to meeting Ferdinand about my ability to meet challenges. After seeing Ferdinand and his colleagues make life-or-death decisions and perform highly complicated procedures on a daily basis, I had a total mindset shift and actually believed I could do anything, too. That self-confidence helped me face many challenges after Ferdinand's death.

On my wedding day, my father started getting nervous once he saw Ferdinand standing at the altar. He noticed the very long aisle we would have to walk down for him to give me away in marriage. The groomsmen and bridesmaids had already escorted one another to the front of the church. They were followed by the maid of honor, who entered alone since the best man was already standing next to the groom at the front. My father told me how proud he was of me and expressed how much he loved and respected Ferdinand.

He also made it clear I will always be his baby girl, no matter if I was married or how old I was. That statement touched my heart and brought tears to my eyes. My father was an excellent dad and provider, and he treated me like a queen. I love my dad. He helped raise me to become the woman I am today. After fumbling around a bit and trying to decide how we would link arms to walk down the aisle, we felt we were ready. He practiced lifting my veil up and over my head a few more times and off we went. Ferdinand looked handsome and had the biggest smile on his face as he waited for me to join him at the front of the church. I felt like I was the luckiest woman in the world. It was an honor and a joy to become Mrs. Cynthia Marie Ukah.

The ceremony was lovely. We said our vows, exchanged rings, and had a candle-lighting ceremony at the end. After greeting our guests and spending a little bit of time with them after the ceremony, the wedding party took additional photos at a nearby park. Ferdinand and I had champagne in the limo, where I only took a sip in celebration because I don't drink. We discussed how flawless everything went and basked in the fact that we were now husband and wife.

Our wedding day was one of the happiest days of my life. Not only was I making a lifelong commitment to the love of my life, I was also joining my best friend on our lifelong journey. Our wedding reception incorporated both American and African traditions, and I couldn't wait to arrive there to celebrate with our family and friends.

We started our wedding with a libation ceremony, a ritual of pouring liquid on the floor as an offering to spirits and beloved people who are deceased. It is a beautiful way of honoring and celebrating our heritage and ancestors. It is also a way of acknowledging our loved ones who are no longer with us.

Another Nigerian tradition involved the kola nut. The kola nut comes from a plant that grows as big as a tree in West Africa. In Nigeria, the kola nut symbolizes hospitality, respect, and friendship and is offered to strangers or other visitors during special occasions. There are usually between two and 16 kola nuts in one plant. Once they are blessed, the nuts are broken, removed from their inner shell, and shared among the guests. This and other wonderful African traditions made my wedding day extra special. Our Nigerian guests were so warm, kind, and eager to share their traditions with us. Because of the beautiful mixture of American and Nigerian traditions and, most especially, the love that was present in everyone and everything, we enjoyed the day like one big happy family. Many guests shared the same emotions that Ferdinand and I felt. Afterward, they stated that our wedding was one of the most wonderful and uplifting weddings they ever attended.

One of my favorite parts of the entire day were the speeches at the reception. I've been to weddings in which it was a struggle to get a single person to make a speech. Inspired by the feeling of love and community among all who attended, our wedding was very different. Once the floor was open for speeches, people were lining up to express their love for us. It was such a humbling and moving experience. We felt loved and supported by everyone in attendance. We eventually had to end the speech portion because it seemed like the compliments, advice and praise would have gone on all night. Family and friends had wonderful things to say about us and our relationship. My heart overflowed with joy.

The DJ was outstanding, and the dance floor was packed the duration of the reception. The DJ had so much fun, he offered to stay longer, free of charge. Our wedding day was flawless. I only forgot one major detail. When I woke up the next morning in the honeymoon suite, I realized I didn't pack clothing for the next day. As embarrassing as it was, I had to wear my wedding dress to go home.

There was no time to rest and soak everything in, either, as we started our life together as husband and wife. Because of our busy schedules and other commitments, Ferdinand and I had to work the following day. We decided to postpone our honeymoon for a later date.

CHAPTER 13

FERDINAND'S INTERNSHIP AND ADANNA'S BIRTH

Ferdinand taking a break from his never-ending studies

Everything quickly went back to normal after our extravagant wedding. We both went back to work and continued our daily routines. Ferdinand was entering the third year of his five-year postgraduate medical education in General Surgery at Howard University. I was working on my master's degree in Special Education at Howard while working at Cora Kelly Magnet School as a kindergarten teacher in Alexandria, Virginia. I was fortunate that I interviewed for three teaching positions after graduating from Howard and was offered a position at all three schools.

Magnet schools were becoming popular by the time I graduated from Howard. They are public schools that offer specially designed instruction and programs not available elsewhere. Their goal was to attract a more diverse student body from other areas in the school district. I accepted the job at Cora Kelly because the school was in a low-income neighborhood, it specialized in the sciences, and I would be able to teach kindergarten students. My student-teaching experience was in a kindergarten classroom, and I knew I had the tools to make a huge, positive impact on my students.

While I have fond memories of all the children, I have had the privilege to teach, there was one in particular who stood out at Cora Kelly. Her name is Sahara Henry, and she will always have a special place in my heart. Sahara's older sister was a student in my class. Although Sahara was four years old and too young to attend kindergarten at that time, she accompanied her sister to the classroom every day with a huge smile on her face as she carried a backpack full of books. Sahara beamed with excitement every time she peeked in the classroom. Day after day, she waited for a chance to attend school. Sahara had a natural zest for knowledge and learning, and she always had a book in her hand.

I couldn't deny Sahara an opportunity to experience the classroom, even if it was only going to be a little while longer. I eventually let Sahara spend time in my classroom during the first fifteen minutes of our opening lesson as the students got settled. Her parents waited patiently for her outside of the classroom. I wanted to keep Sahara motivated, engaged, and excited about attending school. "Once an Ukah student, always an Ukah student" is my motto. Sahara is thirty-six years old now and working on a master's degree in library science. Making and maintaining connections with students is important to me, and my relationship with Sahara has grown over the years. I continue to send her a morning text message daily.

Ferdinand and I had a big goal after getting married. We wanted to save enough money to purchase our first home and start living the American Dream. We viewed ourselves as a young successful couple and wanted the house, backyard, white picket fence and many children playing in an affluent neighborhood, as we grew our loving family together.

My brother got married a month after our wedding and his wife Thelma became pregnant immediately. That was such exciting news, and I must admit I was envious and jealous. I always wanted children and assumed Ferdinand and I would start planning our family right away. When I brought this up to him after learning about Thelma's pregnancy, I was saddened and disappointed when Ferdinand replied, "Not yet Cynthia, we're just not ready"

Not ready?

What does he mean, "Not ready"?

We've been talking about having children throughout our entire relationship.

What does "not ready" mean?

Ferdinand believed in being prepared and organized. He knew raising a child would be expensive and if we started having children before we purchased our first house, the added expenses of having a child, such as purchasing diapers and food, might delay our plan of buying a home. We knew the homes in Washington and Maryland were very expensive. Because of that, we decided to look at new developments farther outside Washington. We found a beautiful three-story townhouse in Bowie, Maryland. The view from our deck included a horse stable with several horses in clear view. We purchased an end unit because it was slightly bigger and not sandwiched between other townhomes.

Our commute to work was less than 30 minutes and we were ecstatic about owning such a large townhouse. The bottom level was unfinished, and we used most of that space for storage. The main level had a sunken living room with high, recessed "tray" ceilings, in addition to windows that extended from the bottom of the floor to ceiling. I loved our picturesque view, and I didn't want to purchase curtains that would obstruct the sight of the horses throughout the day. The main level also had a bedroom, a formal dining room, and a large kitchen. It felt like I was living in the country, and I loved it. It was such a stark contrast to where I grew up in Queensbridge.

We also had three bedrooms upstairs, where one room was converted into a study for Ferdinand and another was used as a guest bedroom. It soon became obvious I had no experience living in a multi-level home. I fell down the stairs more times than I care to remember. I just wasn't accustomed to living in a house with stairs. It's a miracle I didn't break any bones. I have vivid memories of my hand clinging to the banister, holding on for dear life in an effort to shorten the fall or try to stop the inevitable.

Ferdinand wanted me to furnish the house because he was so busy with medical school and didn't have time for it. I didn't have any idea how to furnish a home. Ferdinand knew I didn't like shopping and had no experience with this at all. Yet, Ferdinand made me responsible for picking out all the furniture. I appreciated his confidence in me; however, that was a big mistake. We probably had the most sterile living room imaginable. I selected white, old fashioned Queen Anne furniture, and our color scheme was fairly generic, with everything being white and peach. I don't know where the heck that came from. It's certainly not what I grew up with.

I purchased furniture wanting it to be timeless and classy enough so Ferdinand would feel proud when he invited his colleagues and friends to our home. Washington was a popular place for people to visit. We entertained quite a bit and often hosted out-of-town guests during the weekend. To my surprise, I was pleased when many of our guest commented on how nice the house was.

Ferdinand and I were elated when we found out we were pregnant fourteen months after we got married. Once we started trying, I took pregnancy tests every other day. When the big moment came, I was so excited. I couldn't wait to become a mother. Years before that, I remembered the two of us sitting at the dinner table in our College Park apartment. Out of curiosity, I asked Ferdinand to translate the phrase "Daddy's Girl" into Igbo.

"Adanna," he replied.

"Adanna?" I repeated. "I love the name Adanna!"

I instantly fell in love with that name. I told Ferdinand; we would name our first daughter "Adanna," and that is exactly what we did.

As an educator, I knew how important it was to establish a bond with my child in utero. I read the same book to my baby every day. I even remember the title. It was called *Bunny Rattle,* and when I shook it, the book made a rattling noise. I did this because I wanted my child to hear something very familiar as they entered the world. I frequently talked to my child, too, and sang alphabet and counting songs. I loved that I was carrying our baby, and I enjoyed my pregnancy to the fullest. Thankfully, my pregnancy was flawless, and I couldn't wait to meet my bundle of joy.

I also felt that having both of our families living a long distance from us was an asset. I had married friends with in-laws that meddled in their lives, causing all types of conflict. Ferdinand's family communicated with us by phone. My parents lived in New York, and we traveled to visit them occasionally.

Once I became pregnant, though, my perspective changed completely. Ferdinand's mother came to live with us for a year. I found out this is customary in the Nigerian culture. I couldn't believe how fortunate we were. I was elated to know my newborn would be cared for by his or her grandmother. I didn't have to worry about sleepless nights or childcare. Having my mother-in-law living with us was a tremendous help. I was able to enjoy my pregnancy without a worry in the world. Ferdinand's mother had raised nine children and I knew I would learn a lot from her.

Even though Ferdinand was very busy during my pregnancy, I wanted to go to Lamaze Childbirth Education Classes where I would be taught relaxation techniques and breathing patterns to help ease the discomfort of labor and birth. I knew Ferdinand wouldn't be able to join me, however I felt it was important. My mother kept asking if I told the instructor or couples in class that I wasn't a single parent but, instead, the wife of a doctor. She was worried about how others would perceive me. I told Mom I didn't care what other people thought and I didn't have anything to prove. It broke my mother's heart for me to go to these classes by myself because she thought

I felt alone. I gently told her I knew what I signed up for when I married Ferdinand. I knew I would face many challenges alone and I was prepared for it.

My cousin Karen was in law school at Georgetown University at the time, and she offered to be my Lamaze partner once she found out I was going to class alone. She also offered to go into the delivery room with me if Ferdinand couldn't make it. I believe she made these offers because she felt sorry for me as well. Despite my assurances, my mother and cousin couldn't wrap their heads around the fact that this was the life I chose.

Ferdinand and I didn't want to know the gender of our child; however, we couldn't wait to find out. The day I went into labor, I tried to walk as much as possible to speed up contractions. Because of the classes I took and the reading I had done, I felt I was very prepared, and I wasn't nervous. That was until I arrived at the labor and delivery unit at George Washington Hospital. It was then that I heard a woman in labor screaming at the top of her lungs, stating she was dying and couldn't do it. Her screaming was starting to affect me. Seeing the fear creep into my eyes, Ferdinand kept saying "It's not that bad."

How would he possibly know?! He's not the one who's in labor. I am!

A nurse finally came out of the delivery room and told me not to worry. She told us the woman in labor was on drugs and her experience was not typical. I was escorted to a room and given an epidural injection to relieve the pain. Soon I felt like I was on top of the moon. The medication worked. I was laughing, talking, and not feeling an ounce of pain. I couldn't believe it. Going into labor wasn't bad at all.

A few minutes before I was going to start pushing, a group of five residents walked toward my room during evening rounds. The physician in charge asked if the residents could observe me giving birth. Even in my medicated state, as an educator and wife of a doctor I knew this experience would be invaluable. I gave them permission to observe, and they respected my privacy by keeping their distance. I tried to ignore the six adults in white coats crowding the entry way of the door, each eagerly awaiting the birth of my child. They appeared in various poses. Some were on tip-toes, and some were kneeling. Others were observing on bent knees, practically losing their balance in an effort to witness a live birth.

Ferdinand was in husband mode, hugging me, kissing me and encouraging me the entire time. He periodically rubbed my forehead as we anticipated the birth of our first child. Everything was going as planned until my baby fell asleep during contractions. The doctors decided to blow a horn close to my stomach in an effort to wake my child up. Minutes after that, I gave birth to Adanna Lewe Ukah. Adanna had a full audience when she entered the world, including her dad and my mother. The residents at the door gave us a round of applause.

The doctor said, "It's a girl." My heart overflowed with joy.

"She's so beautiful" were the first words that came out of my mouth.

"Ferdinand, she's so beautiful!"

We were both in complete awe. Adanna, "daddy's girl," was born in September of 1989. She was perfect in every way. She was happy, calm, and content most of the time. She almost always slept throughout the night and only cried when she wanted something to eat, was wet, or felt tired. I thought Adanna was choking when I nursed her for the first time. I cried and went into panic mode. I didn't want to hurt or harm my daughter in any way. My mother reassured me that Adanna would be okay and once the nurse taught me how to burp Adanna, I was able to relax.

My mother-in-law taught me how to swaddle Adanna, the age-old practice of wrapping infants in a blanket tightly to provide a soothing and calming effect. This was a major game changer because it made Adanna feel safe and secure whenever she wasn't being held, which wasn't often.

Adanna sucked her pointer and middle finger constantly. People often made comments and tried to persuade me to stop the habit. I felt it served as a security blanket for Adanna, and if sucking her fingers made her feel happy, I wasn't going to stop her. I read to

Adanna constantly. I think I purchased a book every week from the time I found out I was pregnant until she graduated from junior high school.

Adanna's middle name, Lewe, is Ferdinand's mothers' name and it emphasizes the very close connection we have with his family and especially with his mother. Our beautiful daughter Adanna's birth, of course was such a profound moment in my life. The emotions were overwhelming. She made Ferdinand and me parents for the first time.

CHAPTER 14

SURGICAL RESIDENCY IN PITTSBURGH AND THE ARRIVAL OF NNEKA AND OKEY

University of Pittsburgh Medical Center logo
(Source: upmc.com)

Once Ferdinand completed his internship and residency in the General Surgery Program at Howard University Medical School in 1990, we anxiously waited for him to find out where he would go for his fellowship. This critical decision would determine what area of surgery he would specialize in. Just as important, we would find out where our next move would be. Ferdinand mentioned he was applying to fellowships at various programs in the country. Fortunately, I had already spent a lot of time with Ferdinand and his colleagues throughout the years and was familiar with the routine of doctors moving every two to four years.

Our physician friends moved frequently, often relocating to another state for internships, residencies, fellowships, or simply their first job as a doctor. It was a way of life for us, and we embraced it. All of Ferdinand's colleagues were thriving, elevating, and advancing in their new roles. We knew without doubt we would thrive as well. I didn't have a preference when it came to where we moved. I truly was completely neutral about where I moved next because I was just excited about the adventure that we were embarking on. We discussed the issue of relocating at the beginning of our relationship. The issue of his frequent moving as a doctor would always come up. As a teacher, I knew I could find a job wherever we moved, and we agreed that most of our geographic relocations would be primarily based on Ferdinand's training or profession. I supported him one hundred percent.

Although Ferdinand applied for various fellowships in several places, I was ecstatic when he came home and announced he was awarded a University of Pittsburgh Medical Center (UPMC) Fellowship. The UPMC Fellowship was a multi-organ transplant program, and I knew this was exactly what Ferdinand was hoping for. The Thomas E. Starzl Transplantation Institute at the University of Pittsburgh was world-renowned and we both felt honored that Ferdinand was going to be a part of it.

I was extremely proud of Ferdinand and understood that getting accepted into this highly selective and nationally recognized program was a huge accomplishment. Ferdinand felt like he was on top of the world, with all of his hard work and sleepless nights under extreme pressure having paid off beautifully. Not only was he going to become a transplant surgeon, but Ferdinand was also going to train under the "pioneer of transplantation," the highly esteemed Dr. Thomas E. Starzl, an Iowa native.

Ferdinand knew he would have his work cut out for him and understood this residency program would be even more demanding than medical school or his internship. We didn't know anyone who lived in Pittsburgh at that time. However, Ferdinand did his research and befriended Dr. Velma Scantleberry, a previous recipient of the UPMC Fellowship. Dr. Scantleberry was an excellent resource to find out what the fellowship program entailed. She had just completed her residency in transplantation at the University of Pittsburgh and was able to share her experiences and give Ferdinand lots of valuable advice. She also became a dear friend.

It soon became apparent that she must have stressed how important it was to perfect his surgical knotting technique. The surgeon's knot needs to be strong and it's critical that it be done properly and in a continuous line. In addition, Ferdinand started practicing his suturing technique by using a needle and thread every spare minute he had. He wanted to continuously improve this skill so he would be automatic, quick, effective, and efficient whenever he needed to suture a patient. We soon had surgical string hanging from just about every object in our house.

Each weekend, I purchased pigs' feet at the local grocery store so that Ferdinand could practice suturing skin together. He used pigs' feet because they have tough skin like humans. Ferdinand would diligently cut the pigs' feet in several places and then tie the skin back together. This was all designed to increase his efficiency and speed at performing this critical task.

Our daughter Adanna was eighteen months old at the time we found out about our move to Pittsburgh, and I was four months pregnant with our second child. In the midst of all of this, we knew moving a family of three would be challenging. Ferdinand still had to complete four months of his residency before his program at Howard officially ended. This meant we didn't have a lot of time to secure a place to live, pack, and move our small family.

Just a few months before we had to move, Ferdinand took one weekend off and flew to Pittsburgh to go house hunting. Unfortunately, he didn't have much luck. The real estate agent forgot he was showing up and only had two homes to show him. Ferdinand came home discouraged, but knew we had to find a place to live as soon as possible. We felt like we were running out of time.

We didn't have a lot of money at the time, yet Ferdinand wanted to live in a prestigious neighborhood. He was going to be a transplant surgeon and wanted his home to reflect that status. Ferdinand had dreams of living in a beautiful home in an upscale neighborhood. We loved to entertain, and he wanted to be proud of where he lived when he invited friends and colleagues over for much-needed downtime and relaxation. Since Ferdinand didn't have success finding a home during his first trip to Pittsburgh, he asked me to go there to follow up on three potential houses the real estate agent suggested through email. Ferdinand's fellowship program was going to begin in a few months and finding a place to live had become our top priority.

I give Ferdinand a lot of credit for believing in me and trusting me with tasks and responsibilities where I don't have much experience. I don't focus much on material things. As a result, I'm not very skilled at selecting or purchasing expensive or fashionable items. I prefer to invest my time and energy on developing relationships with people, not things. Name-brand items, expensive homes, and fancy cars have never impressed me. As a result, I don't have any real experience choosing or buying them.

Ferdinand also knew I didn't know much about buying or renting houses and I had little experience working with real estate agents. I had lived in apartments most of my life and Ferdinand was the mastermind behind finding and purchasing our townhouse in Maryland. Because Ferdinand enjoyed those areas, I hadn't paid much attention to details when it came to material things.

Since everything was moving rather quickly, we didn't attempt to sell the townhouse. We had a one-track mind, and our priorities were finding a home and moving to Pittsburgh. We decided we would focus on what to do with the Maryland townhouse once we were settled in Pittsburgh. We were confident the townhouse would sell quickly, considering it was newly built, in a nice location, and reasonably priced. We put the townhouse on the market two months after we moved to Pittsburgh, and it sat there empty for two and a half years. While this clearly wasn't what we wanted to happen, it wasn't a disaster either. The continuing townhouse mortgage payment wasn't an overwhelming financial burden because the home we rented in Pittsburgh wasn't expensive at all. We were happy to hold onto it, since it looked like it might be a good investment, too.

I guess you get what you pay for.

Although we had the additional expense of a townhouse, Ferdinand's salary made it easy for us to handle without causing too much stress or financial strain. We eventually rented the townhouse years later when we moved to Alabama. We felt that at least we would be able to put some extra money toward the mortgage. Our tenants were responsible and paid their rent on a consistent basis for the first couple of months. Unfortunately, Ferdinand decided to make a friendly visit to our new tenants during one of his trips to D.C. He watched a Washington Redskins game with them, shared a couple of beers with them and eventually felt comfortable enough to befriend them. We learned a valuable lesson from this: Never mix business with pleasure.

Our tenants decided they could take advantage of this situation and they simply refused to pay rent from that day forward. We ended up having them evicted after a long, drawn-out struggle involving court filings and legal fees. The tenants basically trashed the townhouse and, after spending a great deal of money on repairs, we sold the house for a very low price. We just wanted to get rid of the added expense.

Ferdinand wanted to live in an area in Pittsburgh called Squirrel Hill because it was near the hospital. It was also known as a prestigious neighborhood where many of the hospital's physicians lived. Once I arrived on my house-hunting trip, I contacted our real estate agent and he had once again forgotten our appointment with him. I was frustrated because it was becoming apparent Ferdinand and I were probably his first clients. Ferdinand found his number in the yellow pages, and we were either too desperate to find housing and not thinking or just too naive to realize who we were dealing with at the time. The agent took me to see one home that needed a whole lot of work. It was the worst looking house in all of Squirrel Hill. The outside looked decent compared to most of the houses in the neighborhood. The inside, however, was a totally different story.

As soon as the agent unlocked the front door, I saw piles of scraps, old furniture, torn up tiles and rugs stacked in random places throughout the house. It was a complete disaster and that's putting it mildly. As soon as I saw the inside, I should have asked about the history behind the house. Why on earth was it this way? Instead, I was overcome by the situation and just let things happen rather than take control.

The house was huge. It had a large formal dining room, living room, long narrow kitchen, two and a half bathrooms and three large bedrooms upstairs. The agent promised he could have it all cleared out, power washed, painted, and upgraded with new carpets and tile before we moved in. He presented a perfect picture of what the house would look like once he added the finishing touches. He was so very convincing. I'm pretty sure he could tell I was gullible and had little experience picking out a home. As a result, he proceeded to take advantage of my naivete.

I knew Ferdinand really wanted to live in Squirrel Hill and since the price was right and the home was big enough for our growing family I gave the agent a rental deposit. In return, he gave me a verbal promise of having the trash completely cleared out of the house. He also promised to have the house painted, with new wall-to-wall carpeting, and new tiles installed in the kitchen.

I learned several important lessons from this experience. I learned how important it was for Ferdinand and me to take time to go through all the things we wanted in a house and to list the critical aspects of what we were looking for. In this way, I could have been better prepared before undertaking this task.

With my lack of experience and knowledge, I made several major mistakes that day. The biggest one was trusting our agent to look out for our interests, which he clearly did not. I didn't sign a contract or get anything in writing. I also didn't go into the basement to see its (terrible) condition. Additionally, I failed to open the back door of the kitchen leading to a backyard infested with jumping worms. Instead, I simply made the decision to rent the house, trusting our agent to fulfill his part of the bargain. I felt that as long as everything went as planned, this could be the house of our dreams.

Unfortunately, I was totally wrong.

On the day of our move, Ferdinand departed our townhouse in Maryland an hour before me. He wanted to get a head start driving to start setting things up before Adanna and I arrived. He was exhausted but very excited at the same time. He used a pay phone to call my mother just about every hour, stopping along the way to find out how Adanna and I were doing. There were no cell phones at that time, so we used my mother as the middleperson. This worked perfectly because I had to stop periodically for Adanna's feeding, diaper changes and much-needed stretching. I would call my mom, using a pay phone to let her know where I was and how far I was from Pittsburgh. Ferdinand would check in with my mother hourly and she would relay my messages. I'm the slowest driver alive, so I was still a long way from Pittsburgh when my mother told me Ferdinand was only thirty minutes away from his destination.

Ferdinand was shocked when he saw our new home in Squirrel Hill. He could not believe the disaster he was looking at. Not only that, he also couldn't understand why I would have given the agent any money at all for us to live in a house in such deplorable condition. All the trash that was piled up in the house when I visited was now in clear view on the porch.

By the time he got there, the moving truck was parked in front of the house. Ferdinand felt so overwhelmed, he just sat in his parked car and cried. The house was an eyesore. Instead of being cleaned out with a new paint job, carpeting, and tiles, it was filled with debris, broken furniture, and old appliances.

Ferdinand called me in pure shock and disbelief. It appeared the contractors had just realized new tenants were arriving and they had started working on the home that very day. The agent hadn't done any of the work he promised. As Ferdinand described the horrible situation, I was upset for a lot of reasons. I hadn't signed a contract, I didn't remember the name of the person that showed me the house, and I didn't have contact information for the agent. Because I felt I failed in so many ways, I expected Ferdinand to be very angry with me. I kept waiting for the anger to set in and I cringed. I knew it would only be a matter of time before it did.

"Cynthia, how could you rent such a place?" He was upset, as I expected, expressing more disappointment than anger. Ferdinand was referred to as a "Gentle Giant" for a reason. His tone was always calm, rational, and controlled. Ferdinand had never before raised his voice in the entire time I'd known him.

"The real estate agent promised to have the house cleaned up and ready for us on our move-in date," I explained, all the while knowing I had let us down.

Once I made it to the house, I saw Ferdinand had tears in his eyes. It was the first time in the ten years we had been together I saw him cry. Nothing had been done inside of the house. In fact, it looked much worse than it did when I first saw it. It now looked like an abandoned house in desperate need of repair and cleaning. There was nothing to be proud of.

Ferdinand told me he would handle everything and managed to get in touch with the real estate agent. We stayed in a hotel for a week while contractors and handymen worked on the house. After a week of intense activity, the house was ready to be moved into. The place wasn't perfect by any means, but it was at least habitable by that point. Despite being in a very nice neighborhood, it still wasn't the kind of place we felt comfortable inviting coworkers, family members or friends.

The floors on the first floor were tilted and the bathroom was wallpapered with old newspapers. The basement was so creepy, I hated going downstairs to do my laundry. In my mind, we lived in the worst house in the entire neighborhood, and I felt it was totally my fault. I couldn't believe Ferdinand forgave me. He was disappointed that day but had to begin his fellowship the following day. Ferdinand didn't hold this mistake against me, nor did he mention it after that day. I couldn't undo the damage that was already done. Although I knew I had made a terrible mistake I wasn't going to dwell on it. We were only going to live in Pittsburgh for two years and I made a personal vow that I wouldn't attempt to rent or purchase a home on my own or without proper planning.

I learned the importance of finding a reputable Realtor, getting contact information, and securing details in writing. I trusted Ferdinand more than I trusted myself in that area of home rentals and purchases. From that point on, Ferdinand oversaw securing housing, and I continued to improve in the area of home décor. I am very practical, and I think we all have strengths and weaknesses. I still feel my home is where my family is — it's not the structure or place. With a lot of effort and patience, we eventually settled into our new home

Years later I realized that while this experience was difficult, I understood that I needed to take responsibility for these types of decisions in my life, especially after Ferdinand's death. Having this experience early in my marriage taught me a lot about responsibility and standing up for myself, especially when dealing with people like real estate agents or making big purchases.

Prior to moving, Ferdinand and I decided I would be a stay-at-home mom during our first year in Pittsburgh. Pittsburgh is known as the Steel City, and I would describe it as an old industrial town. I found people were not openly friendly, and my impression was that people who grew up in Pittsburgh rarely left. In addition, the neighborhood was very insular from a cultural and religious perspective, which helped create a feeling of isolation for me and my family. Almost everyone I met outside of the hospital setting was born and raised in Pittsburgh and not many of them had ever been on a plane. This shuttered perspective and insularity really surprised me. The communities were close-knit, and everyone seemed to know one another. Although I felt like an outsider, I was still very happy taking care of my family as I lived there. I had a lot to keep me busy as I awaited the birth of our second child.

Ferdinand worked nonstop and seemed to be thriving at the University of Pittsburgh. He passed the Medical Board Exam, and that was such a huge milestone. Ferdinand enjoyed transplant surgery and loved sharing his experiences as he learned more about liver and kidney transplants. Dr. Starzl was heavily invested in animal research and performed non-human animal research on dogs, pigs and baboons. The intent of this program was to perfect surgical techniques on other animals before using them on people.

As part of this program, Ferdinand was responsible for taking care of a baboon in the basement of the hospital that was being used for research. He went to the hospital rain or shine like clockwork every four hours, even in the middle of the night when he was on rotation to feed, provide snacks, or turn a television or movie on for the baboon's entertainment. I couldn't believe Ferdinand actually helped take care of a baboon.

Animal Rights Organizations made sure animals used for research were treated humanely. Hence, Ferdinand had to treat the baboon with extreme care. Because baboons closely resemble humans, Dr. Starzl wanted to research and prepare the organs for human transplants. The results were astounding. In 1992, a thirty-five-year-old individual underwent the first animal to human liver transplant from a baboon. The patient was walking and eating within five days of the surgery but unfortunately passed away seventy days later. Although caring for the baboon was challenging at times, Ferdinand embraced his role as he understood the importance and value of animal research.

Meanwhile, I enrolled Adanna at Tender Care Learning Center to provide her with opportunities to interact with peers and learn basic skills. I spent most of my spare time putting our house in order and getting acclimatized to Pittsburgh. For some reason, Ferdinand assumed our next child would be a boy. He bragged to all his friends that he was expecting baby number two, and when he talked to them on the phone, he would tell them he knew he was going to have a son.

I don't know what makes him feel so confident. We have a 50/50 chance.

Since Adanna was named after her father, I asked Ferdinand to translate "mommy's girl" into Igbo.

"Nneka. Nneka means mother is greater," Ferdinand responded.

I loved that name. It sounded beautiful and I especially loved the meaning. I diligently practiced pronouncing Nneka correctly, "NEH-kah." I found saying the name was very tricky with the double N. It's something I never really perfected.

If by some chance we had a boy, I wanted to name our son after his father, Okechukwu Ferdinand Ukah, Jr. I always admired children who were named after their dad. Ferdinand, on the other hand, was not a fan of the idea. Ferdinand had decided to use his middle name as his first name when he moved to the United States because he felt it would be easier to pronounce.

"Nigerians don't name children after their fathers," Ferdinand stated. "That's an American tradition."

I was disappointed he felt this way because I loved Ferdinand and felt he deserved to have a namesake. We thought about alternative boys' names like Nnamdi and Okoye. Much to Ferdinand's surprise, in May of 1991, I gave birth to a beautiful baby girl at the University of Pittsburgh Hospital. Ferdinand finished up a transplant just in time to make it to the delivery room to witness our daughter entering the world.

While we named her Nneka, we gave my mom permission to come up with a middle name since we had incorporated Ferdinand's mother's name into Adanna's name. She came up with the name MeShelle and Ferdinand initially hated it. He eventually got used to it and we were blessed with our beautiful, feisty daughter, Nneka MeShelle Ukah. My mother definitely made the right decision coming up with Nneka's middle name because my daughter loves it and often introduces herself as Nneka MeShelle instead of Nneka.

Nneka had the cutest little face and tight black curly hair. She was constantly moving her hands and kicking her feet up and down. She tried to wiggle herself out of almost anything, including my arms, a blanket, or my lap. When she was awake, Nneka was constantly in motion. Some things never change.

Nneka was a quiet baby and took lots of naps throughout the day, making it easy for me to get things done around the house. I read to her consistently, sang alphabet and number songs just as I did when Adanna was born. I'm thankful I studied education and read a lot about caring for, raising, and educating children. Between that and advice from my mom and mother-in-law, taking care of two young children was a piece of cake. We were both pleased with the day-care center Adanna attended, and we felt comfortable sending Nneka there as well.

We decided I should start looking for a job and three months after giving birth to Nneka, I found the perfect position at Community College of Allegheny County as a Vocational Rehabilitation Specialist. In that job, I worked with students in vocational programs who had special needs. I taught, tutored, read exams, and taped content to ensure student success. Working was extremely fulfilling, and it was nice to spend some time outside of my home. In addition, I only worked part-time. This gave me an opportunity to pursue my professional career and an opportunity to devote time to take care of my family. I spent most of my time taking care of Adanna and Nneka while making sure I was available to assist Ferdinand during this busy time. Ferdinand enjoyed his fellowship position. He loved learning about liver and kidney transplants and always came home with interesting stories to share.

Three months after I started working, I found out I was expecting my third child. My mother thought I was insane and couldn't understand why I was having so many children, especially since they were coming so soon after one another.

She would say, "Cynthia, why are you having so many kids? You're ruining your body. Give your body a rest. You're not a machine. It's just too much."

Too much for whom?

I felt perfectly fine, and I had everything under control. Ferdinand and I planned to have a big family. I was young, healthy, and wanted my children to be close in age. This is one of the best decisions Ferdinand and I ever made. I also had ample time to coax Ferdinand into naming our son after him. It wasn't too much longer before we were blessed with our amazing son. During the month of November in 1992, Ferdinand and I became the proud parents of Okechukwu Ferdinand Ukah Jr. He was so proud to have a son.

The evening we arrived home from the hospital, Ferdinand asked me to join him on the porch as he lifted Okechukwu up to the sky and thanked God for blessing us with a son. There is an old African tradition of holding a newborn baby up to the starry night sky and saying 'Behold, the only thing greater than yourself." This was an emotional moment for the both of us. Okechukwu was healthy, we had three young children and our family was growing. The meaning of Okechukwu is God's portion or God's gift. We felt our family was blessed beyond measure.

Okechukwu was a happy baby as well. He loved to be held and rarely fussed or cried. He sucked his pointer and middle fingers, and he was able to console himself like his sister Adanna. I spent just as much time reading and singing to Okechukwu as I did with my other two children. I was able to spend quality time with him when I sent Adanna and Nneka to day care.

Ferdinand spent time with all his children as soon as he walked in the door. He loved and adored them. He made every moment with them count; often speaking to them in Igbo. Ferdinand was an excellent husband and father. He made me feel special every day and often told me how much he loved and appreciated me.

One day, I remember Ferdinand bursting through the door of our home saying he had fantastic news. He had a letter in his hand and the biggest smile on his face.

'Cynthia, guess where we're going?"

I had no idea what Ferdinand was talking about. Honestly, I thought we might be going on some sort of vacation.

Instead, he shouted, "I received an offer for a job and accepted a position as a Transplant Surgeon at the University of Iowa!"

University of Iowa?

Of course, I was happy for Ferdinand. He worked tirelessly for that past fifteen years of post-college education and rigorous training and all of his hard work was coming to fruition. Ferdinand reached his goal. Dr. Ferdinand Okechukwu Ukah was going to be an assistant professor and transplant surgeon at The University of Iowa Hospitals and Clinics. I was extremely happy and proud of Ferdinand. We didn't have drinks in our house to celebrate, so we celebrated by toasting each other with lemonade in wine glasses. We couldn't be happier. I kept focusing on the word Iowa; so many thoughts crossed my mind.

Iowa?

Really?

Where on earth is Iowa?

Who lives in Iowa?

I asked Ferdinand if there were any Black people in Iowa.

We both laughed and looked at the large map we had hanging up in our home. We studied the map and did a little research on the demographics. At that time the population of African Americans in Iowa City was 1.3%. We both tried to think of people who had ties to Iowa, and I came up blank. Ferdinand had a cousin, Kem Obashi, who attended the University of Iowa. Although it was very late we were both very curious and decided to call him.

Kem basically said we would love living in Iowa. Iowa City was a college town with lots of professionals. It was a highly educated family-oriented community, and the public schools are excellent. I had three young children at the time and after researching the public schools in Iowa City, I became even more excited. Ferdinand flew out to find a home in close proximity to the hospital and public school we wanted our children to attend. Each time we moved, Ferdinand's responsibilities increased, which required spending more time at the hospital. Ferdinand trusted me to handle almost all family matters, as he saved lives and provided for our family.

During our time in Pittsburgh, Ferdinand, Adanna, Nneka, and I had the opportunity to visit Ferdinand's family in Nigeria. I enjoyed it as much as I did my first trip, but this time it was easier because Ferdinand was with me. I also had the opportunity to introduce two of my beautiful children to Ferdinand's entire family.

Here we are with Ferdinand's entire family in this group photo.
I am in the center of the picture with the yellow headdress.
Ferdinand is in the upper right corner in light blue.
Papa is on the far left in the gray robes.

CHAPTER 15

ESTABLISHING OURSELVES IN IOWA CITY AND CHIKE'S BIRTH

University of Iowa Hospital (Source: uihc.org)

I remember taking my children to a play at Riverside Theater in Iowa City. As I stood in the back corner of a jam-packed room, I couldn't help but notice an African-American woman entering the building with two young children. I hadn't seen a woman of color in the community up to that point, and we instantly locked eyes from afar. We stretched out our arms toward each other like we were long-lost friends. We hugged each other for dear life because we were so happy to find one another. I'm pretty sure we shed a few tears of joy, too. It was such a relief to see someone who looked like me. Our kids were ecstatic, too. They played together like they had been friends all their lives.

We simultaneously asked, "Where did you come from?"

We also asked, "Where have you been?"

Her name was Monique Washington and at that time, she had two sons, Ralph and Jasper. She had two more children, Djimon and Nia a few years later. I met her husband Ralph a few weeks later and the two of them have played a major role in my family's life ever since. We were inseparable from that time on. It wouldn't be many more years until I discovered just how critically important the beautiful friendships I made in Iowa City would be as I desperately tried to navigate life with my four young children after Ferdinand's tragic death.

Ferdinand traveled to Iowa City twice before our family actually moved there from Pittsburgh. The first time was to attend a conference and meet colleagues at the University of Iowa Hospital, and the second time was to secure housing. Ferdinand selected a lovely, eclectic, two-story home on a cul-de-sac within walking distance of the hospital. The photos of the house were impressive, and I couldn't wait to move in. I felt confident this moving experience would be much better than the previous one.

Although Ferdinand and I were excited about our new chapter, preparing for the move to Iowa was exhausting. The moving company arrived at our Squirrel Hill home two days before we moved. The first day, they took five hours to pack and box everything up. They then arrived at our home the following morning to load the truck with all our belongings. It all seemed so rushed and almost chaotic with movers in all the rooms and people constantly walking in and out.

We decided to drive our family to Iowa City and planned to leave at 6:30 at night to avoid rush hour traffic in Pittsburgh. We also wanted to stick to the children's normal routine, with dinner being served to them at five o'clock, as usual. I bathed the kids and put on their pajamas, while Ferdinand put our luggage and last-minute items into the trunk of the car.

I tucked two baby bags between the front and back seats of the car – we only had one car by this point, as I had been driving Ferdinand to and from work. One of them contained necessities such as diapers, bottles, and baby food. The other contained books, crayons, small toys, and a stash of children's tapes to honor their music requests. We felt that by listening to music and singing along in the car we would make our trip more enjoyable, and it would help time pass by.

We drove our family directly from Pittsburgh to Iowa City, splitting the trip into two days. We knew full well our children wouldn't be able to sit patiently in a car for 12 to 15 hours, constricted in three car seats with hardly enough room to move. I predicted the children would fall asleep by 8:30 that evening. Thankfully they proved me wrong and were all fast asleep by 7:00.

Our two years living in Pittsburgh had gone by rather quickly. I was so consumed with my family that I hadn't paid much attention to the area's rugged urban landscape. As we drove away, I took one last look at the house, reflecting on our first week in Pittsburgh and how challenging it had been. I also remembered we had arrived in Pittsburgh as a family of three and we were now leaving as a family of five. We had created a beautiful life and home within the confines of that troublesome Squirrel Hill house. We had also created many wonderful and fond memories.

I knew I wasn't going to miss Pittsburgh, though, because everything that represented what we loved about our time there was inside our vehicle. Ferdinand, Adanna, Nneka and Okechukwu were my world and I wanted to love, nurture, and provide a wonderful life for each one of them. Pittsburgh will always have a special place in my heart because it is where two of my children were born. Ferdinand and I spent the majority of our time as we departed Pittsburgh on our way to Iowa talking about how happy and blessed we were as the children slept soundly in the car.

Driving in the car was both scenic and symbolic. I hadn't really noticed Pittsburgh's rugged landscape before, with its hillsides and steep climbs. At times I felt like I was on a rollercoaster as Ferdinand drove through the darkness. The winding roads were narrow with a number of steep hills and inclines. The drive for me became symbolic of life in general.

Life is like a rollercoaster, there will be many ups and downs.

Ferdinand and I realized we were both extremely fortunate. Ferdinand had obtained his dream job, we had a solid marriage, and I was in my element raising three wonderful children. I couldn't ask for anything more.

We stopped in Ohio briefly and spent the night at a hotel, waking up early to finish the last leg of our trip. We gave the kids quite a bit of time to eat, stretch, run around, and play before we got on the road. We had high hopes we'd tire them out for the final leg of our trip. The drive was pretty scenic until we got closer to Iowa. It was then I noticed the flat plains and absence of "civilization." I no longer saw buildings, houses, or businesses for long periods of time. All I could see were endless blue skies, clouds, green grass, and large groups of cows along the way. Occasionally we'd see a car or truck pass by, but not that often. What we did see was evidence of lots of corn in Iowa. I felt like I was entering unknown territory, something of a no-man's-land. It was definitely different from what I was used to in New York, Washington, or even Pittsburgh.

Even though the rural landscape was unfamiliar, it was nice to see the beauty of God's creation, with its flowers, trees, ponds, and a variety of birds. We eventually stopped at a hotel in Coralville, which was only a few blocks from Iowa City and just ten minutes from our new home. I was a little concerned because Coralville appeared to be desolate and very small. Ferdinand got us settled into the hotel while he checked on the movers at our new home. We decided to rent a house for a year because we wanted to take our time finding or building a home if we decided to stay in the community. We had moved around quite a bit by that time, and we wanted to make sure we had stability before we invested in yet another home. We still owned the home in Maryland, and we didn't want to buy a house hastily.

Ferdinand and I officially moved into our home the next morning and I absolutely loved the place. It was perfect for our family and the kids instantly felt at home running all through the house. I loved the large kitchen with its island countertop, wide bay windows, and a wall-to-wall wooden bench for the children to sit down and eat meals or stand on the ledge to peer at the large backyard full of apple trees. The living room was modern; with a marble fireplace in the center of the room, which extended from the bottom of the floor to the top of the ceiling. The house had beautiful dark cherry hardwood floors throughout, a nice sized dining room, playroom, office, and three bedrooms. I also noticed the home must have been designed for a left-handed person. All of the cabinets and doors opened from right to left. I really liked that feature because I am left-handed.

I remember playing with my children outside and hearing a young child screaming at the top of her lungs. The screams became louder and before I knew it, I saw a petite woman marching through our backyard, carrying a young girl in one arm as though she was holding a log. It was the young girl making the noise, and I admired this woman from afar because she wasn't giving in to her daughter's screaming.

I didn't know who she was at the time; however, a few days later she showed up at my doorstep with a plate of homemade chocolate chip cookies. She introduced herself as Mary Panther and her daughter Allie. As time went on, we ran into each other frequently because we had a shared backyard. Her daughter became friends with Adanna, and I continue to have a special relationship with Mary to this day.

I loved being a wife and mother more than anything in the world. I felt it was my calling and I enjoyed every minute of it. Having the luxury of being a stay-at-home mom was a blessing that I didn't take it for granted. I wanted to nurture, teach, and provide our children with a wide variety of experiences. I established set routines for them. Each day involved reading books, watching educational videos and going on at least one family outing every day. In addition to them attending daycare and school, I took advantage of every opportunity presented to us to teach my children something new. I was able to provide them with educational activities and assignments throughout their entire childhood, especially during the summer months.

My goal each day was to conclude the children's activities by 4 in the afternoon. I wanted to make sure I had a hot meal ready for Ferdinand, if by some miracle he had time to run home for a quick bite to eat. More than likely, I ended up dropping his dinner off at the hospital, where I would take the kids to his office on the first floor to stop in for a few minutes to say good night. Sometimes, though, we just drove by his office window to wave at him or see if he was there.

We discovered that although Ferdinand's schedule was insanely busy in Pittsburgh, it was nothing compared to his schedule at the University of Iowa. I didn't realize going into this new job how much time Ferdinand would actually spend at the hospital. He practically lived there. Even when he wasn't at the hospital, Ferdinand's beeper frequently went off throughout the night and day, seven days a week and including holidays.

The amount of coordination and time involved to transplant an organ into a patient was immense and had to be done very quickly. Ferdinand would receive a phone call indicating someone was on life support in another part of the country. A transplant coordinator would then discuss the possibility of organ donation with family members. If consent was given to donate organs, tests were run on the patient to match the new kidney with the body.

Once a match was determined using a database, the recipient was notified and given a short window of time to get to the hospital, tested, and prepped for the transplant. Ferdinand either flew in a private plane to retrieve the organ (or even multiple organs), prepped the recipient for surgery, and performed the transplant, or he cleaned and prepared the organ that was going to be transplanted. Each procedure took several hours. Often, I didn't know in which city or state Ferdinand was actually located.

A typical liver transplant takes 6-8 hours, a kidney transplant takes four hours, and a combined kidney/pancreas transplant takes six hours. The entire process was so complex and time-consuming, it was difficult for me to keep track of what was happening and Ferdinand's role that particular day or night. Because of that, I just decided to not place any expectations on when he would get home when he needed to perform a transplant. I was just happy to see him when he would arrive back home once he was finished.

Ferdinand loved being a doctor and was passionate about being a transplant surgeon. It was wonderful to see him in his element, knowing he was improving the quality of life, or even saving the life of so many of his patients. I continued to admire Ferdinand and felt so honored to be his wife. I wanted to make Ferdinand's life at home as relaxing as possible. He typically fell asleep in the playroom with the kids because he wanted to hear their voices as he slept since he didn't have much time to spend with them. The children would take advantage of the opportunity and jump all over him at that time.

Because Ferdinand practically lived at the hospital, I had to carve out a life for the kids and myself. I refer to Iowa City as one of America's best-kept secrets because my family flourished there. It was the perfect place to raise my children and I met the most amazing and authentic lifelong family-friends there. We instantly became involved in the Nigerian Community, attending monthly meetings, wearing Nigerian clothing, and immersing our children in Nigerian traditions and culture.

I enrolled Adanna at a Montessori school. When I taught kindergarten in Alexandria, Virginia, I was able to identify children who had a Montessori background right away. They seemed so bright, aware, and confident. I decided right then that if given the opportunity, I would provide my children with the same educational experiences. I took my children to the Iowa City Public Library three times a week, where we attended story time, and checked out books and educational videos. The children loved spending time playing at the library playground – it had an amazing water sprinkler.

Adanna befriended a girl by the name of Carolyn during our visits to the library and, before I knew it, I became friends with her mother, Amy Smellie. We started coordinating our meetings at the library together and, after meeting her husband Mark and her other two children Julia and Jordan, we became and continue to be very close friends. Amy invited me to her Bible study session. Before I knew it, I was attending a weekly Bible study group. I loved dissecting the Bible and having discussions to help clarify anything I didn't understand.

I really looked forward to our Bible study sessions. It wasn't long before Amy invited our family to her church, and we became regular members. Our family continued to grow as Christians and our children received an enriched Christian foundation at Sunday school. I learned so much about God's word and grace and was exposed to fine examples of Christian families. I became a solid Christian in Iowa City, and I am forever grateful. My Christian experiences in Iowa prepared and sustained me when devastation eventually reached my home in Alabama.

Iowa City is very much a family-oriented community, with a weekly calendar full of activities for children and families. In that spirit, my friend Monique and I created a group called Play With Color, providing educational, cultural, and art activities for children of color on weekends. We advertised, and children from other areas in Iowa began attending our group. We went on field trips, put on plays, and created our own little community. We basically raised our children together.

The following year Ferdinand and I built a home about ten minutes away from the hospital. The houses in the neighborhood had to be uniform; however, Ferdinand petitioned for a few changes. He wanted brick pillars in front of our house and specially designed numbers to adorn them. He was also particular about the color of our front door. We spent time at many paint stores in search of the perfect color. We even drove through the neighborhood looking at doors to make comparisons in an effort to find exactly what we wanted. Ferdinand tucked notes inside the structure of the house. He wanted the future owner to know the house was built with love.

We had another surprise awaiting us during that time. Soon after Ferdinand began at the university, I found out we were pregnant with our fourth child. I would be giving birth to another baby in

September. Something must have been in the water because my friend Monique was also pregnant, along with all four other members of our Play With Color Group.

As I describe the story of my wonderful life, I want to highlight the women I met in Iowa because they each helped me navigate life without Ferdinand. I can't stress enough how important it is to have solid friendships during times of tragedy and grief. I credit my belief in God, my family, and my solid friendships for helping me to successfully overcome the tragedy of Ferdinand's death.

CHAPTER 16
A BEAUTIFUL NEW ADVENTURE

Ferdinand with our four young children

I remember the day Ferdinand saw an ad in a medical trade journal seeking a Director of Transplants at the University of South Alabama Regional Transplant Center in Mobile, Alabama. Ferdinand circled the ad several times in blue ink, and I could tell by his expression he was really intrigued. Ferdinand had a zest for transplantation and loved the idea of being challenged. Although the opportunity to set up the entire program was an enormous task, I could see that Ferdinand was ready and willing to take on that responsibility. Little did we know our lives would change forever.

I had a relatively smooth pregnancy in Iowa City, but I tired easily since I also had three young children to care for. Although Okechukwu Jr. (we call him Okey, pronounced "Okay") was young at that time, they were protective of me and could sense when I wasn't feeling well or was fatigued. They checked on me frequently; hugging and giving me a kiss whenever I would lie down. Okey reminded me of his father in many ways; they were and still are very nurturing and caring.

I refer to Okey as "they" or "them" because as an adult they have chosen to be non-binary in how others refer to them and how they refer to themselves. I am very proud of Okey for coming to this realization and having the courage to speak up for themselves.

I gave birth to Chike in September of 1995, and we were elated when the doctor announced, "It's a boy!" Ferdinand was so happy to have another son, it would have been easy to think he hit the jackpot. Once he had a chance to hold Chike he beamed with pride and held him for a long time. I was beginning to wonder if he was ever going to let me hold him. It took a while, but he eventually did.

Chike means "God of power and strength" in Igbo. He was adorable and had a head full of curly black hair. Chike was a pleasant baby. He seemed to be content and wasn't fussy at all. As the fourth child, he quickly learned to be a spectator of sorts and was easily entertained by watching his brother and sisters in constant motion. Chike automatically learned to just go with the flow, and has the same personality today.

Once Nneka and Okey saw Chike for the first time, it was love at first sight. They couldn't wait to hold and cuddle him. Nneka acted like mommy Number Two, always stepping-in to hold, feed, and help care for Chike in any way she could. Okey was always in close proximity to their little brother. Chike could be found on a nearby blanket or in a baby seat whenever he was playing, watching a movie, or looking at books.

Adanna, the oldest, was the exception. She held Chike at arm's length the first time she saw him. She wouldn't even look him in the eye. According to Adanna, it seemed like every time she entered a hospital, a new baby was added to the household. She even told my mother to stay home because a visit from Nana often resulted in the addition of a new sibling. As a youngster, Adanna admits she loved her siblings from afar. She was an avid reader immersed in her own world. She spent most of her time reading books in her bedroom, and making mandatory appearances for meals, family movie or game nights. On occasion, she would voluntarily dialogue with her siblings.

Ferdinand did something that was uncharacteristic after Chike's birth. He was well established in his career and felt comfortable taking a week off work to help care for our children. It was the first time Ferdinand was all-hands-on deck and it was great having him around and available 24/7 to help. He was an incredible father and knew I would need additional support managing our new family of six.

I was shocked when I arrived home after Ferdinand picked Chike and me up from the hospital. I saw a huge white and blue banner welcoming our new baby boy hanging across our deck window. Ferdinand had purchased numerous bouquets of flowers and decorated Chike's room with streamers and bells hanging from the ceilings. Ferdinand was able to help bathe, prepare meals, and provide me many opportunities for much-needed naps. It was nice to experience how much more Ferdinand could do when he had the luxury of time. It was a blessing that Ferdinand had a lot of time to bond with Chike in the way he did. We didn't know it at the time, of course, but within a year, Ferdinand would be gone forever.

We gave Chike the middle name Nwosu after his grandfather, Chief Lawrence Nwosu Ukah, and it could not be more fitting. Over time we realized how much Chike resembled his grandfather in appearance, temperament, and communication style. Genetics are fascinating. Both of them were highly respected, mild-mannered individuals who were slow to speak and quick to listen.

I also have fond memories of Ferdinand spending time with Adanna at the foot of her bed, talking about the importance of education, studying, and becoming a doctor. I had to chuckle every time Ferdinand used a pad and pencil to teach Adanna complex math and science concepts at the age of five, as Adanna sat patiently listening, not understanding a word he said. Ferdinand valued education and took advantage of every opportunity to express how important it was to his children.

Okey adored their father, and at the age of two as soon as Ferdinand walked in the front door, Okey instantly ran to him, jumped into his arms and remained glued to his lap as Ferdinand ate, watched the news, or talked on the phone. Ferdinand took Okey on father-and-son evening trips to spend one-on-one time together. He took the girls out individually, too. They would venture to Walmart or Jack's Department Store to pick up children's video tapes, treats, and Power Ranger paraphernalia. They would also head to Dane's Dairy to get ice cream late at night, occasionally going to the playground. Ferdinand loved having a namesake and took Okechukwu with him on outings every opportunity he had.

Nneka was three years old and a ball of energy. She could be found moving from place to place in the house with a caravan of two or three strollers connected by string. They were loaded with at least six dolls, numerous stuffed animals compacted together with everything except the kitchen sink. Nneka was the most outgoing and adventuresome person in our family — she loved nature, animals, and exploring. Nneka was notorious for creating obstacle courses in the basement and recruiting or bribing her siblings to join her. She even coaxed Adanna to join in some of the fun. Nneka believed in having fun at all times. Ferdinand admired her spirit and spontaneous nature. Often, he would just sit and observe her. I remember the day Ferdinand sat me down and spoke to me in a serious tone.

"Cynthia, don't ever let Nneka lose that spirit."

I didn't understand why Ferdinand made that statement at the time. After Ferdinand's death, I remembered those words and tried my best to honor his request, although it was difficult at times.

Having time off also gave Ferdinand an opportunity to reflect on his career and think about next steps regarding his future. Ferdinand felt he was outgrowing his position at the University of Iowa. Everything seemed to be routine, and he did not feel as though he were learning anything new, perfecting his skill, or gaining more experience. Ferdinand wanted to make an impact and he wanted to become even more of an expert in his field. It was right at this time that Ferdinand saw the ad in a medical journal for a qualified doctor to become Director of Transplants at the University of South Alabama Regional Transplant Center.

I knew Ferdinand was an excellent surgeon and I believed in him one hundred percent. While I also knew Ferdinand had three years of experience as a transplant surgeon, I became a little concerned when I read the lengthy description of the responsibilities he would have in that role. I looked at Ferdinand cautiously. With a smile on my face, I approached the subject carefully.

"Ferdinand, this role is huge. What makes you think you can build a transplant program?"

Ferdinand responded with all of the self-assurance I had come to expect.

"What makes you think I can't?"

I knew Ferdinand could do it. I just wanted Ferdinand to understand the magnitude of this position and the sacrifices required to make a new program work. Ferdinand would be responsible for creating a Transplant Center from the bottom up. This meant he would have to convert a maternity ward into a transplant center – a monumental task. He would be the person responsible for making sure all medical equipment, supplies, and personnel were in place. He would also have to recruit, promote, and train people. Ferdinand believed he could do all of it and that was all I needed to know. He was so excited, confident, and ready to embark on this new endeavor. Ferdinand reached out to the University of South Alabama the very next day.

Ferdinand always had an interest in delving into the most challenging projects. He was passionate about what he did and knew his education and training in multi-organ transplantation would make him a great candidate. We did not tell anyone in Iowa he was applying for another position because we knew the competition would be stiff. We also felt people might question his ability to build a program from the ground up and we didn't want any distractions. Instead, we took a leap of faith and relied on God and prayer to help us through the process.

After the first interview, Ferdinand became heavily recruited by the University of South Alabama (USA) to direct their new center. Jay Scannelly, the USA administrator, came to Iowa City to interview Ferdinand personally. He also wanted to tour the hospital and observe Ferdinand in that professional setting. Ferdinand flew to USA several times to complete the interviewing process.

Ferdinand was interested in this position for many reasons. He was concerned about the underserved individuals along Alabama's Gulf Coast who were financially, physically, or emotionally unable to travel a long distance for transplants. This situation reminded Ferdinand of the challenges his family faced when he contracted malaria at the age of six. He remembered how difficult it was to travel interminable dirt roads to a remote Nigerian Hospital, and he didn't want others to experience similar obstacles.

The USA Regional Transplant Center would serve Alabama, the Gulf coast of Mississippi, and the panhandle of Florida. Prior to this, most Mobile patients had to travel two hundred and fifty miles to Birmingham to have transplant surgery. That journey was expensive, inconvenient, and difficult for most patients. At that time, approximately 10,000 kidney transplants were performed yearly in the United States, and more than 40,000 people were on the waiting list.

Ferdinand knew the Southeast region had one of the highest rates of kidney disease in the country and there were as many as 200 people waiting for a transplant in the area that could be served by the USA transplant center. Ferdinand's plan was to heavily promote organ donation and place emphasis on living donor transplants and cadaveric organs (organs from recently deceased donors) from the Alabama Organ Center in Birmingham. Having a transplant center close to those who needed it was practical, cost effective, and less stressful. It could also save lives because those patients who urgently required organ transplants would be able to get the surgery much quicker.

Ferdinand had my full support throughout the entire process, and I was his biggest cheerleader. We prayed through each phase of the interview process while I taped inspirational messages and Bible passages on note cards to help keep Ferdinand focused on his dream and thinking positively about the outcome. Ferdinand passed each phase of the interview process with flying colors. Before we knew it, my wonderful husband, Dr. Ferdinand O. Ukah, became the first Director of Transplants at the University of South Alabama Regional Transplant Center in Mobile, Alabama.

We felt we were headed south for a beautiful new adventure.

CHAPTER 17
GOODBYE, IOWA AND HELLO, ALABAMA

Ferdinand and his staff at the University of South Alabama Regional Transplant Center

We had built an extraordinary, joyful life in Iowa City, full of loving, supportive relationships I treasured deeply. It seemed like every day brought new adventures and reasons to appreciate my family and the wonderful friends who surrounded me. It was all that I could hope for, and I was grateful. Yet, after moving 900 miles and four states away to pursue the incredible opportunity Ferdinand had been handpicked for, my world was shattered in an instant because of his sudden, violent death. One year after moving away, I would come back to Iowa City. I needed every bit of love and support I could find. And I knew exactly where to find it.

I would find out these extremely special relationships I built in Iowa City were absolutely critical to help me through this unbelievably difficult time that I faced. I knew this is what Ferdinand would have wanted. When we left, Ferdinand and I couldn't understand why our home in Iowa didn't sell, although it almost sold three times. As I returned, however, I felt comfort moving back into the house Ferdinand and I had built four years prior. That home reflected Ferdinand's special touch and held great memories, and just being in that loving environment helped with the grieving process. Moving back into the home Ferdinand and I built together felt like the best thing to do. I felt like I belonged there with my children.

When we faced the prospect of our move from Iowa City, there was a mixture of excitement for this new opportunity in Alabama, combined with the sadness of saying good-bye. We had a wonderful and enriching time during our three years in Iowa and we met so many wonderful people. This new position in Alabama was exactly what Ferdinand wanted, and I was excited for him, proud of him, and looked forward to his promotion and new adventures I was going to have with my husband and our children. At the same time, there was a sadness associated with leaving the amazing Iowa community we were involved with and all the deeply held friendships we had established.

We were ecstatic for this new opportunity and couldn't wait to celebrate this major milestone. I kept thinking about Ferdinand's new title. I was so proud of him.

My husband, Dr. Ferdinand O. Ukah, Director of Transplantation at the University of South Alabama.

The day he was offered the job, Ferdinand contacted our babysitter, Adaeze to see if she would be available to watch our children that evening. She was the only babysitter we had used for the three years we lived in Iowa, and we trusted her completely. Adaeze was a wonderful young woman whom our children adored. The feeling was mutual on her part. When Ferdinand died unexpectedly, she showed up at our home in Alabama to help care for our children for a few days. This gave me an opportunity to focus on the memorial service and many crushing responsibilities associated with the death of my beloved husband.

Calling Adaeze to arrange for her to babysit was something special Ferdinand didn't do often. After he confirmed her availability, he asked me to get dressed up because we were going to celebrate at The Lark Restaurant and Lounge, one of the fanciest restaurants in the area. When we found out Ferdinand had been hired, the kids and I made a banner congratulating Ferdinand and displayed it out front. As soon as he burst into the house from sheer excitement, he ran to me, giving me the biggest hug ever and picking his children up one by one to give them a hug and kiss as well.

We cheered, hugged, laughed, and cried tears of joy, chanting "U-S-A, U-S-A" because he was going to the University of South Alabama. We had fun repeating the phrase several times before he quickly ran upstairs to get dressed. We had a 6 p.m. reservation and didn't want to be late. The drive to the restaurant was a joyous one. We held each other's hand and intermittently stared at each other in disbelief as Ferdinand displayed his million-dollar smile. I repeatedly told Ferdinand how proud I was of him, as we prayed, thanked God, and talked about how blessed we were. Ferdinand beamed with pride the entire ride, periodically slapping his hand on the dashboard because he was so excited.

The ambiance at the restaurant was perfect. Each table was covered with white linen tablecloths, pink underlays, and flowers at the center of the table. Ferdinand sipped on an expensive glass of wine as we reminisced about our time in Iowa and talked about how happy we were. We enjoyed a delicious steak and salad dinner as Ferdinand shared details about the final phase of the interview process. He was excited to tell me about his compensation package and with the biggest smile, informed me that he would soon be rewarding himself by purchasing his dream car, a Range Rover. He definitely deserved it and I couldn't have been happier. Ferdinand also mentioned we would have to move relatively soon, and that he would have to make several more trips to the university down south.

I wanted to make sure the transition was smooth for our children, too. Adanna was in first grade at Roosevelt Elementary School in Iowa City. She loved school and had established very close friendships. We felt she would be most affected by the move, and I wanted to make sure she was prepared. The students in her class were researching quails and we knew Adanna would be disappointed if she didn't have the opportunity to see the eggs hatch at the end of the unit. Her close friend, Georgia, promised to call her in Alabama with quail updates once Adanna moved. Georgia kept her promise and called Adanna the day the eggs hatched. Adanna was elated.

Four-year-old Nneka and three-year-old Okey attended Montessori School. The schools in Iowa City are outstanding. Based on what I had heard, schools in the south did not consistently have high ratings and that concerned me. My first priority quickly became researching schools in Alabama. I was fully prepared to homeschool our children if the local schools did not meet my expectations. To support this goal, I wanted to make sure our next home had an extra room I would be able to use as a classroom.

After talking about our three years in Iowa City and remembering all the wonderful experiences we had, we were saddened. We had developed so many heartfelt, meaningful friendships there. I still think of Iowa as one of America's best-kept secrets. It's a wonderful place to live and to raise a family, yet few people pay attention to Iowa on a map. Iowa City is small, safe, family-oriented and kid-friendly. My lasting impression of people in Iowa is that they are genuine, have big hearts, love spending time with friends, and believe in making family a priority.

We knew saying good-bye wasn't going to be easy. I had so many anxious thoughts. For example, how was I going to tell Mrs. Heather (the sweetest woman in the world) and her husband Tim that our family was moving, and we could no longer have our annual pumpkin carving and pumpkin-seed roasting? There would be no more Chuck E. Cheese outings and family movie nights with their kids Erin and Neil, either.

The thought of telling my friend Monique that we were moving tied my stomach in knots. I couldn't imagine not spending time with her family on weekends and special occasions. A few days before we left Iowa, Monique and friends from our play group presented me with a heart-shaped plaque engraved with the name of the group we founded, "Play with Color." We both cried and could barely look at each other. Quite a contrast from our first meeting in which we couldn't take our eyes off each other. It was so very difficult to say good-bye to Monique and all our many, dear friends.

Ferdinand had also developed close relationships with his colleagues and knew they would be shocked to learn he was leaving. I knew his coworkers would be happy for him, because becoming the director of a transplant center is a huge promotion into a very prestigious position. They would also be surprised because Ferdinand hadn't given any indication throughout the hiring process that he had plans to leave the University of Iowa. Ferdinand decided to first share the news of our move with our close friends Dr. Tony Otoadese and his wife, Dr. Claudia Corwin. Claudia was a transplant surgeon and native New Yorker, and we had instantly bonded and became friends when we arrived in Iowa City years earlier. Tony was a Nigerian cardiac and thoracic surgeon.

Ferdinand and Tony spent what little downtime they had sharing stories about Nigeria, discussing Nigerian politics, listening to Nigerian music, and comparing hospital experiences. We developed a close relationship because of our mutual connection with New York and Nigeria. We also traveled in the same social circle, attending the same professional dinners and events together. Claudia and Tony had three children, Max, Ava, and Ben. Our children spent a lot of time with theirs and we considered them family. They were both very happy for Ferdinand and wished him the best of luck.

Once the formal announcement was made by the University of Iowa, we spent most weekends celebrating Ferdinand and saying good-bye to friends whenever he was at home in Iowa City. The Nigerian Community gave us a nice send-off and the transplant department had a going-away party for Ferdinand. We were also invited to our friends' homes and out for dinner practically every weekend once we made the announcement.

Preparing for the move was hectic, as we had fewer than four months to uproot our family from Iowa and settle in Alabama. Once Ferdinand secured the position and signed on the dotted line, everything seemed to be on fast forward. Ferdinand spent most of his time tying up loose ends at the University of Iowa, while at the same time frequently traveling to Mobile to build the Transplant Program and secure housing for our family. He also spent a great deal of time networking with his new colleagues and promoting organ donation in several communities near Mobile. While he was busy with his professional activities, I spent most of my time caring for our children, comparing schools for the kids, and looking for a church to call home.

Ferdinand and I drove my Dodge Caravan to Alabama, dividing the trip into two days. We loaded Ferdinand's new car into the moving truck. It was interesting driving through the Deep South, because it was the first time I had ever seen blatant signs of poverty in the United States. I felt as though we were going back in time, and the sight broke my heart. I knew Mobile was a thriving big city and I waited with anticipation as we drove closer to our destination.

By the time we arrived at our new home, Ferdinand's car was sitting in the driveway and all of our belongings were stacked in their respective rooms. The children had fun running around the house, up and down the stairs, and exploring all of the many rooms. Before I knew it, they were exhausted. We ordered dinner, made up beds, bathed the children and put them to sleep.

Moving to Mobile felt like a dream come true. Once I caught my breath and was able to take everything in, I was able to bask in the magnificence of our beautiful home. Ferdinand had purchased the perfect house for our family on Churchbell Court — a brick two-story, five-bedroom home with a huge backyard. Ferdinand finally had a *study*, too. In our Iowa home, he had a makeshift office with bright lights and a clunky computer situated directly next to the playroom in our unfinished basement. The Mobile study had French doors and wall-to-wall, built-in mahogany shelves. I could visualize Ferdinand displaying framed pictures of his accomplishments, including numerous newspaper clippings welcoming him to the University of South Alabama and advertisements for his new transplant center. These would be displayed because of our deep pride that we — the Ukah party of six — had come so far. We had worked hard to create our beautiful family and this wonderful life. We were so excited to be living this dream.

Next to Ferdinand's study on the main floor was an off-white contemporary kitchen with a huge island and see-through decorative cabinets. The master bedroom was on the same floor with a set of winding stairs that led up to the children's bedrooms. I loved the Jack & Jill rooms – two identical bedrooms connected by a bathroom in between for the kids. I had plans to convert one of the bedrooms into a classroom. Ferdinand toured our neighborhood school, Pauline O'Rourke Elementary, and met with the principal a few times before we decided to enroll Adanna and Nneka in public school. I still felt it was my responsibility to ensure my children's academic success and, at a minimum, I was committed to provide my children with supplemental enrichment activities after school and on weekends to give them an extra boost. I planned on supplementing their kindergarten and second-grade studies with order-by-mail Christian curricula.

Upon arrival in our new home, the major design/building project we undertook was an outdoor swimming pool. Ferdinand was adamant about having a swimming pool in our backyard, and not just any pool, but a kidney-shaped pool to represent his passion as a kidney transplant surgeon. Initially, I thought he was kidding. That was before he hired a contractor and started making plans to build a kidney-shaped pool. I did have reservations — the first being that Ferdinand couldn't swim. Secondly, we had four young children and pool/water safety was a real concern for me. Despite voicing hesitation, I quickly realized how important this pool was to Ferdinand — each of our neighbors had a pool and it was a sign to him that he made it to the big league. After years of training and career navigation, we now had a family home in a wealthy suburb in Alabama. We felt we had it all!!

CHAPTER 18
ALABAMA AND AN UNINTENDED DRESS REHEARSAL

Ferdinand being interviewed by local media at the opening of the regional transplant center

Our first night at the new home didn't go exactly as planned. Throughout our time as a couple — six years of courtship and nine years of marriage, to be exact — Ferdinand had been healthy as an ox. Though he was a deeply anxious person, we soon discovered a good chunk of our social life was full of physicians living with the same tight anxiety and proclivity for success while coping with a highly stressful environment. While he had a few bouts with ulcers, he'd never taken a "sick day" or suffered through something Pepto-Bismol couldn't cure.

It was a real shock then when Ferdinand fell gravely ill the night before he was to show up for his highly publicized first day of work at the University of South Alabama Regional Transplant Center. The sickness came out of nowhere, without warning. I was preparing for bed and thought Ferdinand was already asleep. As I went to turn off the light, he suddenly spoke.

"Cynthia, I'm scared."

Surprised, I gently climbed over him, peered into his face and saw fear in his eyes. That's when I became scared, as well. I was terrified, but had to remain calm because I didn't want to make a difficult situation worse. I also had to maintained control since I had four young children sleeping upstairs.

Ferdinand quietly muttered that he couldn't move and felt like he was paralyzed on the right side of his body. After several attempts to soothe him, I massaged him to try and relax his muscles. I also tried — and failed — to shift his body to another position. It was then my mind started firing off.

The fact that I couldn't shift his body to a more comfortable, mobile position wasn't surprising because Ferdinand was huge. He was a solid 6'3", 200-pound man, and there was no way I could get him to budge by myself. I felt helpless.

After several minutes, I tried to convince him I should dial 911. Ferdinand simply refused, saying "How can a transplant surgeon, who is expected to start the day with a huge reception and welcoming committee, move to Alabama and end up in a hospital bed on the day everyone, including the press, is anticipating his arrival?"

On one hand, I got it. I understood where he was coming from. Appearances were everything, and we were already doing so much to appear steady, solid, and acceptable. On the other hand, as his wife I knew I had to convince him to make his health a priority. Racking my brain, I thought it through.

We didn't have any over-the-counter medicine because we just moved and had barely unpacked.

The option of purchasing meds was out of the question because it was close to midnight, and I didn't have a clue where the nearest pharmacy was located.

In addition, I had four young children — including a toddler — who would be left home alone with an immobile adult if I went searching for medicine.

I also felt I couldn't ask neighbors for help because I didn't know them. They were complete strangers.

We were at an impasse and were getting scared. It was then we chose to proceed with prayer. Ferdinand and I stayed in the bed and prayed nonstop through the night for healing and a quick recovery.

For the first time in my life, as I sat there praying, I thought about the possibility of living without Ferdinand. Between prayers, I ran through scenarios and pondered thoughts that had never come to mind before. I asked myself so many questions:

Who can I call to watch my children if we have to go to the hospital?

How will I move his body, should anything happen to him?

How can I possibly raise four children alone?

I thought about finances, employment, childcare, and how I'll be able to afford to live in this huge house. Where would I go and what would I do?

The hours that night felt like days, and I came up with zero answers. As a stay-at-home mother, with a new mortgage and without a single friend in the area, I felt my only option was to ask God for a miracle.

At the end of that stressful, drawn-out night, our prayers were answered. Miraculously, Ferdinand got up the next morning feeling much more like himself. He was slightly sore and stiff, but mentally agile despite a sleepless night. He was ready for work.

Looking back, I view this distressing incident as a dress rehearsal of sorts. God gave me a small glimpse of what would lie ahead and asked me to ponder questions that had never crossed my mind.

Though I came up with no answers at that time, I had at least asked myself some important, if frightening, questions.

I didn't yet know that a much more tangible, unchangeable shift was coming to our family that would force me to confront the unthinkable, bear the unbearable, move on, and figure life out without Ferdinand by side.

About a month after we moved, Ferdinand's longtime friend Iloba from Portland State came to Alabama to visit for a few days. Ferdinand gave Iloba a tour of the new transplant center, spent time talking about their years in Portland, and talked about God and their faith at length. Iloba is very religious and before he left, he gave me three gospel cassette tapes. I'm a creature of habit and at that time I primarily listened to children's music in my van. It was one sure way to keep the kids quiet and engaged while driving. I decided to try something new, and I listened to each cassette tape. To my surprise the kids and I really enjoyed them.

From that day on, gospel music became our staple and was the only music we listened to the entire time we lived in Alabama. This is another instance in which I think there was divine intervention. I believe I was being prepared for what was to come. Gospel music became a part of my life, as I was constantly being fed God's word. Each song emphasized God's promise of love, grace, support, and mercy. Without knowing it, I was being reassured and comforted by God every time I drove my car. I believe God was setting the stage, subconsciously getting me in the right frame of mind to prepare me for my husband's untimely death.

We were both excited about Ferdinand's new role at the University of South Alabama Regional Transplant Center. Ferdinand was confident in his skill set and nervous because all eyes were on him at the same time. He knew the first surgery had to be a success if he wanted people to take him and his program seriously. Finding the first patient was another challenge. Very few people volunteer to be first to be operated on when a transplant center is just getting started. After carefully screening several candidates, the university decided to transplant the kidney of a man whose sister agreed to be her brother's organ donor. The kidney was almost a perfect match.

I remember the days leading up to the surgery. The media seemed to be ever present because of the excitement surrounding a successful transplant in Mobile, Alabama. Again, I plastered Bible verses on sticky notes all over our home. I wanted to encourage Ferdinand to rely on God and his surgical skills to make the operation a success. Ferdinand went into the operating room at 4:30 in the morning so as not to disrupt the current operating schedule. Thankfully, the first transplant was a huge success and Ferdinand received a lot of media attention and praise.

We also made friends and met some wonderful people as we started our new life in Alabama. These included our neighbors, Clarence and Charlesetta Ball, our insurance agent Mecada, and Olinda, an employee at the Social Security Office. They would all be extremely comforting and helpful as I navigated the tragedy that was about to come.

Ferdinand also befriended the owner of a funeral home. Shortly after our move to Alabama, Ferdinand read a newspaper article about a Nigerian family who lost two children in a fatal car accident. Ferdinand insisted that we attend the funeral as supportive members of the Nigerian community. We arrived late because, of course, Ferdinand had to operate.

When Ferdinand walked up to view the little boy's body, he cried and was visibly upset by what he saw. I wasn't sure why he reacted that way. I was surprised because he didn't know the boy or his family personally. For some unknown reason, Ferdinand also struck up a long conversation with the owner of the funeral home. The conversation lasted so long, I had to interrupt them so I could get my children home.

The day after I found out my husband died, that same funeral director showed up at my front door. He said he saw the news of my husband's passing in the newspaper and wanted to assist with funeral services. This is just one of the many examples where God provided the help I needed at the exact time I needed it.

CHAPTER 19
OUR LAST GOOD-BYE

The two of us at a black-tie fundraiser for the University of South Alabama

I'll never forget the last time I saw his face. Ferdinand was notorious for being late whenever he had to travel. He typically stayed at work until the last possible minute, rushing home to pack and quickly saying good-bye to the kids and me before darting out the door 30 minutes before his flight was scheduled to take off. It used to drive me crazy until I realized it was a recurring pattern. This particular trip was more hectic than most. Ferdinand was traveling to Nigeria with large boxes of medical equipment and supplies. There was no room for error and Ferdinand couldn't be late.

He had made arrangements to operate on his father and time was of the essence. I asked a neighbor's daughter to watch our children for an hour so I could help Ferdinand transport boxes to the airport. Thank goodness, the airport was only 15 minutes away. We made one trip together, carrying the heaviest boxes first. Ferdinand had to stay at the airport to keep an eye on the boxes, while I made two more trips to get the remaining boxes. I was exhausted by the time I completed the third round. I had been carrying boxes and placing them strategically in the car, all while trying to beat the clock. I couldn't believe it when Ferdinand made one last request.

"Cynthia, will you go home and bring the children to the airport? I want to see my children one last time before I leave."

Are you serious?

You must be kidding.

Do you realize how much energy I mustered up just to get your medical equipment and supplies to the airport?

And now, you want me to load the children in the van, park the car and walk to the airport just to wave good-bye?

I couldn't believe Ferdinand had the audacity to ask me to make a fourth trip to the airport. I didn't have any energy left and was looking forward to sitting down and relaxing. I loved Ferdinand; however, I didn't want to make another trip. I felt it would be meaningless because I knew he would be at the gate and ready to board the plane by the time I returned to the airport. I did consider lying and telling him I drove the kids to the airport, but he was already gone by the time we arrived. That made perfect sense and it certainly sounded plausible to me. Thank God, I made a decision that ended up having far more meaning than I gave it at the time.

Although I knew Ferdinand's request was unreasonable, I loaded the children in the car and took them to the airport based on a good-faith effort. When I arrived, I was surprised to see Ferdinand standing behind a Plexiglass window, waving, blowing kisses to our four beautiful children, and playing games by matching their hands from opposite sides of the glass. They were so excited to see their father and I'm glad I decided to make that fourth and final trip. Of course, I had no idea that was going to be the last time our family would see Ferdinand alive. I'm so proud of myself for making the right decision, even though I didn't want to at the time. When Ferdinand died, I didn't have any regrets. I felt I gave him my all and we didn't leave anything unsaid.

While I realize what happened afterward was not my fault, I'm pretty certain I would have regretted not bringing my children to the airport and I probably would have felt guilty for the rest of my life. I'm sure it was a little easier handling the death of my loving husband because I didn't have regrets.

My mother recalled the evening she received that chilling phone call from my brother-in-law Clem on that fateful night. The phone rang shortly after my mom returned home from work. She answered the call and heard somebody screaming on the other end. She could barely understand him, he was yelling as he was telling my mother "Ferdinand is dead." He repeated those words over and over again in very blunt terms.

"Ferdinand was in a car accident, and you have twenty-four hours to get to Alabama to tell Cynthia before she goes to the airport to pick Ferdinand up. I'll call her tomorrow at midnight. Tell her to expect my call."

Clem had gotten straight to the point and abruptly hung up the phone. My mother was in a state of shock. She didn't have time to emotionally process what she had just heard, much less break down or cry. She had so much to do with just a small window of time. There was no chance to be sentimental; she had to take action immediately because time was of the essence.

The first thing she did was call my brother, Darryl. Like everyone else who received the terrible news, he couldn't believe Ferdinand had died. Despite his shock, he made arrangements for my mother to fly out of New York first thing in the morning. Amidst all of the chaos, my mother remembered me talking about our neighbors, the Balls, and looked their names up in the telephone directory. She called them and shared the devastating news. She then asked Charlesetta to pick her up from the airport once she arrived in Alabama. My mother also asked them to keep the information confidential. She didn't want the news to get out until she had an opportunity to talk to me first.

She had asked Darryl to pray that I wouldn't call her that evening. My mom didn't think she would be able to compose herself or control her emotions once she heard my voice. She immediately started packing, not knowing what to pack or how long she would be gone. She realized her prayers weren't answered when the phone rang that evening. My mother froze as soon as she heard it and prayed that God would give her the strength she needed to get through the phone call without crying or divulging too much information.

The saving grace was that we had just come home from a fun-filled event at Pauline O'Rourke Elementary School. The kids had so much fun and were excited to share the evening events with their Nana. Adanna and Nneka were basically fighting over the phone to determine who would share their experience first. Talking to the children broke the ice for my mother and served as a well-needed distraction. After talking to the girls and Okey, it was finally my turn. I couldn't talk long because I had to get my children to bed since we were going to pick their daddy up from the airport.

The last thing I said to my mother was "God is so good."

After hanging up the phone, she later told me so many thoughts ran through her head.

I wonder if I'll ever see Cynthia smile again.

I wonder if I will ever hear her say "God is good" ever again.

Will she say God is good after I tell her Ferdinand is dead?

I wouldn't blame her if she didn't.

She has a right to be angry with God.

Once my mom delivered the horrible news and I had time to talk to and console my children, the next thing we had to do was extremely painful, but necessary. We needed to contact family members and friends to inform them of Ferdinand's premature death. Thankfully, my mother volunteered to handle the phone calls and I made an initial list of important people she should contact immediately.

After that, my mother used Ferdinand's phone book and went down the list, starting with the letter A and going in alphabetical order to disclose the terrible news. Although my mother was in the kitchen making calls, I was in the next room and could hear the screams on the other end of the line as my mom talked to each person. So many people thought my mother was confused.

"Hello, this is Roberta, Cynthia's mother. I'm calling to tell you, Ferdinand died."

I could hear the screaming, yelling, and crying from the adjoining room.

"No, I'm not talking about Ferdinand's father. I'm talking about Ferdinand. He died in a car accident."

Almost everyone was in complete shock and denial. Responses often resulted in screams, yelling, and loud crying. People would argue with my mother because they simply couldn't believe what they were hearing. My mother was my rock, my anchor, and my biggest supporter during that time. She sat at the kitchen table making call after call, looking defeated and totally worn out. I so very much appreciate all that she did for me. I couldn't have gotten through those difficult days without her.

Our insurance agent, Mecada, came as soon as she heard what had happened. She walked into our home and asked where Ferdinand's important papers were. She immediately went into our beautiful study, closed the French doors, and meticulously went through all of Ferdinand's paperwork. I didn't have to do anything except care for my children. It was as if God had the perfect plan, and all the people I needed were already in place. This lessened the burden and reduced my stress immensely.

Ferdinand talked about insurance all of the time. He was constantly dealing with life-and-death situations with families who had children, and he saw the devastation that occurred when a spouse didn't have insurance. I didn't pay too much attention to it at the time, because it didn't affect me, and I thought it was a non-issue for our family. Ferdinand and I were both very healthy and we expected to live a long time. Meanwhile, Ferdinand encouraged everyone he knew to get insurance.

He would always tell family and friends, "If you love your family, you better get insurance and look out for them in the event something happens to you."

I heard Ferdinand say that often throughout the years. I knew he had insurance, but I didn't know how much. The University of South Alabama was expeditious and generous. They provided a large check to help sustain our family immediately. Mecada located all of the insurance papers and reassured me Ferdinand had looked out for our family and left us in good financial shape.

Ferdinand having insurance was the greatest blessing. Because of his wisdom and love for us, I was able to focus on our children without the burden of wondering how I was going to pay bills. Ferdinand's close friends, Dr. Okori, Dr. Odocha, Dr. Ukoh, and Iloba, helped us out financially right away as well. Ferdinand's close friends have always been supportive of me and our family in so many ways.

My friend Olinda, who worked at the Social Security office, had Social Security checks distributed to our family within days. Because of all this loving and generous support, I was able to still be a stay-at-home mom and raise Adanna, Nneka, Okey, and Chike without having to worry about housing or where our next meal was coming from. I am forever indebted to Ferdinand because he cared for our family in his life — and after his untimely death. I have always made sure I give Ferdinand credit for everything we did as a family. Ferdinand provided the funds for rent, food, clothing, and school supplies, Ferdinand's money paid for family vacations, extracurricular activities, birthday celebrations, and Christmas gifts. I always emphasized that Mommy wasn't working, and I didn't have income.

I made sure my children understood what their father provided for them on a daily basis.

Ferdinand's oldest sister Mary called a week after Ferdinand's death and kept repeating the word "Biko," which means *please* in Igbo. She strongly encouraged me to honor Nigerian traditions and rituals regarding widows. I listened carefully to her because I wasn't familiar with any of the traditions, and I was in total shock when I found out what they entailed. Throughout it all, Mary was very sweet and well-intentioned. She spoke to me in a delicate manner and knew this was a sensitive subject.

I was already having difficulty coming to terms with the fact that I was a widow at the age of thirty-five and now was faced with these Nigerian traditions. According to Mary, I would be required to shave my hair, as well as my daughter's hair, and keep it shaved for an entire year. When I asked what the purpose was, Mary simply explained it was a way to let everyone know I was a widow in mourning.

While I honored Nigerian customs whenever I could, my perspective on this was completely different. My children had just lost their father. I wasn't going to turn their world upside down even more by changing my appearance, or theirs, for that matter. I respect Nigerian traditions; however, I kept remembering what Ferdinand always told me.

"Cynthia, don't do anything you don't feel comfortable doing. I trust your judgment."

It was not simply about my level of comfort. My children would also be traumatized all over again after we already experienced a major shift in our lives. There was no need to compound our problems.

Next, Mary also told me I should wear black garments for an entire year. As much as I respected my sister-in-law and Nigerian customs, walking around with a shaved head and wearing black for a year would lead me to severe depression. I had already lost my husband. I couldn't bear losing myself also, in the process. I felt like following these traditions would mean I was the one being punished for being widowed.

When the topic of scarification (scarring) of our faces with a knife or razor was mentioned, I gasped as I responded to Mary.

"I'm sorry, but I can't commit to any of these rituals."

While I appreciated Mary sharing the information with me, I had to explain how challenging it would be to adhere to such traditions under my current circumstances. The thought of causing my children an ounce of pain under these circumstances was incomprehensible to me. Making the slightest mark on each child's face would be out of the question and there was absolutely no way I was going to consider that. I respectfully thanked my sister-in-law and told her I didn't feel comfortable doing any of it.

Throughout this ordeal, I saw God's hand in my life in numerous ways. God prepared me to raise our kids almost single-handedly from the start. Because Ferdinand spent so many hours at the hospital, I knew in my mind that Ferdinand was married to his life-saving work at the hospital first. He was always dealing with life-and-death situations, and I understood his patients would always be his first priority. I was fully prepared to raise our children in the manner Ferdinand expected, even though he wasn't physically with us. I decided to keep his memory alive by talking about Ferdinand in the present tense as much as possible. I remember often thinking of how much I appreciate Ferdinand, so much so that my thoughts became something of a mantra for me.

Ferdinand will always be their father.

He provided for us, even though he suffered an untimely death.

I will always be indebted to him, and I'll make sure my children will always remember him.

The fact that Ferdinand spent the last three weeks of his life with his family in Nigeria was a blessing, too. Spending time with his mother, father, brothers, and sisters was a rare and special gift. They hadn't seen or spent time with Ferdinand in years. He was able to express his love to all of his family members. He totally immersed himself in Nigerian culture, ate delicious traditional foods, and gave everyone an opportunity to enjoy his company for what would be the last time.

Successfully operating on his father was the greatest honor. If Ferdinand had to pass away, spending his final days in Nigeria with his family was the best way to go. Ferdinand left this earth as a trailblazer, hero, loving son, and treasured family member. Although I miss him terribly, he died at the height of his career. He had accomplished so much during his short time here on earth and was loved by many.

I realized how lucky and special I was a few days after Ferdinand's death. Once I was able to take a breath and pause, I was able to think about everything and process what had transpired in my life. I felt extremely blessed to be the woman who was fortunate enough to be Ferdinand's wife. Of all the women in the world who could have married this amazing man, I was the chosen one and I will be forever grateful.

Ferdinand was a planner, and we talked about every aspect of having kids before we got married. I knew exactly what Ferdinand expected me to do in his absence and it was my goal to continue to make him proud. It was at this time I made a decision that "the show must go on" and nothing was going to deter me.

Based on our conversations over the years, Ferdinand had provided the map and blueprint in terms of how we would raise our children. My job was to execute and put our plan into action and that is exactly what I did. We would continue to work together as a team, and we would raise the children exactly as we planned. Over the years of raising our children, I also learned an extremely valuable lesson: when in doubt, pray.

CHAPTER 20
FUNERAL PLANS

In loving memory of

Ferdinand Ukah

Born into life
July 26, 1957
Born into eternity
October 8, 1996

Memorial Service
November 3, 1996

University of Iowa Hospitals and Clinics

The program from Ferdinand's memorial service at the University of Iowa.

My mom kept having recurring dreams that she described as pure chaos. She constantly heard phones ringing, people yelling, and children crying. She could sense something terrible was going to happen to me. She was afraid for my life.

Once the memorial service in Mobile concluded, it was time to prepare for the funeral in Nigeria. I asked my mother if she would take care of my children for a week while I traveled to Nigeria. She wasn't happy about the idea but hesitantly said yes. I knew my mother would do anything for me; she just wanted to make life easy for me. Mom made it perfectly clear she didn't think I should leave my children at such a critical time. My children were one, three, five and seven years of age at the time of Ferdinand's death. In my mom's mind, not only did my children lose their father, she was concerned they would also lose their mother if I traveled to Nigeria, as well.

I had already asked Ferdinand's best friend Iloba to accompany me to Nigeria for the funeral. He was the only person I felt comfortable and safe with as I traveled as a grieving widow. I felt comforted when he said yes. I made arrangements to renew my passport, paying the extra fee to get it back as soon as possible. I was relieved when I was told the passport would arrive within three weeks. This meant it would get to me a day or two before my flight. I was cutting it close but was reassured it would arrive on time.

Clem highly encouraged me to travel with two specific people. Although I told Clem Iloba was my first choice, I followed Clem's directives because I knew I would have to make a few compromises. Clem insisted that I only travel with his two choices. He said that, according to Nigerian tradition, I would have to travel only with family members. Kodo was a cousin who often referred to Ferdinand as his brother. Peter, as far as I knew, was a close family friend. While I wasn't sure what his familial relationship was, I felt I had to comply with Clem's instructions because I had already opted out of the mourning recommendations my sister-in-law Mary made previously.

Clem made it clear he specifically wanted me to travel with just Kodo and Peter. I knew Kodo because he lived with us in Bowie, Maryland for six months. I also knew Peter. He was a shy, quiet friend of Ferdinand's. While I would have preferred to have Iloba come with me, I was okay with Kodo and Peter as my escorts. As the time to travel got closer, my mother became more anxious and was convinced I shouldn't go.

"Cynthia, I have a very bad feeling about this trip. How could you leave your children and travel overseas for an entire week?"

I explained to her that Ferdinand was a model husband and an amazing father. He had a loving wife and family who adored him. There was no way I would allow Ferdinand to be laid to rest without being there to personally say my good-byes. I wanted to show the Nigerian community how much I loved and cared for him. The only way to do that was to attend his funeral, no matter where it was.

I added it would be a huge embarrassment and dishonor to Ferdinand if his wife didn't show up for his funeral. I felt I owed Ferdinand that much and I wasn't going to let him down. I couldn't imagine any wife not attending her husband's funeral. Not only that, Ferdinand and I would be the talk of the town and I could just imagine what the Nigerians would say.

"You see, he never should have married that American woman. She didn't have the decency to attend her own husband's funeral." I could hear it clearly.

I also thought people might focus more on my absence and not Ferdinand's brilliance and contributions to his hometown in Nigeria. My mind was set, and nothing was going to stop me. Ferdinand deserved to have his wife at his send-off and I was determined to be there.

Three days before I was supposed to travel, one of Clem's escorts called and told me he couldn't accompany me on the trip. He didn't provide a reason and I didn't worry because I still had another person to travel with. Even at that point, my mother couldn't understand how I could leave my children alone for a week after my kids had just lost their father. I just wrote it off that my mother didn't understand how much I loved Ferdinand.

When my mom returned to New York to pack enough clothing to stay with my children for a week, she was astounded when she opened her front door. Upon entering her apartment, she found on the floor a shattered frame with my picture in it. There were tiny pieces of glass dispersed throughout her entryway. To her, this represented what she saw in her dreams and was confirmation I was in danger. My mom decided to try her best to convince me not to go.

My mother returned to Alabama a few days before my departure, and I told her Peter, one of Clem's escorts, had bailed on me. I wasn't too worried or bothered by his backing out. I was more concerned because my passport had not arrived as promised. I'm sure my mother was secretly hoping it wouldn't arrive. That way it would be impossible for me to travel to Nigeria.

After making several phone calls to determine what the holdup with my passport was all about, I was told it was mailed to my mother's address in New York. I was devastated. I couldn't believe it. How could something like this happen? I had used my mother's address when I got my initial passport, but it made no sense that I would have put that same address on my renewal application. I didn't understand what had caused this.

Because there was no way I would be able to fly to New York to retrieve it in time for my reserved flight, I immediately flew to Chicago to get a same-day passport. Even though I had a one-track mind, I questioned why I was coming up against all these obstacles. More to the point, my mother's concerns became louder and more pronounced.

"Can't you see what is happening? God is trying to tell you not to go to Nigeria. Cynthia, don't you understand? Clem's escort bailed on you. Your passport didn't arrive.

"Cynthia, your children need you! God keeps putting obstacles in your way and you just keep jumping through all the hoops to get around them.

"I am not going to be the one to tell your children they lost their mother, too. Before you leave, make a tape recording explaining why you left them and why you are gone. I am not prepared to deliver any more bad news, Cynthia, especially to your children."

This was the first time I can remember my mother and I ever having a heated disagreement. I knew my mother was looking out for my safety and I understood her concern. I also knew I wouldn't be able to forgive myself if I didn't go to his funeral. That was the biggest reason why I was so persistent. Ferdinand loved me like no other and I wanted to return the same sentiment.

Kodo, my other escort from Clem, and I made plans to meet at Kennedy Airport. I arrived two hours early and called him several times. My calls all went to voicemail. However, on the fifth try, he answered the phone.

"Kodo. Where are you?"

"I'm here."

"Where?"

"At the airport, waiting for you at the airport. I'm at the gate."

"I am too. I don't see you."

I confirmed where I was and asked him to describe what he was wearing. He tried to convince me that he was also waiting in the same area. Yet, I didn't see him at all. I was so confused.

That is strange, why is he telling me he is at the gate when he clearly is not?

Kodo was nowhere to be seen. He lived with Ferdinand and me for six months and I knew exactly what he looked like. There wasn't anyone at the gate fitting his description. After communicating with him by phone, paging him on the loudspeaker twice, and confirming the airport, airline, and departure gate, I came to the chilling conclusion that Kodo wasn't at the airport at all. He had no intention of accompanying me to Nigeria. I realized Kodo had flat-out stood me up and he had stopped answering the phone altogether.

I called my mother to tell her I had been stood up and would have to travel to Nigeria alone. Once again, my mother pleaded with me to come home, reiterating that my children needed me and traveling to Nigeria just wasn't meant to be. Referencing her dream and all the chaos associated with it, she implored me once again.

"God was showing you all the signs to prove you shouldn't travel. God is giving you so many chances to change your mind. Why are you being so unreasonable and stubborn?"

Before hanging up the phone she told me she loved me. She also left me with a final, chilling warning.

"Cynthia, if you get on that plane, you will not make it back home to your children."

I was faced with the reality that once again I was left all alone. I didn't have anyone to depend on and I would have to fly to Nigeria by myself to bury my husband. I knew I would not have any support. At that point, I was in a state of shock and disbelief. There were so many unanswered questions, beginning with the most urgent one.

Why would someone say they would accompany me to Nigeria and flat-out lie about being at the airport?

Although I didn't feel at all comfortable traveling to Nigeria alone, I knew my Ferdinand deserved to be honored in a respectful manner. I felt I had no other choice, and I was going to do everything in my power to make Ferdinand proud.

Before I knew it, all the passengers at my departure gate were on the plane. I kept hearing my name on the loudspeaker, yet I couldn't stand up. An airline attendant walked up to me and asked if I was Cynthia Ukah. She told me I had to get on the plane immediately because the doors were going to close in three minutes. She literally had to help me stand up and walk with her as she held my arm to assist me as I slowly went down the jetway. As soon as I approached the entryway to the plane, my body totally froze. I couldn't take another step. I couldn't walk, talk, or respond to any questions. It wasn't that I was afraid, it was more that I was confused but calm at the same time. As I found myself in a situation where I couldn't move forward, and I couldn't move back, the doors closed without my getting on the plane.

My mind was in a fog as a long time elapsed. I remember being seated in a wheelchair alone in an empty airport. I was disoriented and I walked around the airport in a zombie-like state for a few hours. I didn't comprehend what had just happened to me. By the time I was coherent enough to call my mother, she was both relieved and very concerned. I couldn't account for the elapsed time and didn't know what to do next.

Knowing I didn't have the capacity to make decisions at that point. My mother made me hand the phone over to an airport employee. With their help and assistance, my mother made arrangements for a taxicab to take me to the closest hotel where she prepaid for a room.

My mom realized I didn't have the capacity to do much of anything at that moment, including attempting to get a room at a hotel. I forgot to call my mom once I arrived at the hotel. I was so exhausted and emotionally drained, I fell asleep as soon as I entered the room.

I was awakened the next morning by several loud knocks on the hotel room door. I heard the voice of two people shouting my name. Once I opened the door the hotel manager asked me to call my mom immediately. They said they called my room several times without a response and were doing a wellness check because they thought I was either ill or unresponsive.

I woke up just in time to catch a return flight back home. I was still in a daze and to this day, I remember hardly anything about the flight to Alabama. I started feeling more like myself and at peace once I made it home safely and saw my mom and four children.

I know in my heart that I did everything in my power to travel to Nigeria to attend my husband's funeral. God protected me that day by incapacitating me so I couldn't get on that plane. I had been ignoring all of God's cues and I became physically incapable of getting on that plane. God clearly intervened and I had to accept the fact that attending Ferdinand's funeral just wasn't meant to be.

As a woman of faith, I wasn't terribly concerned with why God didn't want me to go to Nigeria. I knew it was divine intervention in an extremely profound way and I was satisfied with that. I wasn't looking forward to sharing the news with Clem about Kodo's no-show and my inability to get on the plane. Even though I knew he would be upset with me, I had to let him know.

Once I gathered the nerve to call my brother-in-law to let him know I wouldn't be attending the funeral, Clem simply said, "Oh really," in a soft, relaxed tone. He told me not to worry about it, and that he had everything under control. In fact, he told me he was relieved. With so much going on, he said it would have been added stress trying to support and comfort me under the circumstances. I was shocked. I expected Clem to feel anger and disappointment. In retrospect, I should have known there was a lot more going on in Nigeria that I didn't know about — but would later discover.

Although I didn't attend the funeral, Ferdinand's family sent videotapes of the service. To this day, I have no desire to view the tapes because I prefer to remember Ferdinand and the many years we spent together while he was alive. I do not want to focus on the tragedy of his death.

My mother, cousin, and sister-in-law wanted to see the videotape because they needed closure. The only thing they disclosed to me was they had never seen a funeral in which all the attendees had such a look of utter confusion, bewilderment, shock, and disbelief on their faces. They all seemed to be wondering how this phenomenal doctor, son, brother, husband, father, and dear friend could be taken away from us so soon?

Little did I know I was eventually going to find out much more about the day Ferdinand died. It would confirm my worst fears, and I would be devastated.

CHAPTER 21

"FERDINAND WAS MURDERED"

American flag flown at half-staff in honor of Ferdinand at the Old Capital Museum in Iowa City October 1996

After Ferdinand's death, I knew almost immediately I would move my family back to Iowa once I got things squared away in Alabama. I felt confident that is where Ferdinand would want his children to grow up. That's where I wanted to be, too. We already had a church home, the schools were outstanding, and we had a network of supportive and dear friends. For the first time, I understood the reason our house in Iowa didn't sell each time a family was so close to signing on the dotted line. God had a plan for our family and knew we would find comfort moving back into the home Ferdinand and I had built.

There were seemingly insurmountable legal matters to attend to. I had to locate his birth certificate in order to get Ferdinand's death certificate in Nigeria. So many legal issues needed to be taken care of and I had to have both of those documents. For example, I wanted to sell our home in Alabama and sell Ferdinand's Range Rover. In addition, I wanted to make plans for a memorial service. The responsibilities were never-ending.

I was also surprised to learn the American flag was flown at half-staff in honor of Ferdinand at the Iowa Old Capitol Building in Iowa City. That was such a huge honor; I continue to swell with pride each time I think about it. Ferdinand's coworkers at the University of Iowa were also organizing an elaborate memorial service. The overflow of love, kindness, and support certainly helped keep my spirits up during this devastating time.

Although we only lived in Mobile for a short time, Ferdinand had made his mark and accomplished a great deal. I felt it was important to have a memorial service there, as well. It would be one way for my young children to have some type of closure and help them to understand the finality of Ferdinand's death. It would also be an opportunity for the children to say good-bye to their father in their own way.

God's protection was evident in a myriad of ways. Because Ferdinand died in Nigeria, we were far removed from the reality of what actually happened. I didn't know specific details, wasn't exposed to rumors, and didn't have an opportunity to view Ferdinand's body. While understanding the magnitude of what had happened, at times his death seemed unreal.

I was able to remember Ferdinand as a happy, doting father, playing with his children behind the Plexiglass window at the airport before traveling home to Nigeria. All my memories of Ferdinand were happy, fond ones. I didn't have to take my mind to that dark place of his death, especially if I didn't want to. I sometimes played mind-games with myself, pretending Ferdinand was out of the country for an extended period of time, or working long hours at the hospital as usual. I felt God protected our family and my heart as much as possible. I had a marriage made in heaven and nothing was going to disrupt that.

Imagine how surprised I was when my doorbell rang and the funeral director from Mayberry Funeral Home that Ferdinand had a long conversation with just a few months prior appeared in front of my door. I couldn't believe it.

This man looks familiar. What is he doing here?

The funeral director reintroduced himself and expressed his condolences, as he described how he read about Ferdinand's death in the newspaper. He recalled the lengthy conversation he had with Ferdinand and felt compelled to stop by and offer his help. He remembered our young family and told me how much Ferdinand adored us.

After outlining several options for a memorial service, major details were worked out from the comfort of my home. I couldn't believe this funeral director showed up at my doorstep without me having to make an inquiry, phone call, or request for his services. God knew what was on my mind. Any and everything I needed appeared to be right at my fingertips. God always has a plan.

God is so good, I remember thinking often.

My neighbor, Charlesetta, was a huge help, too. She checked up on our family frequently and insisted on taking me shopping to get a dress to wear for Ferdinand's memorial service. She also made an appointment with her personal hairstylist to get my hair and nails done, something I rarely did.

I remember it raining profusely the day I took the kids shopping to purchase their outfits for the service. While walking in the pouring rain, Nneka stopped in the middle of the parking lot, looked toward the sky, and spoke.

"Daddy must be using the bathroom in heaven and the toilet is overflowing."

I simply chuckled as my other children burst into laughter. Children process death in so many ways. I was just happy Nneka made a correlation between her father and heaven.

I had so many important decisions to make within days of learning about Ferdinand's death. My phone rang constantly. Some people called out of concern and others, including people I didn't know, called to give me unsolicited advice. Strangers called and tried to convince me they were Ferdinand's long-lost friends or relatives. They told me Ferdinand promised to give them financial gifts, or loans for school and business ventures.

Don't these people realize I just lost my husband?

Why are they asking me for money when I have four mouths to feed for the next sixteen years?

Suddenly, people I spoke to on the phone and hardly knew were financial experts, as they offered to handle my finances or sell my property. My intelligence was insulted when a lawyer told me he found someone who was interested in purchasing my home for cash. He had the audacity to offer me $35,000 for our $250,000 home. Did he really think I was that naive?

I wasn't sure whether I was being taken advantage of because I was a widow, a single woman, or perceived as an uneducated woman. Bankers tried to take advantage of me as well, as they provided misinformation and charged exorbitant fees. One lawyer had the nerve to ask if all my children were Ferdinand's biological children.

There wasn't a question of paternity when Ferdinand was alive. Why is it an issue now?

I concluded that people will probably try to take advantage of me for the rest of my life. Based on my introduction to widowhood, I soon discovered women without husbands are often taken advantage of and belittled. As the wife of a doctor, I was treated like a queen. As soon as Ferdinand died, all of that changed.

I also discovered it was easy to make a distinction between those who cared and people who didn't. I was saddened and disappointed, and missing Ferdinand more and more with each passing day. I no longer had Ferdinand to confide in or stand by my side. I felt there wasn't anyone around to protect me or look out for my best interests. I had to set boundaries and create a new normal.

After spending sixteen years with Ferdinand, I knew all of his close friends and relatives. I made the decision to keep in contact with and only accept phone calls from people in Ferdinand's and my close circle of friends and family. I didn't need the additional stress of strangers or unknown relatives talking down to me, belittling me, and asking for money.

I decided we would stick together as a family, all five of us, and I wasn't going to let anyone else in our circle. I was going to rely on God and Ferdinand's wisdom to navigate my life as a widow. I knew I had to face the reality that I was alone and had to develop a thick skin. I had to act like the head of the household, and it was imperative for me to speak up, exert my authority, and start standing up for myself.

I was in total shock and felt honored and privileged when I received a telephone call from the world renowned Dr. Thomas Starzl. He was known as the father of transplantation, and Ferdinand had studied under him in Pittsburgh. He greeted me and told me how much he admired Ferdinand and his work ethic. He also told me how much Ferdinand loved and talked about his family. Dr. Starzl was also the first person to imply there was something suspicious about Ferdinand's death. He found it hard to believe that Ferdinand died in a car accident. He felt something didn't seem quite right. He strongly encouraged me to investigate further.

Initially, I felt he was simply sharing his opinion and I didn't think much of it. Once I was able to process what he said, though, I realized I had minimal knowledge regarding the automobile accident. All I knew was some vague information I had been provided. I didn't know exactly what happened, but I believed what my brother-in-law told me. After Ferdinand's death, I put all my energy into raising my young family and continued to focus on what I had instead of what I didn't.

I was fortunate that my children went to bed at eight o' clock every evening like clockwork. After they went to sleep, that gave me an opportunity to rest, relax, and reflect on the day's events. I typically went to bed around 11 o'clock, and I can still remember that one Sunday evening around midnight. I was awakened by the telephone ringing and received the most horrific news.

Who would be calling at this time of night?

I hesitantly answered the phone as the voice on the other end spoke.

"Hello, Cynthia."

"Yes?"

"This is Dr. Ukoh." Dr. Ukoh was a colleague of Ferdinand's and our close family friend in Washington. His tone was very serious, and he had my attention.

"Tell me, how do you think Ferdinand died?"

"He died in a car accident in Nigeria." I wondered why he would even ask this question. This is what I had been told by Ferdinand's family.

"Cynthia, that is not true. It's a lie. Ferdinand was murdered."

Then there was silence. I didn't know how to even respond to this.

"Cynthia, did you hear me?" Dr. Ukoh finally asked.

"How do you know that?" I was confused and in shock. My head was spinning.

"Everybody knows."

"What happened to my husband?" I whimpered.

"I can't tell you, Cynthia. You must ask your brother-in-law when you talk to him on the phone. I can't share any details. I just thought you should know the truth."

It was at this instant that sheer terror encompassed me. After hanging up the phone, I ran into my children's rooms to make sure they were okay. I double checked the locks on the doors and closed all the curtains and blinds.

I was afraid. I didn't know who murdered Ferdinand or why. I was paranoid, constantly peeking out of the windows. I called my mother to tell her what I just learned. She couldn't believe it. We were both speechless. So many thoughts raced through my mind.

How could people be so mean?

Everyone else knew!

Why is everyone lying to me?

I was terrified at that point. If someone murdered Ferdinand, our family could be next. I was scared and perplexed, too. I didn't trust anyone at that point. I spent every moment on eggshells, taking note of every sound in the house, peeking out of windows and securing the locks. Paranoia definitely set in.

I was anxious and couldn't wait for Clem to call. I rarely called Clem in Nigeria and typically waited for him to call me. I knew Clem would call within a few days. He was consistent when it came to keeping in touch during that time. Waiting was agonizing, I just wanted to know the truth. I would lie in bed at night thinking about Ferdinand's final moments. I just prayed that Ferdinand didn't suffer. He was an amazing husband, father, and friend. Whatever had occurred, he didn't deserve any of this.

Waiting to find out whether this information was true was like torture and I wanted to know the truth as soon as possible. I feared for my life as well as my children's. I didn't know whether someone from Nigeria was responsible for his death or whether it was someone in the United States. This sudden turn of events turned my world upside down. I couldn't eat or sleep because I was constantly on guard, peering out the windows, peeking through the window panels of my front door, taking note of suspicious people and vehicles in front of my home or in the neighborhood. This was insane.

How could this be my life?

I basically slept with one eye open; every creak, sound, or thump in the house caused me to panic. I would get out of bed several times during the night to make sure my children were unharmed and safely tucked in bed.

I didn't share this news with anyone except my mother. This news was both horrifying and unbelievable. The thought of someone hurting Ferdinand was incomprehensible to me. Ferdinand was often referred to as "a Gentle Giant." Although he was tall in stature and a solid 200-plus pounds, he was the kindest, sweetest, and gentlest human being with the biggest heart. If someone felt the need to kill a man like Ferdinand, I felt we were all susceptible. When Ferdinand died, I made a deal with God, fully knowing I didn't have the right to do so. I also remembered the Bible says, "Ask and you shall receive."

"God, if you would give me the wisdom and strength to raise these children the way Ferdinand and I want them to be raised, I promise I won't be angry with you. I just want to make Ferdinand proud, and I want to fulfill our hopes and dreams for our children."

I also promised I would read my Bible daily, which I continue to do to this day. Along with that, I made a vow to pray on my knees each night. Prior to this promise, I prayed lying down comfortably in my bed before going to sleep. I wanted to show reverence, humility, and my desperate desire for the help I knew only God alone could provide. I wanted to humble myself before God to show that I was depending on and fully leaning on God for help and support, keeping in mind Psalm 68:5: "God is a father to the fatherless, and a defender of widows."

After receiving the call from Dr. Ukoh, I had to remain calm and in control. I had four young children counting on me to be their rock. I couldn't crack under pressure or share any of my fears. My children thrived with consistency, routine, and a safe environment. I wasn't going to let this news affect them in any way. Everything had to appear normal. My losing control was not an option. I had to keep it together for my family's sake and there was only one way to do that. I relied on God and prayed more than I ever had before.

Four days later, Clem finally called. And when he did, I didn't waste time before asking him how Ferdinand really died.

"Clem, what really happened to Ferdinand? I received a call from his close friend and was told Ferdinand didn't die in a car accident. What happened to my husband?! Was he murdered?!"

"Cynthia, I can't tell you what happened until I see you in person. It's our tradition. I must discuss this matter with you face to face. I have to prepare for the funeral and tie up loose ends. I promise, I will come to the United States as soon as I can."

That's where the conversation ended. I didn't expect I would have to wait five more months to learn the entire truth.

Clem's response didn't satisfy me at all; however, I didn't have any option but to wait. At that point, I wondered if anyone in my close circle was being transparent or sharing information with me. I felt numb, abandoned, and alone. At the same time, I didn't want to open a can of worms by asking questions or trying to pry information out of the wrong people. I also didn't want to stress myself out any more than I already was. Additionally, I didn't want to start unnecessary rumors, tarnish Ferdinand's name in any way, or take the chance that the information might leak to my children

Deep in my heart, I knew Dr. Ukoh was telling me the truth. If it wasn't true, I knew Clem would have made it perfectly clear that Ferdinand did in fact die in a car accident. As I lay in bed thinking about this new revelation, so many thoughts ran through my head.

What if it is true, and Ferdinand was murdered?

Would God be able to bring Ferdinand back?

All I want is for Ferdinand to come back home to me.

Despite my fervent desire to have things be very different than they already were, I knew nothing was going to bring my husband back, even if he was murdered. Still, despite my misgivings, I wanted to know the truth. I had to know what happened to my husband.

CHAPTER 22
GOING HOME AGAIN

Our home on Weeber Street in Iowa City

Six months after Ferdinand's unexpected death, Clem finally traveled to the United States to talk with me about what he knew. I had deeply mixed emotions about what he had to tell me. I wanted to know the truth. More than that, I *had* to know the truth. At the same time, I knew what he was going to tell me would be upsetting beyond words. And I was right.

When Clem arrived, he walked into our home and solemnly greeted me. He sat his suitcase in our foyer, carefully opening it to retrieve an envelope. He walked slowly to our kitchen table and sat with the envelope in his hand. Barely looking me in the eye, he finally spoke.

"Cynthia, what can I say? It is true."

My head was spinning. I felt sick to my stomach. The rumors and innuendos I had heard must be true. I wanted to hear what had happened, yet I was afraid to find out more.

"Your husband, Ferdinand was killed. He was murdered."

There it was. Clem had confirmed my worst fears. I was angry and afraid beyond anything I've ever felt.

"I'm sorry, Cynthia."

My children and I had moved back to Iowa City and reestablished ourselves in this loving community. We were getting on with life as best we could. And now this.

Part of me wondered, *What next? How much more can I take?*

Another part of me didn't even want to know.

That long-awaited day of Clem's visit finally arrived. Six months after Ferdinand's death, he was coming to the United States. I finally was going to hear the entire truth regarding the circumstances of Ferdinand's death. While I was anxious to hear what he had to say, I braced myself for what I expected to be horrible news.

After Clem told me Ferdinand had been murdered, I could barely catch my breath as he continued to describe what had happened.

"Um, Ferdinand went to the market to get last-minute gifts for you and the kids before he was to return home to Alabama."

My mind was racing as Clem continued.

"Cynthia, I tell you, I transported Ferdinand everywhere, every place during his visit home. But because I was tired, only this one time, I asked Mathew to drive Ferdinand back home to the village when he was done at the market."

I was in a state of shock and disbelief when Clem confirmed what I already believed to be true. Hearing the words killed and murdered took on a whole new meaning at this point. As Clem shared more details, my mind started drifting because I wasn't prepared to receive it. How could I be prepared for this? Even today, my memory of the details is a bit murky. I just could not believe what I was hearing.

While Ferdinand was at the market shopping, apparently the driver left and came up with a plan to have someone join him at the site of a particularly large and well-known pothole. On the way home, the driver ran over the pothole and stopped the car on the side of a bush-filled road. That is where the crime occurred.

I was told it was most likely a robbery that had gone wrong. All of Ferdinand's personal items, such as his wallet, cash, computer, and cell phone, were missing. His body, with a huge gash in the back of his head, had been shifted from the passenger seat to the driver's seat, making it appear as though he were the driver.

Ironically, the items he purchased at the market, including beautifully carved African sculptures and bracelets, eventually made it to my home in Iowa. I remember I was emotional when I opened the box because while Ferdinand's gifts made it back home, Ferdinand did not.

The day of Ferdinand's death, Clem continued, he received a call indicating his brother was in a car accident. When Clem arrived at the scene, he found Ferdinand dead in the car with a huge gash in the back of his head due to the brute force impact of a sharp object. The driver had left the scene.

I didn't want to listen to any more details after that. I just couldn't bear to hear it and my heart couldn't take it. Again, I didn't shed a tear. A part of me died when Ferdinand did and the ability to feel vulnerable and show the true emotions I was feeling disappeared that day.

My role had changed, and I felt I had to always remain stoic. Before Clem's visit, I already rationalized in my mind that whatever had happened to Ferdinand, nothing was going to bring him back or give me any type of resolution or closure. I knew Ferdinand was gone forever, and it was up to me to be strong enough to carry the torch and provide our children with the loving, secure environment we envisioned.

I subconsciously took all of the information I learned that day and tucked it down into the deepest recesses of my mind. I erased that part of my life from my brain. I heard what Clem was telling me about the events of October 8, 1996, but I couldn't allow it to take up too much space in my head.

I shared the specific details of Ferdinand's death with my mother and brother. People in the Nigerian and medical communities already knew bits and pieces of what had happened to Ferdinand. Thankfully, most people respected my privacy and didn't probe too much. I was able to shut the door on that part of my life and continue to live as though the murder never happened.

I knew that obsessing over the details could cause incapacitating anguish, severely affecting my mental state, and preventing me from living a productive and fruitful life. The information Clem shared wasn't going to add any value to my life. I felt it could only hurt me, stifle what progress I could make, and haunt me even more than it already had. I knew I had no choice other than to move forward and pretend Clem's conversation never happened. I didn't discuss details of Ferdinand's death with anyone because I knew it would feel like I was reopening a wound each time I had to revisit that terrible day.

I had four children to protect. They were under the impression their father died in an automobile accident. How was I going to tell them their father was murdered? My children had already been through enough and I wasn't going to add any more stress and trauma to their lives. I didn't have any idea how or when I would tell them the truth. The children were very young, and I felt I had time to figure that out.

Another reason I didn't share details about Ferdinand's death is because we lived in a close-knit community. I feared my children would find out the cause of Ferdinand's death from someone other than me if I discussed it with anyone else. That thought scared me enough to make my stomach turn. I knew I would have to be deliberate about how to approach them with this information. I knew I would have to find a way to tell my children in the right place and at the right time.

Because of this, the increased use of the internet in schools frightened me. I was afraid my oldest daughter Adanna would become curious and look her father's name up on the internet. I thought my children might accuse me of lying to them all these years by not telling them the truth. I also feared losing their trust. In my heart I felt they were too young to handle such news. I wanted to shield them and protect them as much as possible.

As Clem sat at our table after he had finished telling me what he knew about Ferdinand's murder, he handed me the envelope containing photos from the accident scene and asked if I wanted to see them. Without hesitation, I said, "Absolutely not

"I have nothing to gain by looking at photos of my deceased husband."

"Cynthia," he insisted. "You have a decision to make. They have arrested the suspected murderer and he is in custody. As Ferdinand's wife, you can determine this man's fate. You can have him stoned to death or you can have him sent to prison for the rest of his life."

This can't be real, I thought. *Since when is stoning a form of punishment?*

"Cynthia, I'm serious."

He waited for my response as I collected my thoughts.

"Clem. I don't believe death is a punishment. I want this guy to suffer in jail and think about what he did to my husband. Stoning him would be the easy way out."

CHAPTER 23
GUILTY AS CHARGED

MATHEW NWALU v. THE STATE

(2013) JELR 35294 (CA)

Court of Appeal • CA/E/207C/2009 • 23 Dec 2013 • Nigeria

Title page from the Appeals Court document recording the trial of Ferdinand's murderer

After my brother-in-law Clem told me about Ferdinand's murder, he explained the accused had been arrested and was in police custody. He also told me there was going to be a trial. I couldn't believe how much had taken place in Nigeria since I last heard from Clem, just six months before. I felt as though my life was split between two different worlds, both filled with sorrow and grief.

It was easy for me to pretend everything going on in Nigeria was a figment of my imagination, which allowed me to cope and go on with my day-to-day life in Iowa. I knew the Nigerian community was outraged by the sudden loss of my husband — their hometown hero — and the catastrophic events leading to Ferdinand's death. I knew Ferdinand and his family were highly regarded and had the financial resources to hire excellent lawyers. I felt confident justice would be served.

I felt emotionally detached, because the reality of the circumstances regarding Ferdinand's death were too much for me to bear. Because I was so far removed and not involved in the legal aspects of the case, I didn't follow it closely. I continued to focus on my children and the daily challenges I faced. I did not have the energy or legal background to follow the trial but was thankful and reassured because Clem promised he would attend all court hearings. He also said he would do everything in his power to make sure the person responsible for Ferdinand's death remained behind bars.

It took years for the case to go to trial. Clem gave me brief updates during his yearly visits to Iowa. He took care not to share too many details, since he knew conversations relating to the trial took an emotional toll on me. Based on court documents and testimony from the trial in Nigeria I have just recently read, I now have a more complete understanding of what actually happened on the day my world was turned upside down.

As I decided to write this book, I knew I would have to find out more about what happened in Nigeria that day and the months that followed. I needed to do this for my own well-being. I also wanted to tell a more complete and accurate story of what happened. I realized I would have to research something I had been afraid of looking at for such a long time.

After 25 years of healing and finally finding the strength to read court documents, I found out exactly what happened to Ferdinand. I also learned how utterly cruel people could be. Reading the documents brought me to tears, not just for myself, but for my beloved Ferdinand. He did not deserve any of this. Throughout this entire journey, God's grace and mercy was able to get me through this very difficult stage in my life. Here is what I have learned about the day my world was turned upside down.

On November 8, 1996, Clem gave Mathew Nwalu, our trusted family driver, his vehicle and asked him to pick Ferdinand up from the market in Enugu and drive him to his family home in Mgbowo. According to Mathew, both he and Ferdinand left the village of Enugu in the same car. Mathew drove, while Ferdinand sat as a passenger.

As they traveled out of town and joined the highway, Clem happened to pass them on the road. He remembered seeing his brother sitting in the front passenger seat as Mathew drove Ferdinand in his Mercedes Benz 230 diesel. Less than an hour later, Clem received a chilling phone call indicating Ferdinand was lying inside his car on the expressway with head injuries.

Clem went to the scene immediately and found Ferdinand's lifeless body in the driver's seat. Apparently, someone shifted Ferdinand's body to the driver's seat to make it appear as though he was the driver. Ferdinand was found all alone. The driver, Mathew Nwalu, had left the scene. Once the police officer and police photographer arrived to investigate the accident, an off-duty police officer noticed Mathew standing nearby behaving abnormally. The photographer took photos at the scene, as well as taking additional pictures of the vehicle and corpse the following day. After questioning Mathew Nwalu and recording voluntary statements, which were later used as evidence in the trial, Clem put Ferdinand's lifeless body into his car and took him to the hospital to be identified. Clem knew the severe injuries were incompatible with an accident. Assuming there was foul play, Clem insisted on a thorough investigation.

In the course of the investigation, abundant evidence was uncovered that Mathew was the person who was last seen with Ferdinand when he was alive. Although no one saw Mathew or anyone else deliver a fatal blow, it was Mathew's responsibility to prove his innocence in court beyond reasonable doubt. The law is different in Nigeria from that in the United States, where people are presumed innocent until proven guilty.

Mathew pleaded not guilty to the murder charge and insisted the fatal automobile accident claimed the life of Ferdinand. Mathew gave sworn evidence in his own defense and did not have any witnesses. According to Mathew, the Mercedes somersaulted and caused Ferdinand's death. Mathew said he was driving on Port Harcourt Expressway headed toward Mgbowo, at approximately 4 p.m. when he came upon a pothole. As he was trying to avoid hitting it, he lost control of the vehicle. The car swerved and hit a tree, after which the car somersaulted. Mathew stated that drivers in other vehicles came and assisted him out of the car. He also indicated other drivers helped turn the vehicle upright, back on its wheels. He continued to insist Ferdinand's death was the result of a fatal motor accident.

The prosecution, on the other hand, believed the alleged accident was staged. They felt they could prove Mathew murdered Ferdinand and tried it make it look like an accident. The prosecution called seven witnesses. An autopsy had been performed, and it was confirmed that the injuries on Ferdinand's' body could not have been caused by an automobile accident. They proved the injuries could only have been caused by a hard, heavy, sharp object.

The Deputy Director in the Road Traffic Department examined the vehicle after the accident and concluded there was no accident at all, let alone a somersault. They confirmed the dents on the vehicle were calculated, as they noted several discrepancies between the ghastly nature of the injuries on the head of the deceased and the minor damage to the car. The damages and dents on the vehicle were simply not commensurate with the nature of the alleged accident. For instance, the dents on the roof were so minor, they could not have been the result of a somersault. The dents were also evenly distributed and of the same dimensions, as though someone used the same object to deliberately make a few dents on the car.

When the investigator went to the scene of the accident, he saw grass around the accident area carefully rolled down as if someone used their hands to deliberately flatten the grass out. However, all the shrubs and trees were still standing. Even though eyewitnesses and other direct evidence are important when trying to establish guilt, there are situations in which circumstances clearly suggest that the accused, and no one else, must have committed the offense. There was enough evidence to prove Ferdinand did not die as a result of a car accident. After evaluating the evidence and carefully considering the statement of Mathew's counsel, the judge found Mathew Nwalu guilty of the offence of murder and sentenced him to prison.

The judge was infuriated with Mathew Nwalu and made the following closing statement:

"The blood of Professor Ukah must continue to haunt him and his cohorts and confederates till doomsday. He deserves to be hanged by the neck until he is certified dead for the dastardly act of murdering in cold blood a rare brain in a country like ours where the deceased would have contributed to the revitalization of our comatose health sector."

The news of Ferdinand's murder was devastating both then and now. However, I knew at the time I couldn't let that news or anything else deter or distract me from being fully present for my children. I had to remain focused. I didn't have time to sit and wallow in misery. I needed to put every ounce of time and energy into taking care of my four children and creating the life both Ferdinand and I desired for them. I kept myself so busy I didn't have time to face the reality of what had happened many thousands of miles away in a foreign country. In the years that followed, I learned that I was strong, determined, and capable of almost anything, especially when it came to providing for, supporting, and protecting my family.

This was an extremely difficult chapter for me to write. Even years after the tragic murder of my late husband, much of this information was completely new to me because until now, I did not have the heart to read transcripts from the trial. I have had the videotape of Ferdinand's funeral in my possession all these years and still haven't gathered the strength to view that, either. Even now, I fear I will be forced to face the truth and stop living my life as though Ferdinand went away on a long journey. As I write this book, I am realizing I never really faced the truth. Until now.

CHAPTER 24
ADANNA AND NNEKA

Adanna and Nneka in 1997

Although we moved back to our Iowa home and into familiar surroundings, I wasn't prepared for the stark differences I would experience living as a widow with four young children. Initially, I was afraid of being in our house alone. The back side of our home faced a large, wooded area and long, rectangular windows encompassed the back of our living room and dining room area. The potential to expose onlookers to everything and everyone in our home made me uneasy. What used to be a favorite feature in our house — a picturesque view of greenery, beautiful trees, and wildlife — all of a sudden made me nervous and paranoid. That physical transparency into our lives became my greatest fear and resulted in many sleepless nights.

I often felt someone was watching our family from the wooded area. I could tell my mind was playing tricks on me as I sorted out various scenarios. I even created emergency and get-away plans in case something tragic happened. Sometimes I felt faint, and I called my friend Mary, a nearby nurse and neighbor, to let her know I was worried I was going to pass out. When that happened, Mary suggested getting a brown paper bag and breathing slowly into it. I would leave my door unlocked with emergency numbers written in large letters just in case someone needed entry into my house to provide medical assistance. I was afraid I would get sick and there wouldn't be anyone in my home capable of helping me.

I realized the easy solution would have been to simply purchase curtains or blinds to cover the windows. Even that straight-forward decision took quite a while because of all the daunting tasks and household responsibilities I had suddenly taken on. I had to make all the major decisions regarding our family. I had to do research, take measurements, compare prices, and discuss specific details with interior designers. That was Ferdinand's territory, and he had assumed all those responsibilities years ago. Now that I was faced with everything I had done previously and Ferdinand's tasks as well, I was overwhelmed. While eventually I adjusted, incorporating what used to be Ferdinand's role into my new normal took some time.

I believe in routine. Everyone woke up at the same time, ate all meals together, and traveled together as a team. I rarely had a babysitter and felt all the children should contribute to our well-being as a family. It was a very "all hands on deck" perspective. I had high expectations for all my children and made sure they complied the first time I asked them to help with something. I knew raising four children alone would be a greater challenge if they were disorderly and unruly.

I ran a loving, tight ship with lots of room to grow as individuals. My children quickly learned to accept what I had to say the first time, and that I wasn't interested in their opinions regarding what they believed was and wasn't fair. Everything I did was timed and I didn't have room for error. We even had family meetings on weekends if there was an issue or issues that needed to be discussed.

Our house was big enough that we had enough bedrooms for each child to have his or her own room. I, however, wanted my children to develop close relationships, learn how to compromise, and settle differences between themselves, so I made sure they shared a room with a sibling. My children didn't have a television in their bedrooms because I wanted them to spend time communicating and playing with each other.

I also provided supplemental education throughout their lives. I felt education inside and outside the classroom was critical. My children knew at an early age that college was an expectation for them. They attended Montessori preschools and public elementary schools. I was heavily involved in their schooling, making sure all class and homework assignments were complete and on time. Extra-credit assignments were not optional in our home. They were mandatory.

I didn't purchase anything for my kids unless they did research on what they wanted to buy. They had to explain why they wanted a particular item or object, along with the price of what they wanted. They also had to list the pros and cons of different alternatives and where to find them. This informed perspective proved to be valuable, because my adult children research just about everything before they make important decisions and purchases.

Each of my children has distinct personalities and varied interests. When they were growing up, my Dodge Caravan resembled a motor home of sorts. I spent most days after school, shuffling kids from one activity to another, changing clothing for specific events, and eating our meals and snacks in the car. Because the children were so young and I frequently had no one else to watch them, they had to accompany their siblings to every lesson, practice, sporting event, or recital.

Adanna was a quiet child and keen observer. She started reading at the age of three and always had a book in her hand. I remember taking her to a Backstreet Boys concert when she was eleven years old. I should have left her books in the car because she read a book throughout the entire concert. Whenever scholastic book order forms were given out at school, Adanna routinely ordered six or more books each time.

She would read each book front-to-back and reread them until we purchased new books or checked out another huge stack from the library. Adanna was in the gifted and talented program in elementary school and took many Advanced Placement (AP) classes in high school. She was also a huge Harry Potter fan. Each time a new book came out, our entire family would go to a local bookstore named Prairie Lights. We would arrive around 10:30 at night and stand in line until midnight to get one of the first copies. Adanna would then stay up all night, reading the entire book in ten consecutive hours.

Early on, it became apparent that Adanna was having some difficulty with her coordination. I can recall walking as a family, looking back, and finding Adanna had tripped or fallen for no apparent reason. I also remember parking in front of a dance studio and thinking dancing school might help Adanna with coordination. Fortunately, Adanna excelled at dance and ended up at Kate Carol Dance Studio for more than eight years. She often worked as an assistant as well.

All my children had to play an instrument. Adanna played the violin at Preucil School of Music for two years and piano at West Music, a store that provides private music lessons. Adanna took school very seriously and was always hard-working and responsible. Early on, she knew she wanted to leave Iowa after graduating from high school. She applied early to Yale and joined the class of 2007. After graduation with a degree in Political Science, Adanna got her MBA at Northwestern University's Kellogg Business School and currently resides in New York City. She is currently working as Senior Director of Business Development at an education technology company in New York.

Nneka was always the life of the party in our home. She has so much personality. Our house would have been extremely boring without Nneka because she was the most outspoken, comical, adventurous, and creative child in the Ukah family. Nneka's interests changed like the weather, too. Nneka expressed interests in and was an avid collector of snow globes, loved manatees, beanie babies, Polly Pockets, trolls, foreign currency, and much more.

She was always creating homemade mazes or some other adventurous project. She also loved preparing for any eventuality. For example, Nneka had a blow-up raft under her bed for years as well as a fire-escape ladder. She took singing, violin, and piano lessons, too. She did dance, gymnastics, and horse-riding, also. And Nneka loved animals.

Nneka always had expensive taste. She was interested in name-brand clothing from the time she was in elementary school. She started earning money early in life. Her first job was as a cat sitter at the age of seven. She made 25 cents a day caring for a neighbor's cat three times a day. I believe this is where Nneka developed her love for animals. Through this and other jobs growing up, Nneka learned the importance of working, being responsible, and managing money. We laugh now about how little money Nneka made at the time.

That wasn't the main reason she did this, though. Through these different jobs, even as low-paying as they were, she learned the value of a dollar and saved her money to purchase higher-priced items such as video cameras, Nintendo game systems, exotic birds, and intricate bird cages.

I wasn't the only one who saw Nneka's potential, either. My friend Claudia noticed how responsible Nneka was and hired her as a mother's helper when she was just 11 years old. She compensated Nneka extremely well and Nneka learned how to manage and save money. Nneka essentially became financially savvy at a very young age, refusing to pay full price for anything. It's no surprise Nneka majored in Business at Western Illinois College. She is the owner of Nneka MeShelle Agency. Nneka is an events strategist; she hires Brand Ambassadors for a variety of events in big cities. She is also Sports Event Marketing Manager at Red Bull. Her motto is "Never Not Working," meaning every interaction has the potential to result in a networking opportunity.

Nneka (front) and Adanna in 2021

CHAPTER 25
OKECHUKWU AND CHIKE

Okechukwu (Okey) in 1997

Chike in 1999

My primary goal as a parent was to raise intelligent, confident, well-rounded children who would be able to navigate this world and achieve their goals despite the many obstacles they would face. I wanted to teach my children about their proud Black heritage and expose them to as many positive Black role models as I could. We lived in a community that was 1% Black at that time, so this was a real challenge since there weren't many role models nearby and Black history and culture wasn't emphasized. Nonetheless, I wanted my kids to have pride in who they were and to believe they could achieve anything they set their minds to.

As a child, Okey was tactile and enjoyed hands-on activities. They loved playing with K'NEX building sets, Transformers and Power Rangers action figures. Okey took piano and drum lessons for several years. I wasn't surprised that they were passionate about music, especially since we come from a musical family spanning three generations. A great deal of Okey's spare time was spent in our basement creating music and making mixtapes.

Okey loved reading books about culture and history, too. They preferred to read books about famous African Americans, the African and Black diaspora, and issues affecting the lives of Black people. Books such as *Roots* and *The Autobiography of Malcolm X* by Alex Haley were very influential. Okey grew up knowing the truth about our history and racism in America. Whenever Okey felt an individual or minority groups were being targeted or treated unfairly, they weren't afraid to speak up and would sign petitions, protest, address leaders in the community, and go to the city council to address important issues and concerns.

Somewhat to my surprise, Okey expressed interest in visiting Nigeria when they were thirteen years old. I believe this was their way of warning me that it was just a matter of time before that dream would become a reality. Although the thought of Okey traveling to Nigeria scared me, I was thankful I wouldn't have to worry about it until they were at least 18 years of age.

Growing up, it was very clear that Okey was sentimental, compassionate, and strong-willed. They always made me feel special and consistently showed affection. It was not uncommon for Okey to open doors for me, escort me to and from my car, and carry groceries into our home. They held my hand with pride whenever we were in public, especially after observing the way his Uncle Jimmy, a retired judge, held his wife's hand during their yearly visits to Iowa over the Christmas holiday season. I was both shocked and impressed that Okey would take note of that and treat me in such a special way.

They played basketball and experienced a great deal of success in high school. Selected as team captain, being chosen for second team all-state at Iowa City West High School, and helping to lead Iowa City West to a fourth-place finish at the 2011 Iowa state high school tournament were major accomplishments.

As a non-scholarship walk-on, Okey played basketball for the renowned University of Iowa Hawkeyes, appearing in games during the sophomore, junior, and senior seasons (2013-2016). They earned the team's Appreciation Award and even appeared in the NCAA Tournament that season, where the University of Iowa's basketball team made it through to the second round.

Chike is the youngest and favorite among his siblings. He's a quiet observer and man of few words, just like his grandfather, Chief Nwosu Ukah. Chike is easy going and extremely levelheaded. He has always kept his eye on everything that was going on in the Ukah household. He fully understood all the do's and don't's in our house, as well as knowing the expectations I had of him. Chike has always been obsessed with cars. As a child he had an extensive collection of John Deere construction trucks, Hess toy trucks, and Hummer vehicles. Once he purchased a toy vehicle, he did research to find out as much about it as possible.

Chike specifically loved steering wheels. I'd look through catalogs and purchase the most realistic steering wheels I could find, complete with gears, turn signals, a horn, and more. He also had subscriptions to several car magazines. Chike can provide details on any type of car. He kept his most prized steering wheel in my car and pretended to drive with me from the age of three to nine years old. I was shocked when I discovered one day that Chike had been pretending to follow all the driving rules, mimicking me at all times.

Chike was an excellent student and avid reader. He particularly enjoyed the Artemis Fowl Adventures series and sports-related books. He loved writing stories and always had a journal nearby. Chike enjoyed playing video games, and I was thankful for that. His love of video games meant he was something of a homebody. Because of that, I didn't have to worry about his whereabouts, which gave me an opportunity to keep track of my older children and their extracurricular activities.

Chike was a magnet when it came to making friends, too. He always had a solid group of friends, and we hosted overnights at our home with two or three friends practically every weekend. They would stay up all night, play video games, eat snacks, order pizza, and enjoy each other's company. Chike also played the saxophone for a short time and ended up taking guitar lessons. He didn't want to play the piano like the rest of his siblings.

A neighbor recruited Chike to play on a basketball team when he was in elementary school. I agreed because it was a form of structured exercise. Initially, Chike didn't enjoy playing the game. He hated practicing and his team constantly lost. Chike hated losing but eventually realized teams that won spent a great deal of time practicing.

His interest in basketball peaked when he was in junior high school. Chike went to the recreation center after school each day and, because of his height, he dominated on the basketball court. Chike enjoyed playing on the Northwest Junior High School team and excelled as a player. During his time at Iowa City West High School, the basketball team won sixty consecutive games. They had the eighth-longest winning streak in Iowa history. West also won two State Championships. Chike thoroughly enjoyed the game of basketball.

Okey wanted to join the University of Iowa basketball team because Chike was obsessed with Hawkeye basketball. If Okey was on the team, Chike would have access to all basketball games and get preferential seating. Chike would also have an opportunity to meet all of Okey's teammates. Although it was an honor and privilege to be on the team, Okey quickly discovered there was a stark difference between the way our community treated them as a resident and how differently the perception was after becoming a Hawkeye basketball player. Prior to becoming a Hawkeye basketball player, Okey didn't feel they were treated fairly by the Iowa City community.

Okey was determined to leave Iowa City immediately after graduating from the University of Iowa with a bachelor's degree in Political Science. The primary goal was to move to a city that was diverse. After graduating from Iowa, they moved to Washington, D.C., and worked as a community organizer for a non-profit organization.

Chike enjoys spending time with all of us in his family and he also values alone time. He graduated from the University of Iowa with a bachelor's degree in Sports Management. Chike currently works in Chicago as a technical recruiter for a large education company.

Okey and Chike have become wonderful, productive, loving young individuals and I am extremely proud of them. I believe Ferdinand is always with us and I see characteristics of Ferdinand in them whenever we're together. I thank God for helping me raise such amazing human beings.

Okey in 2019

Chike in 2022

Chapter 26
Unfortunate Events

After moving back to Iowa City, our family continued to make adjustments living our lives without Ferdinand. Yet, I still wanted to keep his memory alive. One day, the perfect answer appeared, as if by magic. Of course, I knew it wasn't magic at all. As with everything in our lives, it was a gift from God.

Becky, the woman who cleaned our house once a week, mentioned a beautiful console table she saw at a boutique that would fit perfectly against the wall facing our entryway. I wanted to find a way to remind my children of Ferdinand's values and spiritual presence without deliberately providing verbal reminders. The black marble console table situated in the foyer of our home was a godsend.

After looking at the stainless-steel table with three inserted black marble tiles, I knew it was perfect and purchased it right away. I found three of my favorite photos of Ferdinand, enlarged them, and placed them on the table. I then hung three huge Nigerian masks on the wall above it as a visual representation of our African heritage. There was enough space on the table to add treasured artifacts and we referred to the table as our "daddy table." It was a way for my children to make a connection with Ferdinand, as they saw the table on a daily basis.

I also kept my keys and important documents on the table. Whenever I had something I wanted the kids to look at or take with them, I would say, "It's on daddy's table." When the kids received a medal, trophy, or report card they wished they could share with their dad, they would put it on the daddy table. There were also times the children were upset with me or unhappy about something that occurred during the day. When that happened, I encouraged them to write their frustrations down and place the letter or note on the daddy table as well. I promised I wouldn't read what they wrote, and I never did, unless they specifically showed it to me.

I used the table and photos of Ferdinand as subtle reminders to them that Ferdinand is and will always be their father, even though he wasn't physically with them. In this way, the daddy table provided a connection and engagement with Ferdinand. It also was a source of comfort for all of us.

It's no secret growing up as part of a racial minority in Iowa City — or any city for that matter — has its challenges. Our family experienced racism on many levels: educationally, socially, and emotionally. Like every community, Iowa City has neighborhood schools and Ferdinand and I did our research to ensure we moved into a neighborhood that had a school with an excellent reputation. The school we had our eye on in Iowa City looked very promising, but I was in for a rather rude awakening.

Five minutes into my scheduled visit and tour of our new neighborhood school, I knew I would not subject my children to the environment that was presented. After taking one look at me, the principal made it clear that the school's population didn't include many students who received free and reduced lunch. Without knowing anything about me and my family, she was implying my socio-economic status was low and that I would need assistance paying for my children's lunch.

In addition, she made a point of telling me the school was highly ranked based on the Iowa Test of Basic Skills (ITBS) Assessment. She followed that up by informing me that this particular school had limited resources for students who struggled academically. Whether she intended to insult me or not, the implications were very clear. Why did the principal assume I was low-income, needed free and reduced lunch, and had children who required specialized or remedial services?

It was painfully clear she made several assumptions based on race. It didn't take me long to cut the visit short. I knew I didn't want my children in an environment that judged them solely based on the color of their skin. Instead, we enrolled our children at nearby Roosevelt Elementary School, a multi-cultural, diverse school in which all my children were accepted and thrived.

Sadly, the subtle racism of low expectations emerged even after my children were well established in school. My daughter Adanna, for example, was always an excellent, hard-working student. She was in the Extended Learning Program and consistently earned A's and 100% on assessments and assignments. Whenever she had a substitute teacher, though, she received much lower grades. Her spelling tests were scored incorrectly, and she would routinely get a B even though she earned an A. She would also receive a B on her written essays from the substitutes when she clearly earned an A. When this happened, I resubmitted her work once her regular teacher returned to determine the appropriate grade. I also contacted the substitute teachers to share my thoughts and frustration. It was such an extraordinarily frustrating experience to find that some educators have such low expectations of Black students. They don't believe the students are capable of excellence, even when they clearly demonstrate that level of high performance.

My children also knew there was a high probability they would encounter a police officer whenever they were out in the community, such as when they went to the mall with a group of their Black friends. They were often followed by security officers and store employees at the mall. They would be asked to leave stores and accused without merit of stealing. My son Okey even videotaped an occasion in which they predicted they would be stopped by a police officer because they had four of their Black friends in his SUV.

Unfortunately, they were correct. Within minutes of turning the video camera on, the flashing lights of a police car could be seen from their rear-view mirror. Once again, a police officer stopped them to ask where they are going and, when it was clear Okey and their friends were completely innocent, he let them go. It was another sad example of what Black people in America have known for a long time. Driving while Black apparently gives officers a right to stop innocent individuals for no apparent reason.

I feel blessed because my children relied on each other for emotional support. Having three siblings gave them an opportunity to share their experiences, express frustrations, and problem-solve with each other. I knew living in a predominantly white environment could affect their self-esteem, and I absolutely did not want that to happen. The reality of our situation affected my role as a parent.

Despite all the struggles and difficulty they faced as they grew up in an environment where they were a distinct minority, my children have all blossomed into wonderful adults. I could not be prouder of the men and women they have become. I know Ferdinand is just as proud of them as well.

CHAPTER 27
SPECIAL EDUCATION TEACHER

Teaching in Coralville, Iowa today

The classroom was being destroyed by a second-grade student. Anthony would repeatedly throw desks, chairs, books, and educational tools, scattering them across the room. A room-clear was required whenever this happened, in an attempt to keep the other students safe. Class instruction was immediately halted as the teacher escorted the rest of the class to a safe setting. Typically, the class would go to the cafeteria, library, or playground until the student settled down and the classroom was ready for re-entry.

Young children often have difficulty expressing themselves when they feel overwhelmed or frustrated. It was apparent this student was struggling with feelings he didn't know how to manage or process. I noticed Anthony frequently standing in the hallway, often refusing to go into the classroom. He wasn't completing his schoolwork or assignments and his teacher couldn't determine what his actual reading or math level was, or what if any progress he was making.

Although Anthony wasn't in my classroom; I took an interest in him because it was obvious he was struggling and I wanted to help. Anthony lived with his father and older sister. His father was a mechanic, and I knew he lived in a loving and caring environment. Anthony came to school in a good mood, usually had a smile on his face, and was well-mannered.

I couldn't understand why he was having outbursts that seemed to increase in duration and frequency by the day. I decided to build a relationship with Anthony. Each time I encountered him in the hallway I would speak to him.

"How are you doing?"

No response.

"Are you doing, okay?"

No response.

Even though I didn't get a response, I continued asking the same questions each time I saw him. I explained to him I was asking these questions because I cared about him. I also expressed that I understood if he didn't feel like talking to me. Instead of talking, I asked Anthony to respond by giving me a "thumbs up" or a "thumbs down."

After two weeks he was responding to me and eventually agreed to take a short walk with me once or twice a day. Our school had a huge library in the middle of the building, with classrooms around the perimeter of the building. Anthony and I established a good relationship; however, he still refused to take exams or complete his assignments. When I found out his teacher couldn't get a baseline to find out what his reading or math level was, I volunteered to assess him during my lunch break. Once Anthony and I began, I explained that we would work for ten minutes and take a five-minute break, repeating that process until we were done.

What I discovered was astonishing. It totally explained Anthony's impulsive behavior. Because I was able to work with him in a one-on-one setting without any distractions, Anthony felt very comfortable taking the test. Relying on what I learned at Howard and what I experienced as a teacher, I understood that most children don't misbehave because they want to. There is always an antecedent — a reason why. As a teacher, I knew I must be observant, patient, and willing to use all resources available to meet each student's needs.

As I observed Anthony, I immediately noticed simple tics. These small movements would be difficult to perceive in a large setting. As he concentrated, his eyes blinked more frequently, and he had difficulty holding the pencil steadily. The small muscles in his hands seemed to periodically jerk, too. As time went on, I also noticed involuntary movements of his shoulders.

Although the movements were subtle and I felt he tried to disguise them, what I saw reminded me of a student I had with Tourette Syndrome (TS). While I am not a doctor and it's not my job to make a diagnosis, I felt I might have discovered something very important. Based on my experiences, I had a strong feeling Anthony had some form of undiagnosed TS, which would explain the sudden outbursts.

I'm sure Anthony was frightened each time his body made sudden movements he couldn't explain or control. He didn't understand what was happening and didn't want his peers to notice the tics. In an attempt to avoid being embarrassed or having kids make fun of him, I suspected Anthony behaved in this manner because he didn't want students to notice his tics. Causing a disruption in the class took the focus off him because the class exited the room each time he had an episode.

I also suspected Anthony avoided schoolwork because the more he concentrated, the more prevalent and obvious the tics became. I shared my observations with his teacher, the school counselor, and the school psychologist. After getting parental permission for an evaluation, Anthony was indeed diagnosed with TS. Because of his now-diagnosed condition, this youngster was entitled to an Individualized Education Plan (IEP) and the school was able to meet his needs.

I admired my mother growing up because I thought she had the best of both worlds. As a teacher, she was able to work outside the home and was also readily available for my brother and me by the time we came home from school. My mother worked for a program called "Operation Return," teaching at-risk students with behavioral challenges in junior high school. In this program, students with behavioral issues had to return to an elementary school setting to relearn classroom expectations, practice appropriate behavior, and earn their way back into junior high school.

My school years were difficult, and I didn't have the best experience or attitude toward school growing up. I was extremely quiet and shy. I didn't raise my hand or volunteer to speak in class unless a teacher called on me, which was almost never. Each day, I tried to convince myself to raise my hand or volunteer to speak up during class. However, I didn't have the confidence to be assertive and, in the end, I just didn't have the nerve to do it. I felt pretty much invisible while I was in school, and this drove me to resent my teachers somewhat. I felt they didn't make an effort to help or encourage me to get out of my comfort zone. I saw how they encouraged other students and felt that should have been one of their responsibilities with me, too.

I also knew a few students who struggled in school and could hardly read. They were basically passed from one grade to another, even though they were woefully behind. This was especially true for some athletes. I felt the school took advantage of athletes and was concerned about their athletic abilities and success at winning basketball games as opposed to helping them to succeed academically. I quickly learned school would be smooth sailing for me as long as I was well-behaved, sat quietly, followed directions, and completed assignments.

The teachers I knew clearly didn't have high expectations for us. They accepted students the way they were and didn't encourage them to achieve outside their comfort zone. If a student was smart and outgoing, that was great and the teacher called on them constantly. If a student was quiet, the teachers gave them passing grades and basically left them alone.

Thank goodness I was a decent student and didn't have to work too hard to get good grades. My parents weren't helicopter parents either. For them, education wasn't a high priority. As long as my brother and I didn't fail a class, they didn't have any complaints and they pretty much left us alone.

As I described in an earlier chapter, the teacher who influenced me the most is the one who didn't believe in me. The incident I'm referring to was when my favorite teacher informed the entire class that she believed I couldn't get into Howard University. She may have thought her negative critique would discourage me and I wouldn't even try to go that route. She may have even believed that I, as a Black girl, didn't have the ability to succeed in college. In fact, her cruel remark had the complete opposite effect. I didn't get mad or upset. Instead, I was inspired to show her I could do it, as I chuckled and thought, *She just did me a huge favor.*"

What she said was exactly what I needed to hear. It was the first time I felt motivated to prove someone wrong. Even though I was quiet, I had high self-esteem when it came to accomplishing personal goals. My parents consistently emphasized that my brother and I could achieve anything we put our minds to. My teacher's negative assessment was also the first time I realized I thrived whenever I was presented with a challenge.

Years later, after successfully graduating from Howard, I went to my old high school to address the harsh words and criticism she shared with me on that particular day. Instead of anger, though, I was grateful that her comments didn't negatively affect me. I wanted her to understand that her comment could have affected another student differently. She could have broken their spirit and possibly discouraged them from pursuing their goals or going to college. I understood the importance of having a positive self-image and how the lack thereof could make or break a person. Unfortunately, the teacher had retired, and I wasn't able to talk with her about this. She had done her job, though, as I had learned the importance of changing negative situations into positive ones and I feel I am a better person because of that.

I knew I would love being a teacher as soon as I attended my first education class at Howard University. The school of education was small, which worked to our advantage. Each class had 10-12 students, and we received a great deal of individual attention. The instructors were outstanding and passionate about the field of education and learning. As a result of being in small classes and having wonderful instructors, we received a world-class education.

Our professors also emphasized how important our role as educators would be and they consistently reminded us of the impact we as teachers could have on the lives of children. When I graduated, I felt like I would be able to open doors of opportunity and encourage students to do their personal best at all times. I wanted to make learning fun and provide positive reinforcement and praise as often as possible.

Because of my experience of feeling invisible in elementary school, I understood the importance of establishing relationships with my students. Getting to know my students, making connections with them, and understanding each child's learning style was also very important. As I reflect on my school experiences, I make it a point to ensure every student I interact with feels special.

Even after I graduated from Howard, I loved reading about child psychology, creating educational materials and writing lesson plans to achieve desired class goals. I began my teaching career after I graduated from Howard as a kindergarten teacher in 1987. I loved teaching students how to name and identify alphabet letters, sounds, and basic sight words. Seeing the expression on a child's face when they realize they can actually read is priceless. Teaching students how to identify numbers, count, add, and subtract was also so much fun.

I see education as the greatest equalizer. It is the tool that makes it possible for anyone, regardless of socioeconomic status or background, to become anything they want to be and achieve their desired goals. Education is also the key to financial independence and social mobility. I wanted to become a teacher who could make a difference in the lives of every student I encountered. I knew I had the ability to help every student feel confident, capable, and eager to learn. My goal was to become an excellent teacher. I wanted to inspire my students to reach for the stars and follow their dreams.

Although I was a stay-at-home mom, I had several opportunities to use my teaching skills both at home and in the community. While my children were growing up, I was an active parent in my children's classrooms. I accompanied my children on every field trip, helped with fundraisers and was active in the Parent Teacher Organization (PTO). I was a guest speaker and introduced the other students to Black History in all my children's classes when they were in elementary school. I also taught about the meaning of Kwanzaa, an annual celebration of African-American culture in schools and in the community.

I knew I would eventually have to get back into teaching. When my youngest, Chike, was finishing elementary school, I realized I had to start earning my own income. I decided to get my feet wet by working as a substitute teacher once or twice a week throughout Iowa City. I loved working at different schools in the area and teaching various subjects at different grade levels. It was excellent on-the-job training after being out of the classroom for 13 years.

Whenever I was a substitute teacher at Lucas Elementary School, Brian Lehman, the school principal, made a point to come into the classroom to observe me. On three occasions he asked if I would be interested in a full-time position. He followed that up by telling me he would highly consider hiring me.

Although I wasn't quite ready to take a permanent job at that time, I knew how competitive it was to be chosen for a teaching position in the Iowa City Community School District (ICCSD). I had friends who applied for teaching positions in ICCSD and were turned down. They had to teach in nearby districts. It was very apparent how difficult it was for many teachers to get jobs, no matter where they wanted to work.

After Principal Lehman had asked once again if I was interested, my mother encouraged me to interview for the position, stating "God is blessing you with this wonderful opportunity. You must take advantage of it." I'm thankful I followed my mother's advice. After my interview, I was offered a part-time position as a special education teacher working with students in first through third grade.

"Once an Ukah student, always an Ukah student." That's my personal motto. I've always made myself available to advocate for my students. I've also made a point of supporting former students and their parents whenever needed. For example, I assist former students with college preparation, studying for college admission exams, and completing job applications. I enjoy running into my former students in the community and periodically hearing from them as they've become adults or as college students. These encounters are so enjoyable and such an added perk of being a teacher.

For example, I've had the honor and privilege of mentoring Hashim, a student I've worked with several times a week after school since he was in the fourth grade. I am extremely proud of him and consider him a part of my family. Hashim is 19 years old now and we continue to work together. My philosophy is "Every Child Can Learn" and I will do everything in my power to help each student achieve his or her goal, one step at a time. Hashim graduated from City High school last year, worked at Goodwill in Cedar Rapids and will enroll at Kirkwood Community College in the Fall.

Then there were those times when I was instantly taken aback, and I wasn't sure how to respond to the situation.

"I don't trust you Ms. Ukah," were the words that came out of Rachel's mouth during a reading comprehension lesson.

She was a third-grade student of mine and to say I was shocked would be an understatement. Why wouldn't Rachel trust me? Although the statement surprised me, I continued to probe....

"Really?" I asked.

"Yes."

"Are you serious?"

"Yes."

"Why don't you trust me?"

"Because you always do what you say you are going to do."

I was confused at this point. It didn't make any sense.

"What do you mean?"

"I trust my mama and whenever my mama says she's going to do something, she never does it."

Okay....

I had difficulty processing what Rachel said. More importantly, I knew I wouldn't be able to address the issue on the spot. After I went home that day, I dug a little deeper to find out how I was going to handle this situation. Based on what she told me, Rachel's definition of "trust" was based on her personal experience, which was the complete opposite of how the rest of the world defined trust.

I knew it would be inappropriate for me to tell her she was incorrect, and that she shouldn't trust her mother since she never does what she says she is going to do. Worse, I should never tell her she should actually "trust" me because I always do what's expected.

Teachers make judgment calls all of the time. I knew it's important to remember students come from varied backgrounds and have families with values and morals that might be different than mine. It's my responsibility to teach the meaning of "trust" as it's commonly defined. It is not my responsibility to change the student's view or perspective of the word "trust" based on my personal experiences or upbringing.

It's very important to listen to students, give them a voice, and ask why they feel the way they do or say some of the things they say. Open communication leads to a better understanding for all of us. When students express something that is not my way of viewing things, it doesn't mean I should correct or impose my personal view upon them or insist the student is wrong. It's important that I respect what each student says and remember that I don't walk in their shoes.

The next day I explicitly defined the word "trust" in class and gave several examples of what trust meant in our reading passage. I did this because I knew in my heart Rachel actually did trust and respect me. She also knew I cared about her. I realized my job as a teacher is to educate students. It is not to prove that their understanding of what trust means does not coincide with my definition or society's definition of trust. As an educator I was reminded we all come from different backgrounds and view things through different lenses.

Unfortunately, I was not able to follow up with Rachel, because she moved away from our school district within a couple of weeks. What I learned from my experience with her was the importance of respecting others' perspectives, and not imposing my views on students, while ensuring I help enlighten students regarding what I understand to be correct. Teaching is my passion. I enjoy going to school each morning knowing I'm working with a group of professional, dedicated, and committed teachers and support staff. Our primary goal is to ensure each child is learning, growing, and achieving his or her personal goals. I couldn't imagine doing anything else. Although teaching is becoming more challenging each year as the demands continue to increase, I remain committed to the belief that all children deserve high-quality education.

I often hear the phrase "teachers don't get paid enough." Although that might be true, it depends on how "being paid" is defined. I feel I get paid every minute I spend with a student, knowing I have the potential to improve their life. Whether it involves teaching them a new skill, motivating students to take school seriously, helping to increase their self-esteem, or simply putting a smile on a child's face, that's a wonderful form of payment and I receive those dividends every day. I believe all children can learn. I also believe educators should be constantly learning. Great educators are lifelong learners. Collaborating, taking additional classes, and attending workshops and conferences keep teachers updated on best practices in education. Each child is unique and has his or her own individual learning style. I believe in meeting children where they are academically, socially, mentally, and physically, and working as a team to devise an education plan so they can grow.

My own children often make fun of me by suggesting I talk to them like they are kindergarten students. Whenever I give advice or make suggestions, some of my friends jokingly imply I'm trying to put them on an Individualized Education Plan. Although, while I realize none of them are serious, I feel I am always in teaching mode. I feel I am not as much instructing as I am explaining things explicitly, much like I do with my young students.

Teaching has also taught me how to be a keen observer. To meet individual needs of my students, I must analyze patterns when they read, or solve equations. Then I must adapt each lesson to them. In my personal life, I find I also spend most of my time observing, learning, and gathering information in different settings. Teaching taught me how to problem-solve and find solutions, especially in those situations that involve children.

Over time, I've become well-established in the community and I'm always running into students I've taught throughout the years. It makes my day when I hear a child call out my name "Ms. Ukah!!" and then ask, "Do you remember me?" I remember all my students. I love hearing about what they are doing with their lives, and it warms my heart. We all try to do what we can to help make this world a better place. I know without a doubt that I make a positive impact on the lives of students on a daily basis, and that's a very good feeling.

Along with the joy I feel in doing a job I believe is extraordinarily worthwhile, teaching helped me become outgoing and talkative. As a child I was introverted and quiet. I soon learned teachers must be able to stand up in front of a class with confidence to teach a lesson. Along with that, communicating with parents, administrators, and a variety of school personnel brought me out of my shell. Teaching also taught me to be creative and flexible. As a special education teacher, I work with students who are often several grade levels behind their peers, require assistance focusing in class, and need help completing assignments. Often, they have physical or medical challenges as well.

Many students I work with have behavioral challenges and have difficulty following basic directions or simply sitting in one space for any length of time. I've learned to communicate effectively and have the ability to shift, adapt, and accommodate my students without any prior notice.

I love learning about and teaching strategies to children that can help them achieve success. I love working with students who have learning disabilities, or academic, behavioral, physical, or health challenges. I also enjoy helping children with ADHD and those who are on the autism spectrum. I have discovered that the students I work with have amazing personalities and the biggest hearts. They often have to work harder than most students and demonstrate a great deal of pride and joy when they reach big and small milestones.

Teaching is also about making connections, collaborating with, and helping students learn and grow in various settings. I realize I am fortunate because I have developed many friendships through teaching. My friend Deb is a great example of a friendship that developed after her son Herbie graduated from elementary school. He was a third-grade student in my class six years ago. I didn't know Deb personally at the time; however she contacted me when Herbie was in 8th grade and asked if I would tutor him at the Iowa City Public Library during the summer.

We became acquaintances at that time. Later we ran into each other at my friend Claudia's house on Thanksgiving Day, three years ago. My friend, Floyd DuBois, a proud Haitian and longtime friend, accompanied me to the event. To my pleasant surprise Deb, Herbie and Floyd hit it off immediately. Herbie was adopted in Haiti and didn't know any Haitians in Iowa City. As a result of that connection, Deb gravitated to Floyd instantly and he spent most of the evening teaching the two of them about Haitian history and culture. He shared childhood memories, taught Herbie some basic French words, and established a unique bond with them.

The three of them were inseparable. I was elated because Herbie met someone who could teach him about his heritage. The smile on Herbie's face was worth a million dollars. Deb was excited to meet Floyd because he could help instill pride in Herbie regarding his Haitian heritage. They exchanged numbers and developed a bond that continues to this day. I also gained a friend in Deb. Over the years I've had the pleasure of attending Herbie's football games, roller-derby matches, and choir concerts.

I could go on endlessly about what I have gained from being a teacher. Of course, I've been paid much-needed income. I've also met an incredible number of treasured students, parents, and colleagues. Along with the wonderful people I've gotten to know, I've expanded my horizons as I've grown personally and professionally as a teacher. Mostly though, I'm deeply honored to be associated with such a proud and respected profession.

CHAPTER 28
TRUST IN GOD

With faith, everything is possible

Soon after Ferdinand's death, as I was beginning to move forward in life, it took a couple of days before I realized my wedding ring was no longer on my finger. I woke up one morning, stretched, and extended both arms. I then stared in disbelief at my bare finger. My hand was unrecognizable. I had worn my wedding ring on my finger every day from the time I married Ferdinand. Suddenly, I saw my ring was no longer there.

Initially, I panicked. I jumped out of my bed and rummaged through the sheets and covers as though I was looking for a needle in a haystack. Hoping and praying the ring just slipped off during the night, I grasped for every glimmer of hope as I looked anxiously and fearfully under each pillow. I peered under my bed, and tiptoed carefully throughout my house, as I strained my eyes to check every spot on the floor.

I attempted to trace every step and movement from the day before. After an hour or so, I was finally able to think rationally. I realized I most likely lost the ring days ago and didn't notice. Because of the tremendous emotional toll of everything that had gone on, I had lost a lot of weight and didn't even realize it. Due to my condition, the ring could have slipped off my finger at any time without me knowing it. For example, it could have happened while playing with the kids on the playground, washing dishes, or bathing the children.

As I sat at the kitchen table in disbelief, I reflected on everything that had happened to me. It was then that peace and tranquility came over me. It was another gift from God. I realized the lost ring was symbolic. I knew the ring without Ferdinand was meaningless. I had already lost my husband. It seemed only fitting that I would lose the ring as well. I also realized I needed to take care of myself, too. While losing the ring was sad, I saw that I needed to be healthy to be there for my children. It was time to move forward.

My belief and faith in God are what helped me navigate life without Ferdinand. Because of God's presence in my life, I didn't feel abandoned. Although there were times I felt lonely, I knew I was supported and protected by God in so many ways. Whenever I felt discouraged, I thought back to the events that unfolded at the time of Ferdinand's death. I realized God prepared me as much as possible for this horrible event, and tried to ease the pain by placing specific people in my life. My relationship with Ferdinand was based on joyous times we were together, even though his profession kept us apart frequently. Because Ferdinand spent the majority of his time working at the hospital, I was already accustomed to taking care of most household responsibilities. This included caring for our four children almost single-handedly.

It is no coincidence that the first three friends we met when we moved to Alabama were an insurance agent, Social Security advisor, and funeral director. I didn't realize it at the moment, but these were three key individuals I or anyone else would need to consult in the event of a sudden death. Looking back, it is very apparent God placed Mecada, Olinda, and the funeral director in our lives to help me through this terrible and disorienting time as my world turned upside down.

As a transplant surgeon, Ferdinand was faced with death and grieving families daily. Watching how young widows were emotionally and financially devastated when a spouse died broke his heart. This experience prompted him to think about protecting his family in the event something happened to him. I didn't understand at the time why Ferdinand was so adamant about insurance. He talked about it all the time and even encouraged his friends and families to purchase insurance as well. Due to his extraordinary wisdom, devotion, and love for his family, Ferdinand's insurance policy provided us with a comfortable lifestyle for many years as it enabled me to raise our children in the home we built. For that I am forever grateful.

God also prevented me from going to Ferdinand's funeral in Nigeria. Although my mother tried to convince me not to go, I instead did everything humanly possible to attend his funeral. God intervened once again by shutting my body down and making it impossible for me to move, walk, or talk. I couldn't make myself physically get on the plane to Nigeria even though I had decided this was what I wanted to do. That was divine intervention.

Among an extraordinarily long list of divinely inspired events, the moment that stands out the most to me and continues to melt my heart was my personal good-bye from Ferdinand. The silhouette that appeared in the corner of my bedroom at approximately the same time Ferdinand died in Nigeria was my saving grace through some extremely difficult times. It was confirmation to me that Ferdinand is in heaven and God is in control.

Ferdinand has been gone from this Earth for 25 years now. Each year, within two or three days of our wedding anniversary, no matter where I am (Iowa, New York, Jamaica, Miami, or Hawaii), someone, somewhere plays the song *Always* by Atlantic Star. It's the first song we danced to as a married couple. Two years ago, I heard the song in my friend Ann Kessler's truck when I accompanied her to Sycamore, Illinois to get a generator because her electricity went out during the devastating derecho windstorm that ravaged the region. Last year, I heard the song on the radio while driving in my car. Experiences like these bring me comfort and I remember how extremely blessed I am.

The biggest challenge I faced, however, was having to file for bankruptcy during Chike's last year in high school. I was struggling financially; emotionally drained, and so embarrassed I did not feel I could share this information with anyone. I struggled for two years and confided in my oldest daughter Adanna. Much like almost everyone who files for bankruptcy, there is guilt and shame tied into not being able to support and take care of my family's financial responsibilities.

Adanna had just graduated from Yale, and I had two other children in college at that time. Money was really tight. I didn't want to uproot Chike from his childhood home. Similar to what my mother had done for me, I wanted Chike to live in our home and have the same childhood experiences his siblings had until he left for college. That was a very scary time for me, full of uncertainty and fear. Money was scarce and my financial obligations continued to increase.

I finally realized that my only way out, the only way to get a fresh start and be able to move forward, would be to face the reality of my situation and declare bankruptcy. I knew there would be a stigma surrounding what I was going to have to do. I only had one child living in my house at the time and Chike's well-being was my primary concern. Throughout this difficult and scary time, my daughter Adanna was my rock. She provided comfort, advice, and a much-needed sounding board at a time when that was very important for me. I am forever thankful for the wonderful and loving young woman she has become.

Living in a small community had many benefits. Meeting and getting to know Ferdinand's former patients was always a surprise and welcomed blessing. Our last name "Ukah" is unique and certainly stands out. There have been numerous occasions in which someone would hear our last name and ask, "Are you related to Dr. Ukah?"

This occurred with my children as well as myself. It was always a great feeling when people we didn't even know shared personal memories and experiences they had with Ferdinand. It reaffirmed our sense of pride and was a constant reminder that he made an impact on the lives of others.

Whenever the children had a doctor's appointment at the University of Iowa Hospitals and Clinics; doctors and nurses often recognized our name and would go out of their way to tell the children how amazing Ferdinand was. I felt we were always in good hands and Ferdinand was once again looking out for us even though he wasn't with us physically.

Paul and Julie Olson are perfect examples of people who have come into our lives as a result of being one of Ferdinand's patients. Julie was a transplant recipient and she absolutely adored Ferdinand. After Ferdinand's death we developed a very close friendship. By the time Okey and Chike were in high school, her husband Paul accompanied us to most of my son's basketball games. This was a huge deal because they both knew Ferdinand personally and had many stories to share. Paul was also a godsend because he was a wonderful role model and often volunteered to drive us to out-of-town basketball games. This was a blessing because we sometimes traveled in severe weather, and I was often terrified. God puts the right people in our lives at just the right time. God's timing is always perfect.

I periodically drive past our previous home on Weeber Street to look at the trees Mr. and Mrs. Knabe planted for our family years ago. During one of my visits, I noticed a man working in the yard on the side of our old house. Once I drove by, I noticed the gentleman was African American.

What are the odds that a Black family would move into our former home?

When I moved out of our home, I prayed that a wonderful family would move in and enjoy the home as much as our family did. I was elated, quickly made a U-turn, parked my car and introduced myself.

"Excuse me, my name is Cynthia Ukah, and I am the previous owner of this home."

The gentleman turned around and stood up.

"Ma'am, I know exactly who you are, and I know who your husband is as well. We worked together at the university."

Iowa City is a small town, and I recognized this man Russell, as an X-Ray technician at the university. I also recall his children attending the "Play with Color" group my friend Monique and I started years ago. I felt my prayers were answered because a lovely family did move into our home.

Russell had tears in his eyes and kept telling me I had to talk to his wife. I knew I had seen his wife in the community, however, I didn't know her and didn't understand why he kept repeating the phrase, "Ma'am, you have to talk to my wife."

He explained that his wife had been looking for a house for quite some time. She was having difficulty finding the perfect one. When she found out the history of our home and the occupants that lived in it; she was sold. Her only hesitation was that she was afraid I would resent her because she was living in a home that I lost due to bankruptcy.

I called her and we made arrangements to meet over coffee about two weeks later. She was a wonderful woman and said she purchased the home because she knew we were Christians and heard about our story. After my house sold, my lawyer called and told me the new homeowners paid more for the house than it was worth. He stated this was the first time in his career that something like this happened. After connecting the dots, I believe this family paid more for the house because they wanted me to make a profit from its sale. Our God is an awesome God.

God blessed me with an amazing mother. She has been my rock throughout the years and has been an excellent support system. My mother moved to Iowa when she retired as a schoolteacher five years after Ferdinand died. She wanted to live close by in case I needed her. Mom had so many fond memories of Ferdinand. She realized how much Ferdinand loved me when Ferdinand called my mom to find out if she heard from me when I traveled alone to Nigeria. My mom told him I was fine. Ferdinand wasn't satisfied with that answer, He asked my mother several times, "How did she sound, did she sound like she was fine?" My mother knew at that moment that Ferdinand really cared for me.

My mother remembers the inspirational sticky notes we had displayed on mirrors and walls throughout our house. Each contained Bible verses or positive notes and affirmations of encouragement. Whenever my mother visited, Ferdinand made arrangements for the two of us to go out for dinner. During Ferdinand's memorial service at the University of Iowa, my mother beamed with pride because so many people shared stories and fond memories of Ferdinand. She remembers an anesthesiologist who said. "Most doctors talk shop when they are in the operating room, but Ferdinand always talked about his love for Cynthia and how much he loved his family." My mother believes our marriage was a gift from God, truly made in heaven; a true partnership of love and looking out for each other. According to her, "Ferdinand you're the best."

As I mentioned in an earlier chapter, another major spiritual event in my life was receiving a Bible as a Christmas gift when I was sixteen. I read it front to back and it provided me with a solid religious foundation. I knew God wouldn't give me any more than I could bear. I soon discovered my church family in Iowa City was very supportive, and the members served as excellent role models. I attended church and Bible study sessions weekly to help keep me grounded, focused, and disciplined. This regimen has helped me throughout my life and it remains an important part of my routine to this day.

I try to give back to my community by setting a good example and serving as a Board Member for Faith Academy, which provides a Christ-centered education for students in grades K-6. I also serve on the Crowded Closet Board — a nonprofit thrift store that shares

God's love and compassion in the name of Christ by supporting Mennonite Central Committee world relief, service and development programs, and local community relief agencies. All profits of Crowded Closet support relief and service organizations.

I made the decision not to date soon after Ferdinand's death. I knew raising a young family of four required all my attention. I felt I needed to be dedicated and committed to my children one hundred percent. Experiencing the devastation of Ferdinand's loss at such a young age was as horrible as it was unexpected. Feeling fully supported and guided by scripture and God's promise was my salvation, as it has sustained me throughout the most difficult periods in my life. This knowledge deep in my soul was a constant source of comfort.

Despite the major tragedy my family and I have overcome, I feel truly blessed because I have had a fulfilling and happy life. Adanna, Nneka, Okechukwu and Chike bring me so much joy. I'm proud of myself as well. I know things could have gone terribly wrong after Ferdinand's death if I had succumbed to the fear and despair that welled up inside of me. I know it was my focus, love, and dedication toward my family that sustained me during the hardest of times. Mostly, though, I am proud I have kept the faith. Throughout it all, I believed in a loving and just God that protects us, and I have never had cause to doubt that.

For this and so much more, I am eternally grateful.

CHAPTER 29
MY MESSAGE

Our beautiful family, taken just before Ferdinand traveled to Nigeria

I remember waking up the morning after Ferdinand died and couldn't believe what had just happened.

How could my loving husband, this phenomenal son, father, and renowned transplant surgeon with so much to live for and give others, leave this earth? How could life continue to go on as usual?

Later, as I lay in bed, I watched the sunrise, and listened to birds chirping and the faint voices outside in the distance. Part of me still couldn't believe the world didn't stop and take note of this devastating loss.

Don't you understand? Ferdinand is no longer with us.

I thought about all the people that would be affected by Ferdinand's death. His family in Nigeria, our four children, dear friends, numerous patients who adored him, and even those who would never benefit from his great knowledge, skill, and compassion. Of course, I also thought about myself and my loss. Ferdinand had so much more love to give, wisdom to impart, and many lives he could have saved. Ferdinand was one of a kind and hands down the most amazing person I had ever met. And then he was gone in the blink of an eye.

This book is much more than recalling the pain from his tragic death, though. Far beyond that, my story is one of great love and unshakable faith. This book is about a one-of-a-kind love affair and an extraordinary adventure that resulted in four incredible children. My tale is a story of recovery from a devastating loss and how my life has been so full of love and purpose despite that loss. My story is also a testimonial to how, with God's love, I found the strength to carry on and thrive despite all of the unexpected obstacles that came my way.

It was a complete honor to be Ferdinand's wife and best friend. He blessed me with a wonderful life and four amazing children. I will treasure the memories we shared forever. I think about his humility, intelligence, and how he loved his family tremendously. I learned a lot from Ferdinand and continue to use the lessons I learned from him in my daily life today.

As I reflect on the last 25 years I am constantly reminded of God's presence in my life. As my friend Amy stated:

"Cynthia, you have two options: you can go through this difficult situation with God or without God. This is not going to be easy, but if you decide to go through this with God, you won't ever be alone, and He will guide you through this."

I'm thankful I decided to put my faith in God to help me through this extraordinarily challenging time. Losing a loved one is always difficult, and people grieve in many different ways. I know there isn't a right or wrong way to grieve and there are no rules when it comes to dealing with unspeakable sadness. We all handle situations differently based on our specific circumstances and we should try to respect the way people grieve even if we don't fully understand their rationale.

I became a widow at the age of 35 and didn't have a clue what I was doing. I was living day-by-day and trying to take things one step at a time. I found solace and strength in God. I prayed more than I ever had before. I didn't feel alone because I had always felt God's presence. I also relied on the many conversations I had with Ferdinand to help guide me. We had a "Marriage Made in Heaven" because Ferdinand and I loved each other deeply and we took the time to develop a well-thought-out plan. Although he wasn't with me physically, I still felt we were working as a team because he continued to guide me even after he departed.

Of all the lessons I learned, perhaps the most important is that "love lasts forever." And while my life has been full of joy and compassion since Ferdinand's death, it is my honor to give tribute to the man who meant so very much to me, his children, and all of us who loved him so deeply.

This book is my humble attempt to keep his memory alive as a wonderful example of what is possible for any of us to achieve. I hope you have enjoyed reading it as much as I have enjoyed writing it.

Love and blessings to you all.

ABOUT THE AUTHOR

Alive and well in 2022 (Image by Audree Larson)

Cynthia Ukah was born and raised in Queensbridge, a housing development in New York City. After successfully completing primary and secondary school, which included participating in court-ordered busing to attend white-majority schools, she was accepted at prestigious Howard University, where she graduated with a bachelor's degree in Elementary and Special Education in the spring of 1983.

While at Howard, she met Ferdinand Ukah, a Nigerian citizen and a student at the Howard University College of Medicine. After becoming a doctor, Ferdinand was competitively selected to specialize in transplant surgery at the University of Pittsburgh Medical Center. Ferdinand was later hired by the University of Iowa Hospital where he quickly became a rising star. It wasn't long before Dr. Ukah was chosen to start a regional transplant center for the University of South Alabama in Mobile.

Along the way, Cynthia and Ferdinand fell in love, as they learned to appreciate and eventually embrace their vast cultural differences. Getting married while Ferdinand was in his medical residency at Howard, the two of them soon became the loving parents of four children over the course of six short years.

It was then that disaster struck. Ferdinand died unexpectedly while visiting his family in Nigeria to organize and supervise a kidney transplant for his aging father. Despite this overwhelming tragedy, Cynthia leaned heavily on her abiding faith in God and the support of her community in Iowa City as she dedicated herself to raising her children as a single parent.

As her children got older and went to college, Cynthia rejoined the work force as a special education teacher in the Iowa City Community School District. Cynthia continues to work there today, as she devotes her time to lovingly help elementary school children with special needs.

Cynthia is active in the community, as she enjoys her many close friends, participates in church activities, and is a member of local planning boards. Most importantly, she also maintains loving bonds with her four wonderful children (Adanna, Nneka, Okechukwu Jr., and Chike), and her mother Roberta.

A Marriage Made in Heaven is the first of what Cynthia hopes to be many books.

CPSIA information can be obtained
at www.ICGtesting.com
Printed in the USA
JSHW032227160223
37855JS00001B/3

9 798986 927909